The AI Ethics Advisor

Antonio Carnevale

The AI Ethics Advisor

Methods and Practices for Training and Standardization of Experts

Springer

Antonio Carnevale
DIRIUM Department, Palazzo Ateneo
University of Bari
Bari, Italy

ISBN 978-3-032-05525-5 ISBN 978-3-032-05526-2 (eBook)
https://doi.org/10.1007/978-3-032-05526-2

This Springer imprint is published by the registered company Springer Nature Switzerland AG
The registered company address is: Gewerbestrasse 11, 6330 Cham, Switzerland

Preface

In recent years, the figure of the AI Ethics Advisor has emerged as a key actor in the design, deployment, and governance of digital technologies. This book seeks to explore the reasons behind this emergence and to clarify the deeper meaning of a profession that challenges not only traditional academic structures but also the accelerating pace of contemporary technological production. Situated at the crossroads of philosophy, policy, and engineering, the AI Ethics Advisor is no longer a theoretical abstraction, but a role under active construction—normatively contested, institutionally fluid, and professionally in formation [2, 16, 18].

Methodological Note: Mapping a Moving Target

The selection of sources presented across the chapters is the outcome of a machine-generated literature review, curated and interpreted through the author's own expertise in the field. While computational methods have helped structure the bibliographic landscape, the final composition remains the result of a situated, reflective ordering of knowledge. The decision to focus primarily on the period 2020–2025 reflects the historical density of recent years—from the pre- to post-COVID transformation, to the rise of generative AI and large language models, to mounting geopolitical instability. In certain cases, earlier sources were included when they proved conceptually foundational to ongoing debates.

This hybrid methodology—blending automated retrieval with critical synthesis—aims to illustrate the contours of a rapidly evolving epistemic field, providing a grounded yet provisional overview of a domain still in flux [13].

The AI Ethics Advisor: A Hybrid and Tensional Role

The AI Ethics Advisor is not merely a conveyor of abstract moral rules, but a practitioner tasked with translating ethical reflection into operational forms. Far from a mere compliance officer, this figure inhabits a liminal space between conceptual scrutiny and institutional implementation.

Three defining characteristics mark this role:

- A bridge between theory and practice, where complex normative questions must be rendered actionable without being reduced to simplistic checklists or procedural formalities [3, 4].
- A hybrid actor across academia, industry, and policy, challenging the silos of traditional knowledge domains and professional hierarchies [2, 16].
- A catalyst of interdisciplinarity, operating at the confluence of ethics, law, computer science, organisational theory, and social critique [19, 14].

This very hybridity is both the advisor's strength and vulnerability. On the one hand, the role holds the potential to challenge the instrumental logic of capitalist innovation, advocating for co-creative models of development where economic value is not the sole measure of success [12, 18]. On the other hand, it risks being absorbed into marketing strategies of ethical posturing—what has been aptly termed ethics washing—where ethical engagement is symbolic rather than structural [7, 11].

A Discipline in Fits and Starts: The Fragmentation of AI Ethics

Compounding the ambiguity of the advisor's role is the fragmented epistemology of AI ethics itself. Unlike other applied ethical domains—such as bioethics or legal ethics—AI ethics is still struggling to consolidate its methodological and conceptual foundations. What currently passes under this name is less of a discipline than a contested terrain, characterised by epistemic dissonance, institutional incoherence, and normative inflation [6, 15].

A number of centrifugal forces drive this fragmentation:

- The sociotechnical complexity of AI systems, particularly stochastic machine learning models, resists stable frameworks for ethical assessment [5, 20].
- The demand for pragmatic tools and interfaces has led to a proliferation of simplified evaluation kits and gamified toolkits—what one might call the toolkitisation of ethics [14].
- The pressure from industry and public opinion to move quickly "from principles to practice" incentivises bespoke, often opaque, methodologies that hinder convergence [4, 9].

- The time-constrained nature of funded research fosters operational shortcuts, privileging short-term outputs over long-term epistemic coherence [8, 17].
- The need to satisfy KPIs and achieve visibility often drives actors to prioritise novelty over integration, undermining opportunities for cross-fertilisation and collective learning [13].
- Finally, the symbolic capital now attached to AI ethics has transformed it into a field of strategic differentiation, further fuelling its conceptual and institutional dispersal [16, 18].

The result is a form of knowledge production that advances not linearly but in fits and starts, through rhapsodic bursts rather than coherent paradigms. This dynamic contributes to a deeper problem: the neglect of meta-ethical reflection. In a rush to define what is good or just, little attention is paid to the epistemic and methodological architectures underpinning such judgements. Debates rarely ask how we reason about ethics in AI—what counts as valid justification, what modes of deliberation are appropriate, and what constitutes an adequate normative framework [7, 15].

What's in a Name? Between AI Ethicist, Officer, and Advisor

A further tension lies in the very nomenclature of the role. Competing labels abound: *AI Ethics Officer* denotes an internal compliance function; *AI Ethics Advisor* suggests external consultancy; *AI Ethicist* evokes philosophical reflection and normative scrutiny.

This book adopts the term "The AI Ethics Advisor", positioned as a middle ground between the institutional embeddedness of the Officer and the intellectual independence of the Ethicist. The aim is twofold: to promote the professionalisation and formal recognition of the role while preserving its transversal and critical capacities [2, 13]. The Ethics Advisor is not merely a gatekeeper of acceptable conduct. In an era shaped by probabilistic systems that optimise prediction without understanding, the advisor must cultivate doubt, illuminate alternatives, and resist the allure of cognitive shortcuts. Their vocation is not only to "do ethics" but to enact a vision of technological progress compatible with a broader conception of human flourishing [5, 14].

Structure of the Book

The book is structured in five chapters, each addressing a key dimension of the emerging profession of the AI Ethics Advisor. Chapter 1 explores the identity, competencies, and institutional roles of this figure, analysing the tensions between autonomy, legitimacy, and organisational embeddedness. Chapter 2 examines principlism in AI ethics, unpacking its philosophical foundations, interpretative divergences, and the challenges of operationalisation. Chapter 3 focuses on the concept of trust, scrutinising its relationship with explainability, accountability, and sociotechnical perception. Chapter 4 moves into the pragmatic domain, offering a comparative overview of strategies for implementing ethical principles in concrete settings. Chapter 5 turns to AI governance at national and international levels, interrogating the regulatory, geopolitical, and institutional dynamics that shape the space in which ethics advisors operate.

Each chapter blends theoretical reflection with practical insights, offering a conceptual toolkit and operational perspective for those seeking to understand or embody this profession.

Potential Impact

This book seeks to contribute not only to scholarship but to practice and policy. It offers a structured and critically curated map of a field that is simultaneously nascent, fragmented, and urgently needed. By foregrounding both normative reflection and institutional pragmatics, the volume addresses two key audiences.

For aspiring professionals and educators, it offers a scaffold for acquiring competences and navigating the tensions of an emergent role [2, 10]. For policymakers and institutional leaders, it highlights the structural constraints—regulatory gaps, lack of standardisation, and risks of instrumentalisation—that must be addressed for this role to achieve legitimacy and efficacy [1, 8, 17].

By situating the AI Ethics Advisor at the intersection of theory and action, this book advocates for a future in which ethical reasoning is not peripheral but foundational to the governance of artificial intelligence—and to the shaping of technological futures more broadly.

Acknowledgements This work is partially supported by the project FAIR, Future AI Research (PE00000013), spoke 6, Symbiotic AI, under the NRRP MUR programme funded by the NextGenerationEU.

Bari, Italy Antonio Carnevale

References

1. Cihon, P., Maas, M. M., & Kemp, L. (2021). Should explainability be a fifth ethical principle in AI ethics? *AI and Ethics*.
2. Cocchiaro, M. Z., J. Morley, C. Novelli, E. Panai, A. Tartaro, & L. Floridi. (2025). Who is an AI Ethicist? An empirical study of expertise, skills, and profiles to build a competency framework. *AI and Ethics*. https://doi.org/10.1007/s43681-024-00643-y

3. Dignum, V. (2020). Putting AI ethics to work: Are the tools fit for purpose? *Nature Machine Intelligence 2*, 488–490.
4. Fjeld, J., Achten, N., Hilligoss, H., Nagy, A., & Srikumar, M. (2020). *Principled artificial intelligence: Mapping consensus in ethical and rights-based approaches to principles for AI.* Berkman Klein Center.
5. Floridi, L., & J. Cowls. 2019. *A unified framework of five principles for AI in society.* Harvard Data Science Review. https://doi.org/10.1162/99608f92.8cd550d1
6. Hagendorff, T. (2020). The ethics of AI ethics: An evaluation of guidelines. *Mind and Machines 30*(1), 99–120. https://doi.org/10.1007/s11023-020-09517-8
7. Hagendorff, T. (2022). AI ethics and its pitfalls: Not living up to its own standards? *AI and Ethics*. https://doi.org/10.1007/s43681-022-00173-5
8. Jobin, A., Ienca, M., & Vayena, E. (2019). The global landscape of AI ethics guidelines. *Nature Machine Intelligence 1*(9), 389–399. https://doi.org/10.1038/s42256-019-0088-2
9. Mittelstadt, B. (2019). Principles alone cannot guarantee ethical AI. *Nature Machine Intelligence 1*, 501–507.
10. Morley, J., Elhalal, A., Garcia, F., Kinsey, L., Mökander, J., & Floridi, L. (2021). Ethics as a service: A pragmatic operationalisation of AI ethics. *Mind and Machines 31*(2), 239–256. https://doi.org/10.1007/s11023-021-09563-w
11. Munn, L. (2022). The uselessness of AI ethics. *AI and Ethics*. https://doi.org/10.1007/s43681-022-00209-w
12. Panai, E. (2023). The latent space of data ethics. *AI and Society*. https://doi.org/10.1007/s00146-023-01757-3
13. Panai, E. (2024). Reflections on putting AI ethics into practice: How three AI ethics approaches conceptualise theory and practice. In *AI Ethics in Action*.
14. Panai, E. (2024). The ethico-politics of design toolkits: Responsible AI tools, from big tech guidelines to feminist ideation cards. *AI and Society*.
15. Rességuier, A., & Rodrigues, R.. (2020). AI ethics should not remain toothless! A call to bring back the teeth of ethics. *Big Data and Society 7*(2), 1–5.
16. Sætra, H. S., Coeckelbergh, M., & Danaher, J. (2021). The AI ethicist's dilemma: Fighting Big Tech by supporting Big Tech. *AI and Ethics*. https://doi.org/10.1007/s43681-021-00123-7
17. Smuha, N. A. (2021). Beyond a human rights-based approach to AI governance: Promise, pitfalls, plea. *Philosophy and Technology 34*, 1–20.
18. Steinhoff, J. (2023). AI ethics as subordinated innovation network. *AI and Society*. https://doi.org/10.1007/s00146-023-01658-5
19. Vakkuri, V., Kemell, K.-K., & Abrahamsson, P. (2021). *Beyond principlism: Practical strategies for ethical AI use in research practices. Journal of Responsible Technology*.
20. Vakkuri, V., Kemell, K.-K., Kultanen, J., Siponen, M., & P. Abrahamsson. (2019). *Ethically aligned design of autonomous systems: Industry viewpoint and an empirical study.* arXiv, 1906.07946.

Contents

Chapter 1
AI Ethics Advisor Office: Scope and Purpose

Abstract This chapter explores the emerging profession of the AI ethics advisor, defining its scope, competencies, and the institutional contexts within which it operates. It examines the core responsibilities of AI ethics advisors, from providing ethical guidance and oversight to facilitating organisational dialogue around ethical issues. The chapter further investigates the complex landscape in which these advisors work, noting challenges such as "ethics washing," corporate constraints, and the necessity of maintaining independence and credibility. By drawing from empirical and normative studies, the chapter outlines a structured competency framework for AI ethics advisors, highlighting their crucial role in bridging ethical principles and practical AI governance.

Keywords AI ethics advisor · Competency framework · Professional identity · Professional independence · Ethics washing

Introduction by the Editor

The emergence of artificial intelligence (AI) has brought profound ethical, social, and political challenges, necessitating the presence of specialised professionals capable of navigating the intersection of AI development, regulatory frameworks, and ethical imperatives. The AI ethics adviser (or AI ethicist or AI ethics officer) has gained increasing prominence among these emerging figures. But who is the AI ethics adviser? And in what contexts do they operate? This chapter seeks to answer these fundamental questions by examining the competencies, roles, and institutional settings in which AI ethics advisor function, as well as the challenges they face in ensuring that AI technologies align with ethical and social values.

A. Carnevale, *The AI Ethics Advisor*,
https://doi.org/10.1007/978-3-032-05526-2_1

Who Is the AI Ethics Adviser?

A recent empirical study on the AI ethics profession highlights that, despite the growing importance of ethical advisory in AI, there is still little consensus on what constitutes the expertise and skill set of an AI ethicist [1]. While some conceptualise the role as analogous to that of a health care ethics consultant—providing ethical guidance within an organisation—others view it as a regulatory or compliance-oriented function, ensuring that AI systems meet legal and ethical standards [1]. The study suggests that an AI ethicist must possess moral expertise—akin to bioethicists—capable of bridging theoretical ethical principles with concrete decision-making processes in AI governance [1].

Moreover, the AI ethics advisor is not necessarily a standalone figure but rather part of a broader ecosystem of professionals involved in responsible AI. Job descriptions for AI ethics roles indicate that they often function as facilitators, mediators, and educators within their organisations [1]. Their responsibilities range from conducting ethical risk assessments and drafting ethical guidelines to training employees and engaging with external stakeholders. However, this multiplicity of functions also presents a challenge: AI ethicists may be expected to take full responsibility for the ethical outcomes of AI systems, potentially leading to moral disengagement by other decision-makers within an organisation [1].

The AI ethics advisor operates within a complex institutional and organisational landscape. They may be found in corporations, government agencies, non-governmental organisations (NGOs), think tanks, and academia. However, the institutional context in which they work greatly influences their capacity to effect meaningful ethical change.

For instance, in the corporate sector, AI ethics advisors are frequently embedded within Big Tech companies, where they must navigate the delicate balance between promoting ethical AI and serving the interests of their employers [2]. This dynamic has led to accusations that AI ethics, as a field, is often subordinated to the priorities of corporate capitalism, functioning as a "subordinated innovation network" that ultimately serves the goals of data-driven business models rather than facilitating independent ethical scrutiny [3].

Furthermore, some scholars have raised concerns that AI ethics is being co-opted as a form of "ethics washing", where ethical discourse is employed more as a marketing tool than as a substantive regulatory mechanism [4]. As a result, AI ethics advisors often face the AI ethicist's dilemma—the paradox of trying to reform AI systems from within institutions that profit from ethically questionable practices [2].

In contrast, AI ethics advisors operating in academia and independent research institutions may enjoy greater autonomy but often struggle with limited access to the industry and policymaking circles where key AI ethics decisions are ultimately made. Similarly, within government and regulatory bodies, AI ethics advisors play a role in shaping legislation and governance, though they may face bureaucratic inertia and political constraints [5].

Conclusion: Challenges and Future Directions

The profession of AI ethics advisor is still in its formative stages and faces significant structural challenges. One of the most pressing issues is credibility and independence. Some experts argue that ethics advisors should undergo a process of certification and standardisation to ensure that their expertise is formally recognised and protected from conflicts of interest [1]. Others suggest that AI ethics should move beyond principles-based approaches and adopt more enforceable mechanisms, such as legal regulations, industry-wide standards, and algorithmic auditing practices [6].

Moreover, the role of AI ethics advisors must evolve to avoid becoming a superficial corporate function. Rather than merely producing ethical guidelines that are rarely implemented in practice, AI ethics should focus on building ethical infrastructures—organisational systems that embed ethical reasoning into AI development and deployment [5].

Machine Generated Summaries

Who Is an AI Ethicist? An Empirical Study of Expertise, Skills, and Profiles to Build a Competency Framework [1]

This is a machine-generated summary of:

Cocchiaro, Mariangela Zoe; Morley, Jessica; Novelli, Claudio; Panai, Enrico; Tartaro, Alessio; Floridi, Luciano Who is an AI Ethicist? An empirical study of expertise, skills, and profiles to build a competency framework [1]

Published in: AI and Ethics (2025)

Link to original: https://doi.org/10.1007/s43681-024-00643-y

If you want to cite the papers, please refer to the original.

For technical reasons we could not place the page where the original quote is coming from.

Abstract-Summary

"Only a few studies have taken an interest in this professional profile, and they have yet to provide a normative discussion of its expertise and skills."

"We focus on their specific kind of moral expertise, drawing on a parallel with the expertise of Ethics Consultants in clinical settings and on the bioethics literature on the topic."

"We highlight the differences between Health Care Ethics Consultants and AI Ethicists and derive the expertise and skills of the latter from the roles that AI Ethicists should have in an organisation."

Introduction

"Some critical voices have pointed to the potential for ethics washing related to the emergence of the role of AI ethicists [7], and, beyond that, the subordination of the entire field of AI ethics to the interests of Big Tech [3]."

"Precisely in response to the concrete risks that this critical literature highlights, we argue in the discussion section that the development of clear benchmarks for the competencies of AI ethicists, along with the development of an institutional framework that can support their activities, can serve as a critical factor in minimising the risks associated with ethical washing and facilitating a real ethical impact for these professionals."

"It advocates for a structured competency framework to define and standardise the role of AI Ethicists, emphasising their critical function in bridging ethical principles with practical application in AI development and deployment."

"The role of an AI ethicist is not at odds with other teams that may perform ethics-related functions, but rather complements them to bring specific ethical expertise to the organisation."

Methodology: Empirical and Normative

"We may potentially miss profiles that contain related phrases, such as "I conduct research on the ethical implications of digital technologies—including AI," but do not explicitly mention "AI ethics" or "digital ethics.""

"We looked for online postings for the position by using the keywords "AI Ethicist jobs", "AI Ethics jobs", and "Responsible AI jobs"."

"Specific job titles, such as data scientist, reporter, professor, and research scientist, were deliberately excluded to focus on roles directly relevant to AI ethics."

"Our search ultimately identified 26 active job listings for the position of AI Ethicists."

"In the job postings reviewed, AI Ethicists were assigned several core responsibilities, including creating Ethical AI solutions, conducting research and analysis on AI Ethics, and overseeing AI projects' monitoring, evaluation, and compliance."

"As our preliminary research showed, the description of the AI Ethicist resembles that of a consultant tasked with offering advice, guidance, and expert knowledge to enhance clients' ethical decision-making capabilities within the AI domain."

The Practical Moral Expertise of AI Ethicists

"An important aspect of AI Ethicists' role is improving legal compliance, which often serves to operationalise general moral values into specific legal standards."

"The AI Ethicist is an individual who has the moral expertise to provide correct answers to questions that fall under the domain of AI Ethics."

"Any moral expertise might prompt organisations to offload all ethical decisions onto the AI Ethicist, leading to moral disengagement."

"Let us turn now to the kinds of moral expertise that an AI ethicist may be required to have by drawing on the distinction among the three, possibly overlapping, kinds of expertise identified in bioethics [8, 9]."

"This indicates that an AI Ethicist should have at least the same performative moral expertise as an average individual."

"While the role of researcher fosters the professional development of AI ethicists, it also facilitates their ability to improve organizational awareness and integration of ethical practices."

Knowledge and Skills of the AI Ethicist

"To clarify the knowledge and skills required for an AI Ethicist acting as facilitator, researcher, and educator, we will first link specific tasks to each role."

"Other skills and knowledge areas required of the AI Ethicist were identified indirectly by drawing on the HC Ethicist's core skills and knowledge areas listed by the ASBH."

"Mutatis mutandis, this skill seems necessary for AI Ethicists as well, particularly concerning task Fo-1: how could AI Ethicists facilitate discussions and resolve conflicts on ethical matters without the ability to identify the relevant stakeholders in the first place?"

Conclusion: AI Ethics as a Profession. What's Next?

"Risk management is essential; although it benefits from AI technical knowledge, it draws significantly on established methodologies from fields like finance and climate science, where it is applied to different products or events."

"Credibility and independence are essential for the growth and development of the profession of the AI ethicist."

"To protect AI ethicists, organisations should not reduce their role to mere virtue signalling or ethical washing."

"AI ethicists should validate and standardise their knowledge and skills through recognised certification processes to maintain independence and credibility, ensuring alignment with industry standards."

"Given their exposure to such civil liability risks, AI ethicists, particularly those in consulting or advisory roles, might also benefit from some form of protection."

"Similar developments could strongly incentivise the growth of the AI ethicist profession."

"We outlined the skills and knowledge that together are necessary to answer questions in the domain of AI Ethics correctly and should underpin the expertise of AI Ethicists."

The Latent Space of Data Ethics [5]

This is a machine-generated summary of:

Panai, Enrico The latent space of data ethics [5]

Published in: AI & SOCIETY (2023)

Link to original: https://doi.org/10.1007/s00146-023-01757-3

If you want to cite the papers, please refer to the original.

For technical reasons we could not place the page where the original quote is coming from.

Abstract-Summary

"To avoid the misuse, underuse, and harmful use of data and data-based systems like AI, we should use an ethical framework appropriate to the object of its reasoning."

"In recent years, the space for data-related ethics has not been precisely defined in organisations."

"Ethical issues have, therefore, been dealt with using inadequate levels of abstraction (e.g. legal, technical)."

"If building an ethical infrastructure requires the collaboration of each body, addressing ethical issues related to data requires leaving room for the appropriate level of abstraction."

"This paper first aims to show how the space of data ethics is already latent in organisations."

"It then highlights how to redefine roles (chief data ethics officer, data ethics committee, etc) and codes (code of data ethics) to create and maintain an environment where ethical reasoning about data, information, and AI systems may flourish."

Introduction

"This space has been occupied by experts closer to the issues of data privacy (e.g. the data protection officer (DPO) or the chief data officer (CDO) for compliance with regulations), data processing by artificial intelligence (AI) algorithms (data scientists or, in general, data workers—DW), or more broadly by those in charge of the company's code of ethics (chief ethics officer (CEtO) or board of directors)."

"It will be necessary to integrate into the organisation other decision-making bodies with specific skills to help the chief data ethics officer write the code of data ethics and support data ethics committee decisions about data, i.e. to deal with high-risk algorithms (as an algorithm risk committee—ARC), to regulate the ethical instances of specific protected categories such as children's data (children's data oversight committee—CDOC), etc. The existence of those bodies should be coupled with their knowledge; the expertise of each committee member must be appropriate to the nature and purpose of the data processing and the nature of the AI algorithms and autonomous systems."

Context

"The constant use of high-level ethical principles (human rights, transparency, explainability, privacy, accountability, fairness, non-discrimination, reliability, inclusiveness, etc. [10], which are sufficiently broad to be unachievable when working on the fine-grained level of abstraction of data, shows that there is still a lack of systematic understanding of how data ethics can contribute to making ethical choices about data, the algorithms that process it and the practices that come with the process."

"The c-level members who are more competent in legal aspects of data processing (chief data officer or, in Europe, data protection officer) base their decisions on legal regulations [11, 12] rather than on an ethical framework."

"Making ethical choices about digital technologies, data and ultimately AI systems requires reorganising the debate within an ethical approach concerning data, algorithms and related practices."

Mapping the Data Ethics Space

"At this level, the chief information security officer deals with the lowest layer, that of physical and logical data protection."

"At the legal level, there is the chief data officer (CDO) or the data protection officer (DPO)."

"At the legal level, both the chief data officer and the data protection officer are responsible for compliance with data processing law Yet, there is a substantial difference between the two roles."

"At this level, the chief ethics officer and/or the ethics committee are accountable for the company's code of ethics and assist the CEO and the board of directors in formalising the organisation's ethical principles and values."

"The board of directors and CEO share part of the accountability endorsing the work of the executives below: the chief information security officer, chief data officer or data protection officer and chief ethics officer."

Ethical Gap for Data: On the Latent Space of Data Ethics

"There is a degree of uncertainty around the terminology in Ethics related to data, information and AI, but even greater is the lack of clarity in the roles and competencies required to deal with data ethics."

"In data-based companies (namely, companies where data are the main resource for production), the technical complexity of using data and AI algorithms and autonomous systems requires advanced technical skills and specific knowledge of data ethics."

"While the chief ethics officer works on a higher level of ethical granularity that concerns the company's external relations with society and internal relations with its employees, the data protection officer or chief data officer changes the level of abstraction to deal with the legal aspects related to data and personal data and data workers have a technical and performance-focussed approach to data and algorithms."

"The result is that ethical decisions on data and AI algorithms and autonomous systems are outside a defined ethical framework."

Discovering the Data Ethics Layer

"According to Floridi and Taddeo [13], data ethics is "the branch of ethics that studies and evaluates moral problems related to data (including generation, recording, curation, processing, dissemination, sharing, and use), algorithms (including AI, artificial agents, machine learning, and robots), and corresponding practices (including responsible innovation, programming, hacking, and professional codes), in order to formulate and support morally good solutions (e.g. right conducts or right values)"."

"The ethics of practices [...] addresses the pressing questions concerning the responsibilities and liabilities of people and organisations in charge of data processes, strategies and policies, including data scientists, with the goal to define an ethical framework to shape professional codes about responsible innovation, development and usage, which may ensure ethical practices fostering both the progress of data science and the protection of the rights of individuals and groups." [13, p. 3]."

Missing Bodies

"Sections, I argue for (1) the creation of a detailed code of data ethics as well as for the identification of the person accountable for such a code (that is, the chief data ethics officer); (2) the identification of an algorithm risk committee for assessing the level of risk for algorithms; (3) the establishment of a data ethics curriculum for data ethics officers, data-related committees and data workers."

"It is precisely for this reason that the chief data ethics officer ought to be accompanied by an algorithm risk committee, which can assess the potential and latent risks of AI algorithms and autonomous systems before they are put into production."

"It also highlights the importance of a specific data ethics curriculum for data workers, at an operational level, and for the chief data ethics officer and the algorithm risk committee, at a data ethics level."

The Rise of Committees

"The data ethics committee (DEC) should provide theoretical and technical support for the ethical choices made by the chief data ethics officer or the algorithm risk committee."

"The role of the data ethics committee is relevant because there is currently no regulatory support that defines its role and protects it in its function."

"In specific cases, where data impacting the lives and relationships of protected groups have to be processed, it is necessary to set up ad hoc ethics committees with specific expertise to shape internal governance, paying particular attention to the ethical risks associated with the protected category, such as in the case of children's data, students' data, patients' data, marginalised or minority groups' data, etc. A practical example was raised by the publication of the Age-Appropriate Design Code by the UK Information Commissioner's Office [14]."

Overall Accountability and Endorsements

"The aim of this article is to describe the roles of those directly responsible for safeguarding the information ecosystem and thus the infrastructure of ethics (or infra-ethics) within the organisation."

"Perspective, everyone has ethical responsibilities in the handling of data, albeit to different degrees."

"Continuing with our river analogy, we could state that, similar to how everyone must follow navigation rules to ensure a smooth flow, there are also organisations responsible for controlling speed limits and guaranteeing that the banks, warning indicators, and buoys are operating as they should.. Similarly, although in an organisation other c-level bodies have responsibilities in the handling of data (chief human resources officer (Age appropriate), chief operations officer (COO), chief technology officer (CTO), chief financial officer (CFO), etc), the bodies mentioned in this paper are those that have responsibilities and/or accountabilities for safeguarding the ethical quality of the information environment."

Interactions for a Functional Infraethics

"Each body of an organisation and every process involving data or AI systems should not adhere to absolute principles but rather help create and maintain an environment in which ethical reasoning can flourish."

"The four ethical principles of information ethics that aim to handle informational entropy in an informational environment [15, p. 71] should shape governance and practices in the management of data and AI systems in companies."

"In a company, data ethics works to shape the infrastructure that enables the 'control' and 'governance' of informational entropy."

"The role of data ethics is not to run the business, but to have a power of verification and sufficient decision-making autonomy to create an ethical environment that fosters the flourishing of the informational entities that comprise it (thus, following the previous analogy, also of customers, suppliers, etc)."

Conclusions

"The results of this article support the idea that there is a new ethical space within organisations that concerns data ethics."

"This new space contributed to raising important theoretical questions regarding the internal organisation of companies in mature information societies."

"The reflection is limited geographically and culturally because it begins, is grounded on and evolves within on Western philosophies."

"Notwithstanding these limitations, the study suggests the recognition of a specific ethical space focussed on data ethics with the aim of building an ethical infrastructure (or infraethics) within companies."

The AI Ethicist's Dilemma: Fighting Big Tech by Supporting Big Tech [2]

This is a machine-generated summary of:

Sætra, Henrik Skaug; Coeckelbergh, Mark; Danaher, John The AI ethicist's dilemma: fighting Big Tech by supporting Big Tech [2]

Published in: AI and Ethics (2021)

Link to original: https://doi.org/10.1007/s43681-021-00123-7

If you want to cite the papers, please refer to the original.

For technical reasons we could not place the page where the original quote is coming from.

Abstract-Summary

"Assume that a researcher uncovers a major problem with how social media are currently used."

"This situation routinely occurs as ethicists navigate choices regarding how to effect change and potentially remedy the problems they uncover."

"What we refer to as the AI ethicist's dilemma, which emerges when an AI ethicist has to consider how their own success in communicating an identified problem is associated with a high risk of decreasing the chances of successfully remedying the problem."

"The article concludes that attempting to change the world of Big Tech only using the technologies and tools they provide will at times prove to be counterproductive, and that political and other more disruptive avenues of action should also be seriously considered by ethicists who want to effect long-term change."

Introduction

"Assume that a researcher uncovers major problems related to the increased usage of AI and AI based social media."

"This situation routinely occurs as AI ethicists navigate the choices involved in deciding how to effect change and remedy the problems they uncover."

"The dilemma also extends beyond social media, and entails the ethicist's relation to the major technology companies in general."

"These examples relate to what we refer to as the ethicist's dilemma, which emerges when an ethicist has to consider how their own success in communicating an identified challenge is associated with a high risk of decreasing the chances of successfully facing the challenge."

"Deciding what constitutes a moral problem, and thus determining what decisions should go through such a process, often depends on one's personal ethical implied beliefs."

The Moral Problem: The Ethicist's Dilemma

"Unlike, for example, big tobacco, whose power is mainly linked to its access to resources and networks not directly relevant for communicating the challenges created by the tobacco industry, Big Tech has both resources and control of the tools and digital infrastructure required for communicating and raising awareness about the problems that concern the AI ethicist."

"While some might argue that the problems related to AI are the problems of isolated individuals and contexts, we assume that the issues are structural, and that efforts to mitigate negative impacts require working to change a system, and not just to correct or remove individual actors."

"And simplify the moral problem: AI, and AI based social media in particular, negatively impacts individuals and society in non-trivial ways, and the AI ethicist feels obligated take action to counter these impacts."

The Ethicist's Two Main Strategies

"The first strategy entails somehow working with that which one wants to change."

"Summing up: Strategy 1: Seeking change by allying with Big Tech or actively using their technology and infrastructure."

"This route towards change requires that an ethicist steps outside the system to properly assess and observe how it can be undermined, and which alternative strategies exist."

"By adopting such a strategy, the path of change is no longer necessarily determined by the logic of the existing system, and the ethicist is free to consider radically new and different societies and structures of societal and technological interaction."

"Summing up: Strategy 2: Seeking change through distancing oneself from and marginalizing the sources of the problems and allying with other sources of power to effect change."

Evaluating the Ethicist's Options

"Rather than focusing on the consequences of actions, or a set of duties or rules, the virtue ethicist emphasises the virtues associated with a moral character, as seen in relation to what is conducive to ethos."

"As we will see, Big Tech has the power to directly impact individual AI ethicists, and this gives rise to fears of negative consequences and sanctions, etc, but also to considerations of the gains to be had from cooperating with these companies."

"The first three are particularly interesting for evaluating the consequences of actions, while constitutive power in this context is mainly relevant in relation to the generation of harms illuminated by the AI ethicist."

"A deontologically inclined ethicist who has just written a book about the moral rules we ought to follow to challenge the power of Big Tech, for example, should in theory abide by the same rules themselves, unless some universalizable version of the rules in question justify other avenues of action."

What Should the Ethicist Do?

"The most obvious benefit of strategy 1 is that, when successful, it provides a way to be close to the sources of power and to guide and change the exertion of such power in a beneficial way."

"The success of either strategy will depend on how the AI ethicist's power interacts with the power of others."

"In the first strategy, the ethicist needs to ally with powerful people within the system to reach their goals."

"In the second strategy, the alternative proposed by the ethicist can only find wider implementation in society if the ethicist allies with powerful actors outside the system."

"Power is not dirty; in both strategies, it is needed for enabling social change."

"All three ethical theories, in combination, provide good reasons for seriously considering strategy 2 and working to effect change from without the system."

Conclusion

"Turning to the practicalities of change, some rightly argue that political power is dangerous [16]."

"If they are serious about these dangers, it may be necessary to emphasise the political domain and its power to disrupt the technological system."

"Political power must be bridled, but the constructive power of government must also be accepted, and strategy 2 and the path of stronger political regulation, rather than ethics-from-withining and self-regulation is here advocated as necessary, if not sufficient, to solve some of the foundational problems generated by AI."

"Solutions in which 'humane', 'responsible', and 'trustworthy' technology is not determined by the logic of the industries in power, but by drawing on more fundamental political and moral philosophy and fundamental theories of disruptive innovation and social change."

AI Ethics as Subordinated Innovation Network [3]

This is a machine-generated summary of:

Steinhoff, James AI ethics as subordinated innovation network [3]
Published in: AI & SOCIETY (2023)
Link to original: https://doi.org/10.1007/s00146-023-01658-5

If you want to cite the papers, please refer to the original.

For technical reasons we could not place the page where the original quote is coming from.

Abstract-Summary

"AI ethics is proposed, by the Big Tech companies which lead AI research and development, as the cure for diverse social problems posed by the commercialization of data-intensive technologies."

"AI ethics is itself now the subject of wide criticism; most notably, it is accused of being no more than "ethics washing" a cynical means of dissimulation for Big Tech, while it continues its business operations unchanged."

"I argue that AI ethics is indeed ethics washing, but not only that."

"I argue that ethics washing is better understood as a subordinated innovation network: a dispersed network of contributors beyond Big Tech's formal employment whose research is indirectly planned by Big Tech, which also appropriates its results."

"These results are not intended to render AI more ethical, but rather to advance the business processes of data-intensive capital."

"Because the parameters of AI ethics are indirectly set in advance by Big tech, the ostensible goal that AI ethics sets for itself—to resolve the contradiction between business and ethics—is in fact insoluble."

Introduction

"The ethics washing claim is complicated by the fact that AI ethics is not just something done by Big Tech."

"This paper contends that while AI ethics is indeed ethics washing, it also serves the economic exigencies of data-intensive capital more directly."

"AI ethics functions as a subordinated innovation network [17]."

"AI ethics is wracked by an internal contradiction between capital and ethics."

"I show how ethics washing criticisms point to a contradiction immanent to AI ethics."

"Drawing on this theory, I argue that AI ethics is an example of a subordinated innovation network—a dispersed network of labourers whose research is indirectly planned by Big Tech, and whose outputs are appropriated by Big Tech."

"I argue that existing attempts at operationalization provide evidence of Big Tech's subordination of AI ethics research."

Context

"In the wake of manifold scandals including that involving Cambridge Analytica, Facebook and the 2016 US presidential elections, as well as the exposure of Google's secret plans to produce military drone vision systems, the Big Tech firms at the head of the AI industry grappled with a rising social backlash from diverse sectors of society: the so-called "techlash" [18–20]."

"From 2016 on, AI companies began issuing statements proclaiming their ethical AI principles."

"By 2019, nearly all the US Big Tech companies including Microsoft and Google, some Chinese Big Tech companies and organizations such as Baidu and the Artificial Intelligence Industry Alliance, several smaller but influential AI firms such as DeepMind, as well as several think tanks and industry-adjacent organizations like The Partnership on AI had some form of ethical AI principles on display [20, 21]."

Content and Critique

"According to Big Tech, the production of AI commodities is a profoundly ethical endeavour."

"Microsoft [22] declares that it is "committed to the advancement of AI driven by ethical principles that put people first"."

"Big Tech makes an additional claim, asserting that AI ethics are identical to good business sense."

"One might ask: which values and ethical systems are good for the AI industry?"

"An answer to this question is not provided in the ethical AI discourse of Big Tech."

"AI ethics arises in the context of the AI industry."

"According to Hagendorff's [23] analysis, AI ethics understands ethics primarily in terms of principles of accountability, privacy and fairness."

"Such critics agree that AI ethics is "largely deployed to gain competitive advantage (between firms, industries, nations) rather than initiating a genuine push towards social justice" [24]."

Contradiction

"This industrial context generates a contradiction within AI ethics, between capital and ethics."

"The contradiction between ethics and capital manifests in several ways."

"According to these accounts, the contradiction between capital and ethics is manifest in the formation of opposed factions within AI ethics, in addition to its manifestation in the anodyne content of AI ethics, cognitive dissonance of workers, and ineffectiveness in the application of ethical principles."

"The World Economic Forum even aims to surmount the contradiction between ethics and capital via their programme of so-called "stakeholder capitalism" in which the non-ethical Friedmanian logic of shareholder capitalism will be supplanted by a capitalism in which firms "seek long-term value creation by taking into account the needs of all their stakeholders, and society at large" [25]."

"This view that the contradiction between capital and ethics can be overcome has precedents."

"Like business ethics before it, ethical AI faces an insoluble contradiction because a solution would require AI-producing capital to function sub-optimally as capital."

An Ethical Economy?

"Hu [26] makes a similar point, arguing that "just as Big Tech needs 'ethics' on its side to maintain public goodwill, "ethics" ventures need Big Tech for their own legitimacy" (p. 240–241)."

"These groups and efforts survive only because Big Tech has chosen to engage the ethics discourse while it has blocked most other political movement-building" [26, p. 241]."

"Both rightly point out how AI ethics involves people and institutions outside of Big Tech, and they demonstrate how such external actors—whatever their goals—can be brought into alignment with those of Big Tech."

"I contend that AI ethics serves another function of more substantial benefit to Big Tech."

"Hu's analysis points the way to such a line of thought by contending that AI ethics is an avenue chosen by Big Tech while it blocks others."

Intellectual Monopoly Capital

"While global value chains rely on the outsourcing of labour, IMCs outsource innovation via the creation of "innovation networks" consisting of companies, research organizations and universities which work on research and development in ostensible partnership with a monopoly [17, p. 175]."

"While organizations within an innovation network are ostensibly regarded as partners, they lack the power to influence the agenda of the IMC with which they partner, just as contributors to Apple's global value chain are unable to direct the development of the iPhone."

"The creation and control of subordinated innovation networks is thus an advanced form of planning which depends on the "capacity of certain firms to organize long-term capital accumulation beyond their legally owned capital" [17, p. 11]."

"As an advanced form of capitalist planning, the IMC model does not attempt to enclose innovation commons in a conventional sense, instead it grants them ostensible autonomy while directing its operations and appropriating its outputs—what Rikap calls subordination."

AI Ethics as Subordinated Innovation Network

"The AI ethics phenomenon as a whole performs an innovation function for the Big Tech companies which are capable of productively appropriating the output of this network."

""the plan" for AI ethics is not to resolve the contradiction between capital and ethics, but to maintain it, as this interminable conflict is potentially productive of new ideas which are predisposed not to conflict fundamentally with capitalist AI production, including the making of new commodities or otherwise enhancing business processes."

"The first path is to acknowledge the insolubility of the contradiction between capital and ethics, and thus to render fruitless one's own AI ethics research (and undermine one's chances of funding from industry sources)."

"The dispersed labourers of the AI ethics innovation network are subordinated to the IMCs which lead AI research and production."

Case Studies: The Operationalization of AI Ethics

"IBM has published a report on "AI ethics in action" [27] and Microsoft has established no less than three internal groups tasked with AI ethics operationalization: the AETHER Committee, the Office of Responsible AI (ORA), Responsible AI Strategy in Engineering (RAISE) as well as other groups devoted to ethics more broadly, including the Ethics and Society team."

"In this document, Cussins Newman [28] analyses three attempts at operationalizing ethical AI principles, two of which are relevant to this paper."

"Cussins Newman [28] praises OpenAI for operationalizing AI ethics in the staggered release of their large language model GPT-2."

"Cussins Newman [28] holds that this approach effectively operationalized AI ethics, bucked industry and computer science trends and allowed OpenAI to conscientiously "monitor uses, engage with partner organizations on particular research questions, and promote awareness of impacts" [29]."

Conclusion

"AI ethics recruits capital's enemies to contribute to a subordinated innovation network, but a peculiar one that dares not speak its true purpose, and necessarily fails in its expressed purpose."

"Any interesting AI ethics needs to begin from a perspective which does not prioritize the needs of capital or accept them as given."

"This would be an AI ethics which acknowledges the fundamental and insoluble contradiction between the accumulation of capital and human flourishing in its myriad forms, one of which is the ethical sphere."

"The insoluble contradiction within AI ethics should be brought to the fore and explicitly addressed."

AI Ethics and Its Pitfalls: Not Living Up to Its Own Standards? [4]

This is a machine-generated summary of:

Hagendorff, Thilo AI ethics and its pitfalls: not living up to its own standards? [4]

Published in: AI and Ethics (2022)

Link to original: https://doi.org/10.1007/s43681-022-00173-5

If you want to cite the papers, please refer to the original.

For technical reasons we could not place the page where the original quote is coming from.

Abstract-Summary

"Demands for implementing AI ethics and ethicists into AI organizations, especially corporations, are ubiquitous."

"The assumption that AI ethicists have particular epistemological advantages compared to non-ethicists as well as the idea that AI ethics automatically decreases the likelihood of unethical outcomes are both flawed."

"The compilation of risks comprises psychological considerations concerning the cognitive biases of AI ethicists themselves as well as biased reactions to their work, subject-specific and knowledge constraints AI ethicists often succumb to, negative side effects of ethics audits for AI applications, and many more."

Introduction

"Apart from these advantages, embedding ethicists or AI ethics principles in AI organizations bears a range of specific risks that are hitherto disregarded in the field of AI ethics itself."

"This comment discusses and lists risks that either originate from AI ethicists themselves or from the consequences their embedding in AI organizations has."

"The compilation of risks comprises psychological considerations of thinking about ethics and acting (un)ethically, subject-specific and knowledge constraints AI ethicists often succumb to, the complicated professional role of AI ethicists, the missing impact of AI ethics guidelines, as well as negative side effects of ethics audits for AI products."

Risks

"Several types of risks are discussed that are tied specifically to the inclusion of professional AI ethicists, ethical considerations, or ethical audits in organizations researching and developing AI systems and applications."

"If they do not keep it in mind, non-ethicists like AI practitioners are in no way less competent or versed in reaching morally right and ethically reflective decisions in their field compared to professional AI ethicists."

"Factors of bounded ethicality can, as long as AI ethicists do not acknowledge and address them in AI practitioners, increase the likelihood of unethical decision-making, rationalize it, or reframe it in a misleading way."

"To effectively improve ethical decision-making in AI practitioners, AI ethicists must go beyond simply conveying knowledge about ethical issues."

"Providing behavioral training is not a common practice for AI ethicists, besides its importance in increasing the likelihood of ethical decision-making."

Conclusion

"It seems that AI ethics is a discipline that necessarily reduces the likelihood of unethical outcomes in the AI field."

"These risks relate to psychological considerations about bounded ethicality in ethicists themselves, to considerations regarding the individuals who react to (or ignore) ethical principles and advice, to the complicated professional role of AI ethicists, the lack of impact of AI ethics guidelines, or the potential negative side effects of ethics audits for AI products."

"The comment also stresses that implementing AI ethics is not as straightforward and self-explanatory as it seems to be."

"These side effects should be avoided to turn AI ethics into a discipline that can live up to its own standards."

The Uselessness of AI Ethics [6]

This is a machine-generated summary of:

Munn, Luke The uselessness of AI ethics [6]

Published in: AI and Ethics (2022)

Link to original: https://doi.org/10.1007/s43681-022-00209-w

If you want to cite the papers, please refer to the original.

For technical reasons we could not place the page where the original quote is coming from.

Abstract-Summary

"As the awareness of AI's power and danger has risen, the dominant response has been a turn to ethical principles."

"I argue that AI ethical principles are useless, failing to mitigate the racial, social, and environmental damages of AI technologies in any meaningful sense."

"In a zero-sum world, the dominant turn to AI principles is not just fruitless but a dangerous distraction, diverting immense financial and human resources away from potentially more effective activity."

"I conclude by highlighting alternative approaches to AI justice that go beyond ethical principles: thinking more broadly about systems of oppression and more narrowly about accuracy and auditing."

Introduction

"The public and private sectors have released guidelines, frameworks, and principles that are meant to apply when creating new AI technology."

"There are the Beijing AI Principles, DeepMind's Ethics, and Society Principles [30], IEEE's Ethically Aligned Design [31], the Guidelines for Artificial Intelligence by Deutsche Telekom [32], and the Vatican AI Principles known as the Rome Call for AI Ethics [33]."

"The list of AI Principles at AI Ethicist now stretches to over 80 entries, with more being constantly added [34]."

"This article argues that this deluge of AI ethical principles is largely useless."

"While this view is provocative, it is hardly alone: a growing sea of voices have begun critiquing the de-facto turn to AI ethical principles as ineffective [29, 35–37]."

"The result of this failure is a gulf between high-minded ideals and technological development on the ground—a gap between principles and practice."

"The final section argues that, in a zero-sum world, the obsession with AI principles is not just useless but dangerous in funneling human and financial resources 0away from more productive approaches."

Meaningless Principles

"Mittelstadt [38, p. 501] suggests that work on AI ethics has largely produced "vague, high-level principles, and value statements which promise to be action-guiding, but in practice provide few specific recommendations and fail to address fundamental normative and political tensions embedded in key concepts.""

"Despite the mushrooming of ethical statements, Floridi and Cowls [39] suggest many values recur frequently and can be condensed into five core principles: beneficence, non-maleficence, autonomy, justice, and explicability."

"In the Montreal principles [40, p. 545] for instance, "well-being" is the term used, suggesting that AI development should promote the "well-being of all sentient creatures.""

"In this Statement, beneficence is gestured to through the concept of "sustainability," asserting that AI must promote the basic preconditions for life on the planet."

"If sustainability is ambiguous, so are many of the key terms used in AI ethics frameworks."

"Many key concepts in AI frameworks, then, are overburdened, brimming with contradictory meanings."

Isolated Principles

"If the tech industry lacks ethics, so does the education of the software engineers and technologists who will soon join it."

"There is little to no consideration of ethical challenges—how technology intersects with race, class, and culture and how these might introduce new harms or exacerbate existing inequalities [41]."

"The lack of ethical training in education, combined with the lack of ethical application in the industry, suggests that AI development takes place in an ethically empty milieu."

"The problem-space considered when developing a technology is far too narrow, failing to encompass the ethical, moral, and social impacts of designing a product in a particular way [42]."

"Such an ethical framework, situated "downstream" from company culture, will fail to address the more fundamental inequalities and underlying social issues that shape technological development."

Toothless Principles

"AI ethical principles have failed due to the lack of consequences."

"AI ethical frameworks can set normative ideals but lack the mechanisms to enforce compliance with these values and principles [29]."

"After surveying 22 sets of guidelines, Hagendorff [23] concludes that AI ethics is failing on many levels; they lack any enforcement mechanisms and their values are easily overwritten by economic incentives, often becoming little more than marketing devices."

"Legislation takes time to draft, pass, and enforce, and in this sense, Nemitz [43] describes the focus on AI ethics and the subsequent deferral of regulation as a genius move by corporations."

"Values listed in AI ethics statements and proposed by AI ethics organizations adhere closely to corporate values (or as the first section demonstrated, can be interpreted in ways that align with them)."

The Principles/Practice Gap

"While all the participants acknowledged the importance of ethics, when asked whether their AI development practices took ethics into account, all respondents answered no [44]."

"Building on this empirically based research, the authors suggest that there is a significant gap between the research and practice of AI ethics [45]."

"Hagendorff [23, p. 103] for instance, makes a number of salient points but also suggests that privacy and fairness, which occur frequently in ethical frameworks, are aspects for which "technical fixes can be or have already been developed.""

"Krijger [46] suggests there are two key tensions that apply when attempting to operationalize AI ethics: an inter-principle tension, where competing ethical demands are placed on an AI design; and an intra-principle tension, which highlights the difficulty of materializing a principle into a technological form."

Alternatives to Ethical Principles

"AI justice provides a useful term that productively expands the ethical scope of inquiry and intervention."

"As Gabriel [47, p. 218] notes, AI justice "reframes much of the discussion around 'AI ethics' by drawing attention to the fact that the moral properties of algorithms are not internal to the models themselves but rather a product of the social systems within which they are deployed.""

"AI justice may provide useful ways to problematize a taken-for-granted principle like "fairness" which appears across many ethical frameworks."

"Those who develop AI need to better understand the particular needs of these communities, and then work with them in meaningful ways to ensure that AI contributes to their well-being and does not exacerbate historical inequities."

"Such work does not invoke the grand scope of AI ethics, but often uses more mundane but better-understood terms: accuracy, alignment, mismatch, and impacts."

In Defense of Ethical Guidelines [48]

This is a machine-generated summary of:

Lundgren, Björn In defense of ethical guidelines [48]

Published in: AI and Ethics (2023)

Link to original: https://doi.org/10.1007/s43681-022-00244-7

If you want to cite the papers, please refer to the original.

For technical reasons we could not place the page where the original quote is coming from.

Abstract-Summary

"He argued that ethical guidelines are useless."

Introduction

"Luke Munn argued that AI guidelines are useless."

"I aim to defend ethical guidelines."

"Ethical guidelines for AI development and use are in their methodological adolescence and, as I will argue, there are possible fixes to the problems that Munn identifies."

"I give a brief contextualization of AI ethics and ethical guidelines, aiming to explain how the former can inform the latter, and how both can inform standards and regulations."

"In this commentary, I will rely heavily on a set of guidelines that in turn build on a large survey of guidelines [49], but see also [10] for a recent overview of ethical guidelines for AI."

AI Ethics and Ethical Guidelines

"One of the most fundamental challenges for ethical guidelines for AI is not first-order ethical inquires (i.e., questions of what is right, wrong, permissible, impermissible, and so forth), but rather second-order problems regarding how we can translate known ethical principles into understandable goals."

"In a survey of 84 ethical guidelines for AI the following principles were identified in the majority of the guidelines (number of documents in parenthesis): transparency (73), justice and fairness (68), non-maleficence (60), responsibility (60), and privacy (47) [10], which illustrates that there is at least some international consensus emerging on basic principles."

"This illustrates how ethical guidelines work on a much more practical level than AI ethics and how they must therefore be informed by, and adapt to, the empirical conditions (e.g., as can be seen in the requirement above, the requirement specifies in which development phases the conditions are especially important)."

Responding to the Critique and Munn's Proposal

"As he correctly notes, a problem with guidelines is that they often include fuzzy abstract higher-order principles, which is part of the reason why ethical guidelines should be operationalized (i.e., simply put, turning requirements into conditions that can be properly evaluated)."

"To say, the guidelines must make it clear to the designer (or user) when they have satisfied an ethical requirement, but the guidelines do not need to supply a pathway for how to achieve that goal."

"The problem, Munn, thinks, is that the tech industry has a toxic culture and hence, "Unethical AI is the logical byproduct of an unethical industry." [6] This is not necessarily a problem for guidelines, since guidelines can and do address this by requiring ethical standards among developers."

"As Munn argues, this implies a need for stakeholder engagement, which, as previously mentioned, is already a central part of many ethical guidelines, some of which specifically mention minorities and underrepresented groups (e.g., [49])."

Final Comments

"While Munn is correct in saying that there are limitations to what ethical guidelines and principles can do, most of his critique is based on cherry-picking."

"As I have shown in the article, ethical guidelines are already far more progressed than what is reflected in Munn's critique and his own proposals."

"Such guidelines illustrate both how the critique misses the target and a path forward given the challenges we actually are facing."

"There are clear challenges for ethical guidelines."

"Although contextual differences can be challenging, there are plausible pathways for ethical guidelines to resolve these issues."

"As I have argued, the former is not a problem for the guidelines, but a matter that must be solved by other means (e.g., through regulations or self-enforcement through standards)."

"It arguably should not be, since tying guidelines to particular technical solutions would limit the potential for benefitting from technical progress."

References

1. Cocchiaro, M. Z., Morley, J., Novelli, C., Panai, E., Tartaro, A., & Floridi, L. (2025). Who is an AI ethicist? An empirical study of expertise, skills, and profiles to build a competency framework. *AI and Ethics, 5*. https://doi.org/10.1007/s43681-024-00643-y
2. Sætra, H. S., Coeckelbergh, M., & Danaher, J. (2021). The AI ethicist's dilemma: Fighting big tech by supporting big tech. *AI and Ethics, 2*. https://doi.org/10.1007/s43681-021-00123-7
3. Steinhoff, J. (2024). AI ethics as subordinated innovation network. *AI & Society, 39*(4), 1995–2007. https://doi.org/10.1007/s00146-023-01658-5
4. Hagendorff, T. (2022). AI ethics and its pitfalls: Not living up to its own standards? *AI and Ethics*. https://doi.org/10.1007/s43681-022-00173-5
5. Panai, E. (2023). The latent space of data ethics. *AI & Society*. https://doi.org/10.1007/s00146-023-01757-3
6. Munn, L. (2022). The uselessness of AI ethics. *AI and Ethics*. https://doi.org/10.1007/s43681-022-00209-w
7. Phan, T., Goldenfein, J., Kuch, D., & Mann, M. (Eds.). (2022). *Economies of virtue–the circulation of 'ethics' in AI*. Institute of Network Cultures. https://mediarep.org/handle/doc/20441
8. Brummett, A. (2023). Burying the basilisk of bioethics: What can be resolved, dissolved, and refocused in the ethics expertise debate. *Bioethics, 37*(6), 515–522.
9. Watson, J. C., & Guidry-Grimes, L. K. (2018). Introduction. In J. C. Watson & L. K. Guidry-Grimes (Eds.), *Moral expertise: New essays from theoretical and clinical bioethics* (pp. 1–33). Springer International Publishing. https://doi.org/10.1007/978-3-319-92759-6_1
10. Jobin, A., Ienca, M., & Vayena, E. (2019). The global landscape of AI ethics guidelines. *Nature Machine Intelligence, 1*(9), 389–399. https://doi.org/10.1038/s42256-019-0088-2
11. California Consumer Privacy Act (CCPA) (2019). California Civil Code §§ 1798.100–1798.199. Available at: https://leginfo.legislature.ca.gov/faces/codes_displayText.xhtml?division=3.&part=4.&lawCode=CIV&title=1.81.5
12. European Commission. (2016). Regulation (EU) 2016/679 of the European Parliament and of the Council of 27 April 2016 on the protection of natural persons with regard to the processing of personal data and on the free movement of such data, and repealing Directive 95/46/EC (General Data Protection Regulation), OJEU L119, 04/05/2016. *Official Journal of the European Union*. http://eur-lex.europa.eu/pri/en/oj/dat/2003/l_285/l_28520031101en00330037.pdf
13. Floridi, L., & Taddeo, M. (2016). What is data ethics? *Philosophical Transactions of the Royal Society A: Mathematical, Physical and Engineering Sciences, 374*(2083), 20160360. https://doi.org/10.1098/rsta.2016.0360
14. ICO. (2020). *Age appropriate design: A code of practice for online services*. https://ico.org.uk/for-organisations/guide-to-data-protection/ico-codes-of-practice/age-appropriate-design-code
15. Floridi, L. (2013). *The ethics of information*. Oxford University Press.
16. Chomanski, B. (2021). The missing ingredient in the case for regulating big tech. *Minds & Machines*. https://doi.org/10.1007/s11023-021-09562-x
17. Rikap, C. (2021). *Capitalism, power and innovation: Intellectual monopoly capitalism uncovered*. Routledge.
18. Rosenberg, M., Confessore, N., & Cadwalladr, C. (2018). How trump consultants exploited the Facebook data of millions. *The New York Times*. 17 March. https://www.nytimes.com/2018/03/17/us/politics/cambridge-analytica-trump-campaign.html. Accessed 30 Nov 2022.
19. Foroohar R. (2018). Year in a word: Techlash. *Financial Times*. 16 December. https://www.ft.com/content/76578fba-fca1-11e8-ac00-57a2a826423e
20. Green, B. (2021). The contestation of tech ethics: A sociotechnical approach to technology ethics in practice. *Journal of Social Computing, 2*(3), 209–225. https://doi.org/10.23919/JSC.2021.0018

21. Arcesati, R. (2021). *Lofty principles, conflicting incentives: AI ethics and governance in China*. Mercator Institute for China Studies. https://merics.org/en/report/lofty-principles-conflicting-incentives-ai-ethics-and-governance-china
22. Microsoft. (n.d.). *Responsible AI principles from Microsoft*. https://www.microsoft.com/en-us/ai/responsible-ai. Accessed 9 Nov 2022.
23. Hagendorff, T. (2020). The ethics of AI ethics: An evaluation of guidelines. *Minds and Machines, 30*(1), 99–120. https://doi.org/10.1007/s11023-020-09517-8
24. Sloane, M. (2019). Inequality is the name of the game. Thoughts on the emerging field of technology, ethics and social justice. In *Proceedings of the Weizenbaum conference 2019 challenges of digital inequality – digital education, digital work, digital life* (pp. 1–9).
25. Schwab, K., & Vanham, P. (2021). *Stakeholder capitalism: A global economy that works for progress, people and planet*. Wiley.
26. Hu, L. (2021). Tech ethics: Speaking ethics to power, or power speaking ethics? *Journal of Social Computing, 2*(3), 238–248. https://doi.org/10.23919/JSC.2021.0033
27. IBM Cloud Education. (2022). *AI ethics*. https://www.ibm.com/cloud/learn/ai-ethics. Accessed 23 Nov 2022.
28. Cussins Newman, J. (2020). *Decision points in AI governance: Three case studies explore efforts to operationalize AI principles*. UC Berkeley, Center for Long-Term Cybersecurity.
29. Rességuier, A., & Rodrigues, R. (2020). AI ethics should not remain toothless! A call to bring back the teeth of ethics. *Big Data & Society, 7*, 1–5.
30. DeepMind. (2020). *Ethics & society*. https://www.deepmind.com/about/ethics-and-society. Accessed 25 May 2022.
31. IEEE Global Initiative on Ethics of Autonomous and Intelligent Systems. (2019). *Ethically aligned design: A vision for prioritizing human well-being with autonomous and intelligent systems*. IEEE. https://ethicsinaction.ieee.org/
32. Deutsche Telekom. (2018). *AI guidelines*. April 24. https://www.telekom.com/resource/blob/532446/f32ea4f5726ff3ed3902e97dd945fa14/dl-180710-ki-leitlinien-en-data.pdf
33. Pontifical Academy for Life. (2020). *Rome call for AI ethics*. The Vatican. https://www.romecall.org/wp-content/uploads/2022/03/RomeCall_Paper_web.pdf
34. AI Ethicist. (2021). *AI principles*. AI Ethicist. https://www.aiethicist.org/ai-principles
35. Lauer, D. (2021). You cannot have AI ethics without ethics. *AI and Ethics, 1*(1), 21–25. https://doi.org/10.1007/s43681-020-00013-4
36. Morley, J., Elhalal, A., Garcia, F., Kinsey, L., Mökander, J., & Floridi, L. (2021). Ethics as a service: A pragmatic operationalisation of AI ethics. *Minds and Machines, 31*(2), 239–256. https://doi.org/10.1007/s11023-021-09563-w
37. Vakkuri, V., Kemell, K.-K., Jantunen, M., & Abrahamsson, P. (2020). 'This is just a prototype': How ethics are ignored in software startup-like environments. In *International conference on agile software development* (pp. 195–210). Springer.
38. Mittelstadt, B. (2019). Principles alone cannot guarantee ethical AI. *Nature Machine Intelligence, 1*, 501–507.
39. Floridi, L., & Cowls, J. (2019). A unified framework of five principles for AI in society. *Harvard Data Science Review*. https://doi.org/10.1162/99608f92.8cd550d1
40. Université de Montréal. (2018). *The declaration*. Université de Montréal. https://www.montrealdeclaration-responsibleai.com/the-declaration
41. Reidy, M. (2017). *Lack of ethics education for computer programmers shocks expert*. Stuff. July 1. https://www.stuff.co.nz/business/innovation/93629356/minimal-ethics-education-for-computer-programmers
42. Oswald, D. (2016). From ethics to politics: If design is problem solving, what then are the problems. In *Proceedings of the 18th International Conference on Engineering and Product Design Education* (pp. 620–625).
43. Nemitz, P. (2018). Constitutional democracy and technology in the age of artificial intelligence. *Philosophical Transactions of the Royal Society A: Mathematical, Physical and Engineering Sciences, 376*(2133), 1–13. https://doi.org/10.1098/rsta.2018.0089

44. Vakkuri, V., Kemell, K.-K., Kultanen, J., Siponen, M., & Abrahamsson, P. (2019). *Ethically aligned design of autonomous systems: Industry viewpoint and an empirical study*. https://doi.org/10.48550/arXiv.1906.07946
45. Sambasivan, N., Arnesen, E., Hutchinson, B., & Prabhakaran, V. (2020). *Non portability of algorithmic fairness in India*. http://arxiv.org/abs/2012.03659 [Cs]
46. Krijger, J. (2021). Enter the metrics: Critical theory and organizational operationalization of AI ethics. *AI & Society*. https://doi.org/10.1007/s00146-021-01256-3
47. Gabriel, I. (2022). Toward a theory of justice for artificial intelligence. *Daedalus, 151*(2), 218–231. https://doi.org/10.1162/daed_a_01911
48. Lundgren, B. (2023). In defense of ethical guidelines. *AI and Ethics, 3*. https://doi.org/10.1007/s43681-022-00244-7
49. Brey, P., Lundgren, B., Macnish, K., & Ryan, M. (2019). *Guidelines for the development and use of SIS. Deliverable D3.2 of the SHERPA project*. https://doi.org/10.21253/DMU.11316833.v3

Chapter 2
AI Ethics Advisory and Principlism: Bridging Theory and Practice

Abstract Presented here is the philosophical foundations and practical applications of principlism in AI ethics. It discusses core ethical principles like beneficence, autonomy, justice, and explainability, critically assessing their effectiveness and limitations when operationalised in real-world settings. The chapter highlights the gap between ethical theory and practice, examining issues of enforceability, corporate co-option, and interpretative divergences. It argues for an institutional embedding of ethics, recommending an active role for AI ethics advisors to navigate competing interests and to ensure that ethical reasoning informs policy and practice.

Keywords Principlism · Ethical frameworks · Normative ethics · Moral reasoning · Theory-practice gap

Introduction by the Editor

The growing integration of AI into decision-making processes across domains such as healthcare, finance, law enforcement, and governance has rendered the role of the AI ethicist both indispensable and increasingly complex. As these technologies evolve, they generate novel ethical challenges that call for responses rooted in moral philosophy, social justice, and human rights. But what defines ethical AI, and which normative principles should guide practitioners in their professional engagement? This chapter addresses these questions by examining foundational ethical frameworks, comparing diverse perspectives, and exploring the difficulties of translating ethics into operational practice.

A. Carnevale, *The AI Ethics Advisor*,
https://doi.org/10.1007/978-3-032-05526-2_2

Establishing a Framework for Ethical AI

Numerous AI ethics frameworks have emerged in recent years, often organised around five widely recognised principles: beneficence, non-maleficence, autonomy, justice, and explicability [1]. These values feature prominently in major declarations such as the Montreal Declaration and the Asilomar AI Principles, which stress the importance of fairness, human agency, and collective welfare [2]. Despite their theoretical appeal, such frameworks have been criticised for their vagueness and the lack of enforceable mechanisms, which undermines their impact on real-world scenarios [3].

Autonomy, for example, entails that AI systems respect human decision-making. The Asilomar Principles explicitly affirm that humans should retain control over whether and how to delegate decisions to machines [2]. This reflects a Kantian emphasis on individual agency. Yet in practice, this ideal is frequently compromised—particularly in contexts like hiring or credit scoring—where opaque algorithms make consequential decisions with minimal oversight [4].

Justice is equally central to AI governance. Drawing from Rawlsian theories, many ethical guidelines stress that AI should not reinforce structural inequality [5]. The Montreal Declaration similarly urges the elimination of discrimination in AI design [2]. Nonetheless, algorithmic bias continues to disproportionately affect marginalised communities, exposing the fragility of principle-based approaches that remain largely aspirational [6].

Transparency and explainability are also critical to fostering accountability and public trust. Without them, AI systems risk functioning as inscrutable "black boxes." Frameworks such as AI4People identify explainability as vital for protecting social welfare [2]. Yet, high-performing models—particularly deep learning systems—are often inherently difficult to interpret, creating tension between accuracy and intelligibility [7].

Accountability presents further complications. Many AI systems lack clear responsibility chains, which makes it difficult to assign blame when harm occurs. Effective accountability requires action at multiple levels—developers, executives, regulators—but current governance mechanisms often lag behind technical innovation [8, 9].

Beneficence, the call to design AI for societal good, remains a powerful normative aspiration. It is particularly relevant in domains such as healthcare and climate mitigation. However, concerns are mounting over "ethics washing," whereby companies adopt ethical language superficially without committing to substantive governance reforms [10].

Cross-Cutting Insights

The recurring challenge across all these principles is their limited translation into practice. Although autonomy, beneficence, justice, non-maleficence, and explicability are now standard in AI ethics discourse [1, 2], their impact is undermined by conceptual ambiguity, lack of enforceability, and the risk of corporate co-option [3, 8].

Principles alone cannot structure ethical practice. They must confront institutional, technical, and economic dynamics that frequently hinder meaningful implementation. Autonomy is difficult to preserve when algorithmic decisions operate with limited human scrutiny [2, 4], just as justice is elusive when systems reproduce social bias due to flawed datasets or minimal stakeholder input [5, 6].

Moreover, the push for transparency often collides with the technical opacity of complex models, thereby constraining the applicability of explainability and accountability in real-world settings [7, 11].

Addressing these tensions requires moving beyond high-level declarations towards deeper institutional embedding. Ethical reflection should not be treated as an ancillary exercise, but rather as an operational dimension of AI development—shaping design decisions, distributing responsibility, and informing governance structures throughout the AI lifecycle [8, 9].

This shift demands new professional roles, notably that of the AI ethics advisor. Situated at the crossroads of technical, legal, and organisational domains, the advisor is uniquely positioned to mediate between abstract values and concrete practices. Their task is to surface ethical risks, translate normative commitments into processual safeguards, and facilitate interdisciplinary deliberation. Rather than acting as a passive custodian of principles, the advisor becomes a strategic actor capable of challenging inertia and resisting superficial ethical posturing.

Conclusion: From Principles to Practice

The gap between ethical ideals and practical realities defines one of the central dilemmas of AI governance. Ethicists and advisors must navigate competing interests, commercial incentives, and political constraints to ensure that ethics becomes embedded in policy and practice—not merely invoked in rhetoric.

This is not just a philosophical challenge, but a structural one. AI is developed within socio-technical assemblages shaped by asymmetries of power, disciplinary fragmentation, and market pressures. Ethical principles cannot simply be imposed from above; they must be negotiated, adapted, and institutionalised within the specific logics of AI design and deployment.

In this context, the role of the AI ethics advisor is vital. When empowered and supported, this figure embodies a shift from abstract principlism to embedded ethical competence. Their presence affirms that ethical reflection is not an afterthought, but a constitutive element of responsible innovation.

This chapter argues that such a transition is imperative if AI ethics is to move beyond symbolic affirmation and begin shaping the actual conditions under which AI systems are conceived, built, and governed.

Machine Generated Summaries

A Unified Framework of Five Principles for AI in Society [1]

This is a machine-generated summary of:

Floridi, Luciano; Cowls, Josh A Unified Framework of Five Principles for AI in Society [1]

Published in: Philosophical Studies Series (2021)

Link to original: https://doi.org/10.1007/978-3-030-81907-1_2

If you want to cite the papers, please refer to the original.

For technical reasons we could not place the page where the original quote is coming from.

Abstract-Summary

"Many organizations have launched a wide range of initiatives to establish ethical principles for the adoption of socially beneficial AI."

"We report the results of a fine-grained analysis of several of the highest-profile sets of ethical principles for AI."

"We assess whether these principles converge upon a set of agreed-upon principles, or diverge, with significant disagreement over what constitutes 'ethical AI.'"

"Our analysis finds a high degree of overlap among the sets of principles we analyze."

"We then identify an overarching framework consisting of five core principles for ethical AI."

"On the basis of our comparative analysis, we argue that a new principle is needed in addition: explicability, understood as incorporating both the epistemological sense of intelligibility (as an answer to the question 'how does it work?') and in the ethical sense of accountability (as an answer to the question: 'who is responsible for the way it works?')."

Introduction

"Many organizations have launched a wide range of initiatives to establish ethical principles for the adoption of socially beneficial AI."

"Either the various sets of ethical principles for AI are similar, leading to unnecessary repetition and redundancy, or, if they differ significantly, confusion and ambiguity will result instead."

"We report the results of a fine-grained analysis of several of the highest-profile sets of ethical principles for AI."

"We assess whether these principles are convergent, with a set of agreed-upon principles, or divergent, with significant disagreement over what constitutes 'ethical AI.'"

Artificial Intelligence: A Research Area in Search of a Definition

"AI paradigms still satisfy the classic definition provided by John McCarthy, Marvin Minsky, Nathaniel Rochester, and Claude Shannon in their seminal Proposal for the Dartmouth Summer Research Project on Artificial Intelligence, the founding document and later event that established the new field of AI in 1955: For the present purpose the artificial intelligence problem is taken to be that of making a machine behave in ways that would be called intelligent if a human were so behaving. (Quotation from the 2006 re-issue in McCarthy and others [12] [1955])."

"This is a counterfactual: were a human to behave in that way, that behaviour would be called intelligent."

"It does not mean that the machine is intelligent, or even thinking."

"This is sufficiently general to capture the many ways in which AI is discussed in the documents we analyse in the rest of this article."

A Unified Framework of Five Principles for Ethical AI

"The Asilomar document similarly supports the principle of autonomy, insofar as "humans should choose how and whether to delegate decisions to AI systems, to accomplish human-chosen objectives."".

"The importance of 'justice' is explicitly cited in the Montreal Declaration, which argues that "the development of AI should promote justice and seek to eliminate all types of discrimination," while the Asilomar Principles include the need for both "shared benefit" and "shared prosperity" from AI."

"It complements the other four principles: for AI to be beneficent and non-maleficent, we must be able to understand the good or harm it is actually doing to society, and in which ways; for AI to promote and not constrain human autonomy, our 'decision about who should decide' must be informed by knowledge of how AI would act instead of us; and for AI to be just, we must know whom to hold accountable in the event of a serious, negative outcome, which would require in turn adequate understanding of why this outcome arose."

AI Ethics: Whence and for Whom?

"Each of the six sets of ethical principles for AI that we analyzed emerged either from initiatives with global scope, or from within western liberal democracies."

"In its State Council Notice on AI and elsewhere, the Chinese government has expressed interest in further consideration of the social and ethical impact of AI [13, 14]."

"This has been echoed by claims that ethics may be "Europe's silver bullet" in the "global AI battle" [15]."

"Every company, government agency, and academic institution designing, developing or deploying AI has an obligation to do so in line with an ethical framework along the lines of the one we present here, broadened to incorporate a more geographically, culturally, and socially diverse array of perspectives [16]."

Conclusion: From Principles to Practices

"If the framework presented in this article provides a coherent and sufficiently comprehensive overview of the central ethical principles for AI [2], then it can serve as the architecture within which laws, rules, technical standards, and best practices are developed for specific sectors, industries, and jurisdictions."

"The framework played a valuable role in the work of AI4People, Europe's first global forum on the social impact of AI, which recently adopted it to propose 20 concrete recommendations for a 'Good AI Society' to the European Commission [2]."

"We believe that the framework presented here as emerging from the current debate will serve as valuable architecture for securing positive social outcomes from AI technology and move from good principles to good practices [17, 18]."

AI4People: An Ethical Framework for a Good AI Society—Opportunities, Risks, Principles, and Recommendations [2]

This is a machine-generated summary of:

Floridi, Luciano; Cowls, Josh; Beltrametti, Monica; Chatila, Raja; Chazerand, Patrice; Dignum, Virginia; Luetge, Christoph; Madelin, Robert; Pagallo, Ugo; Rossi, Francesca; Schafer, Burkhard; Valcke, Peggy; Vayena, Effy AI4People—An Ethical Framework for a Good AI Society: Opportunities, Risks, Principles, and Recommendations [2]

Published in: Minds and Machines (2018)

Link to original: https://doi.org/10.1007/s11023-018-9482-5

If you want to cite the papers, please refer to the original.

For technical reasons we could not place the page where the original quote is coming from.

Abstract-Summary

"If adopted, these recommendations would serve as a firm foundation for the establishment of a Good AI Society."

Introduction

"AI4People was set up to help steer this powerful force towards the good of society, everyone in it, and the environments we share."

"This article is the outcome of the collaborative effort by the AI4People Scientific Committee—comprising 12 experts and chaired by Luciano Floridi—to propose a series of recommendations for the development of a Good AI Society."

"The article synthesises three things: the opportunities and associated risks that AI technologies offer for fostering human dignity and promoting human flourishing; the principles that should undergird the adoption of AI; and 20 specific recommendations that, if adopted, will enable all stakeholders to seize the opportunities, to avoid or at least minimise and counterbalance the risks, to respect the principles, and hence to develop a Good AI Society."

"Through this work, we hope to have contributed to the foundation of a Good AI Society we can all share."

The Opportunities and Risks of AI for Society

"AI can be used to foster human nature and its potentialities, thus creating opportunities; underused, thus creating opportunity costs; or overused and misused, thus creating risks."

"If developed thoughtfully, AI offers the opportunity of improving and multiplying the possibilities for human agency."

"Whether by preventing and curing diseases or optimising transportation and logistics, the use of AI technologies presents countless possibilities for reinventing society by radically enhancing what humans are collectively capable of."

"If we rely on the use of AI technologies to augment our own abilities in the wrong way, we may delegate important tasks and above all decisions to autonomous systems that should remain at least partly subject to human supervision and choice."

"The risk is that AI systems may erode human self-determination, as they may lead to unplanned and unwelcome changes in human behaviours to accommodate the routines that make automation work and people's lives easier."

The Dual Advantage of an Ethical Approach to AI

"The value of an ethical approach to AI technologies comes into starker relief."

"Adopting an ethical approach to AI confers what we define here as a "dual advantage"."

"On one side, ethics enables organisations to take advantage of the social value that AI enables."

"Public acceptance and adoption of AI technologies will occur only if the benefits are seen as meaningful and risks as potential, yet preventable, minimisable, or at least something against which one can be protected, through risk management (e.g. insurance) or redressing."

"An ethical approach to AI can also be seen as an early warning system against risks that might endanger entire organisations."

"The clear value to any organisation of the dual advantage of an ethical approach to AI amply justifies the expense of engagement, openness, and contestability that such an approach requires."

A Unified Framework of Principles for AI in Society

"The Asilomar document similarly supports the principle of autonomy, insofar as "humans should choose how and whether to delegate decisions to AI systems, to accomplish human-chosen objectives"."

"It complements the other four principles: for AI to be beneficent and non-maleficent, we must be able to understand the good or harm it is actually doing to society, and in which ways; for AI to promote and not constrain human autonomy, our "decision about who should decide" must be informed by knowledge of how AI would act instead of us; and for AI to be just, we must ensure that the technology—or, more accurately, the people and organisations developing and deploying it—are held accountable in the event of a negative outcome, which would require in turn some understanding of why this outcome arose."

Recommendations for a Good AI Society

"Incentivise financially, at the EU level, the development and use of AI technologies within the EU that are socially preferable (not merely acceptable) and environmentally friendly (not merely sustainable but favourable to the environment)."

"This may include: Curricula for schools, supporting the inclusion of computer science among the basic disciplines to be taught; Initiatives and qualification programmes in businesses dealing with AI technology, to educate employees on the societal, legal, and ethical impact of working alongside AI; A European-level recommendation to include ethics and human rights in the degrees of data and AI scientists and other scientific and engineering curricula dealing with computational and AI systems; The development of similar programmes for the public at large, with a special focus on those involved at each stage of management of the technology, including civil servants, politicians and journalists; Engagement with wider initiatives such as the ITU AI for Good events and NGOs working on the UN Sustainable Development Goals."

Conclusion

"This article—and especially the Recommendations in the previous section—seek to nudge the tiller in the direction of ethically and socially preferable outcomes from the development, design and deployment of AI technologies."

"Building on our identification of both the core opportunities and the risks of AI for society as well as the set of five ethical principles we synthesised to guide its adoption, we formulated 20 Action Points in the spirit of collaboration and in the interest of creating concrete and constructive responses to the most pressing social challenges posed by AI."

"With the Recommendations we offer here, including the creation of centres, agencies, curricula, and other infrastructure, we have made the case for an ambitious, inclusive, equitable programme of policy making and technological innovation, which we believe will contribute to securing the benefits and mitigating the risks of AI, for all people, and for the world we share."

The Ethics of AI Ethics: An Evaluation of Guidelines [3]

This is a machine-generated summary of:

Hagendorff, Thilo The Ethics of AI Ethics: An Evaluation of Guidelines [3]

Published in: Minds and Machines (2020)

Link to original: https://doi.org/10.1007/s11023-020-09517-8

If you want to cite the papers, please refer to the original.

For technical reasons we could not place the page where the original quote is coming from.

Abstract-Summary

"Current advances in research, development and application of artificial intelligence (AI) systems have yielded a far-reaching discourse on AI ethics."

"I give a detailed overview of the field of AI ethics."

"I also examine to what extent the respective ethical principles and values are implemented in the practice of research, development and application of AI systems—and how the effectiveness in the demands of AI ethics can be improved."

Introduction

"The critical question arises: Do those ethical guidelines have an actual impact on human decision-making in the field of AI and machine learning?"

"This paper analyzes 22 of the major AI ethics guidelines and issues recommendations on how to overcome the relative ineffectiveness of these guidelines."

"It is also a reason why ethics is so appealing to many AI companies and institutions."

"Ethics guidelines of the AI industry serve to suggest to legislators that internal self-governance in science and industry is sufficient, and that no specific laws are necessary to mitigate possible technological risks and to eliminate scenarios of abuse [19]."

"This prompts the question as to what extent ethical objectives are actually implemented and embedded in the development and application of AI, or whether merely good intentions are deployed."

"22 of the major guidelines of AI ethics will be analyzed and compared."

Guidelines in AI Ethics

"The list of ethics guidelines considered in this article therefore includes compilations that cover the field of AI ethics as comprehensively as possible."

"I used Algorithm Watch's AI Ethics Guidelines Global Inventory, a crowdsourced, comprehensive list of ethics guidelines, to check whether I missed relevant guidelines."

"The decisive factor for the selection of ethics guidelines was not the depth of detail of the individual document, but the discernible intention of a comprehensive mapping and categorization of normative claims with regard to the field of AI ethics."

"The sampling method used to select the AI ethics guidelines has an effect on the list of issues and omissions."

"What is also largely absent from most guidelines is the issue of a lack in diversity within the AI community."

"Yet importantly, not a single guideline raises the issue of public–private partnerships and industry-funded research in the field of AI."

AI in Practice

"The practice of development, implementation and use of AI applications has very often little to do with the values and principles postulated by ethics."

"Dispensation of ethical principles, AI systems are used in areas of high societal significance such as health, police, mobility or education."

"In the previous sections, the practice of using AI systems is poor in terms of compliance with the principles set out in the various ethical guidelines."

"In other areas, including the issue of hidden costs and sustainability, the protection of whistleblowers, diversity in the field of AI, the fostering of solidarity and social cohesion, the respect for human autonomy, the use of AI for the common good or the military AI arms race, it can certainly be stated that the ethical goals are being massively underachieved."

Advances in AI Ethics

"Ethical guidelines postulate very broad, overarching principles which are then supposed to be implemented in a widely diversified set of scientific, technical and economic practices, and in sometimes geographically dispersed groups of researchers and developers with different priorities, tasks and fragmental responsibilities."

"Regardless of the fact that normative guidelines should be accompanied by in-depth technical instructions—as far as they can reasonably be identified—, the question still arises how the precarious situation regarding the application and fulfillment of AI ethics guidelines can be improved."

"The virtue ethics approach, on the other hand, focuses more on "deeper-lying" structures and situation-specific deliberations, on addressing personality traits and behavioral dispositions on the part of technology developers [20]."

"Those virtues are supposed to raise the likelihood of ethical decision-making practices in organizations that develop and deploy AI applications."

Conclusion

"There is also a wide range of ethical aspects that are significantly related to the research, development and application of AI systems, but are not or very seldomly mentioned in the guidelines."

"Those omissions range from aspects like the danger of a malevolent artificial general intelligence, machine consciousness, the reduction of social cohesion by AI ranking and filtering systems on social networking sites, the political abuse of AI systems, a lack of diversity in the AI community, links to robot ethics, the dealing with trolley problems, the weighting between algorithmic or human decision routines, "hidden" social and ecological costs of AI, to the problem of public–private-partnerships and industry-funded research."

"Such an AI ethics does not seek to subsume as many cases as possible under individual principles in an overgeneralizing way, but behaves sensitively towards individual situations and specific technical assemblages."

"These considerations have two consequences for AI ethics."

Overcoming AI Ethics, Towards AI Realism [4]

This is a machine-generated summary of:

Murgia, Michele Overcoming AI ethics, towards AI realism [4]

Published in: AI and Ethics (2024)

Link to original: https://doi.org/10.1007/s43681-024-00552-0

If you want to cite the papers, please refer to the original.

For technical reasons we could not place the page where the original quote is coming from.

Abstract-Summary

"This widespread surge in AI discussions, both academic and public, underscores a significant gap in normative political theory, a gap that urgently needs addressing."

"Although AI ethics as applied moral philosophy has been criticised as decontextualising AI or as outright useless, there remains a profound lack of understanding the proper political normativity of AI."

"The critique of AI ethics typically focuses only on feasibility concerns or moral harms, approaches that fail to capture the normative sources from which AI as a political phenomenon draws."

"By leveraging the recent realism-moralism debate in normative political theory, I aim to show that the realist tradition can be the unexpected corner from which we can study these consequences and suggest a substantively different approach to AI in future, moving from AI ethics to AI realism."

AI Ethics and the Problem of Moralism

"Let us take a closer look at the differences between these camps before moving on to their common denominator: moralism. (i) Corporatist ethics are what I call the use of broad ethical frameworks, for example by public organisations, corporations, or programmers to temper the (perceived) dangers of AI technologies."

"In reformist ethics, these new lines of thought still base themselves on ethical notions such as fairness, transparency, and accountability. (iii) AI justice turns away from corporatist and ostensibly reformist ethics."

"It shares with the latter an emphasis on the point that AI ethical principles do not exist in an isolated vacuum."

"The idea that AI ethical principles are meaningless can also be extended to reformist ethics."

"This enables AI justice to be posited against a "de facto turn to ethical principles.""

Ethics Is Dead Politics

"What typically attracts realists to the notion of a first political question is, however, not this conservative slant but rather a way of thinking about the political apart from the moral."

"Williams himself introduced the 'Basic Legitimation Demand' (BLD) as a solution to the Hobbesian question: order and stability are necessary but not a sufficient condition for legitimate political power [21]."

"While realists think about political norms such as prudence, security, and trust, recently Williams' notion of legitimacy seems to have gripped their hearts and minds the most."

"This is because it provides a novel way of thinking about the justification of political power that is not based on moral pre-commitments; a shift from the predominant focus within political theory on justice to another norm by which we might understand politics [22]."

"Realism and the non-moral political normativity it is concerned with involve some fidelity to facts, which differ in relevance per realist version."

AI Realism

"These kinds of critical insights benefit from realism insofar as it opens up new ways of thinking about the political nature of AI."

"AI VSD provides us with much-needed work on the contextualisation of AI design and operationalisation of values, but due to its moralist underpinnings stops short at formulating desirable ends and norms that are (radically) politically salient."

"What remains is an AI realism that builds on a non-moral epistemic approach to discern and approximate legitimate AI systems."

"It is in this open space that ensues where further (theoretical) commitments play a key role and where AI realism can draw on the insights and facts pertaining to political normativity, bringing theory into the fold of politics proper."

"A corresponding sensitivity to a non-moral epistemic approach can actually inform and change the design of AI by thinking along these norms."

Putting AI Ethics to Work: Are the Tools Fit for Purpose? [7]

This is a machine-generated summary of:

Ayling, Jacqui; Chapman, Adriane Putting AI ethics to work: are the tools fit for purpose? [7]

Published in: AI and Ethics (2021)

Link to original: https://doi.org/10.1007/s43681-021-00084-x

If you want to cite the papers, please refer to the original.

For technical reasons we could not place the page where the original quote is coming from.

Abstract-Summary

"We review other historical uses of risk assessments and audits and create a typology that allows us to compare current AI ethics tools to Best Practices found in previous methodologies from technology, environment, privacy, finance and engineering."

"We analyse current AI ethics tools and their support for diverse stakeholders and components of the AI development and deployment lifecycle as well as the types of tools used to facilitate use."

"We identify gaps in current AI ethics tools in auditing and risk assessment that should be considered going forward."

Introduction

"To do this, we examine proposed tools to operationalise ethical principles for AI (as opposed to statements of ethical principles), in relation to well-established impact and risk assessment, and audit procedures, that have been used to manage human activities, and new technology."

"This first phase focused on the high-level ethical principles that might best address the impacts of AI and data-driven systems framed as applied ethics and dominated by a philosophical approach as opposed to legal or technical approach."

"Looking at the environmental movement of the mid-twentieth century, in which ethical considerations for many diverse parties, application of technology and societal concerns all converged, there are parallels for best practice in the current AI ethics, impact assessment and audit conversations."

"This paper contributes to the literature by mapping the current landscape of suggested tools for ethical assessment of AI systems, placing these tools in a historical tradition of managing the impacts of technology, thereby exposing possible areas for strengthening these tools in practice."

Background to Impact Assessment and Audit Practices

"Privacy impact assessments developed to meet the need for public trust in information processing by identifying and managing risks."

"While a myriad of processes, tools and applications of these tools at various parts of the production cycle exist across the historical impact assessment and audit activities above, one of the key elements is risk assessment."

"Modern conceptions of risk (risk = accident × probability) became a fully-fledged part of modern societies with the risk assessment practices developed in response to concerns over the impact on the environment and human health from human activity in the form of development, technologies and industrial processes and materials."

"A risk-based approach has developed throughout the latter part of the 20th and into the twenty-first century, taking the methodology and approaches from environmental management and risk assessment and applying them to areas like occupational health and safety, business risk (financial, operational, reputational), quality and information security."

Methodology

"This study draws from the rich impact assessment and audit literature from other domains to develop a typology for comparative document analysis of proposed AI ethics tools."

"Reflecting on the processes used to provide assurance for the environmental impact of organisations, we considered there to be parallels in the need to implement processes to assure the ethical design and deployment of AI systems."

"This was a reflective process where we identified principles and categories across domains and used them create typological sets as follows: The next step was to narrow down the initial large data set of n = 169 documents, which contained many documents that were statements of principles or discussions of AI ethics."

"The terms impact assessment and audit are used in differing ways in the domain of AI ethics tools made coding of these documents complex."

"Across the landscape of AI ethics audit and impact assessment tools, terms are often used loosely, or are used interchangeably."

Results

"A third of the Impact Assessment tools focus on Procurement processes for AI systems from third-party vendors, indicating the need for not only producers of AI products to engage with ethical assessment, but also the customers for these products, who will be the ones deploying the products."

"There were also omissions in these proposed tools for AI which did not include the types of impacts that would be measured in a life-cycle assessment for a product or process, leaving out key considerations like resource or energy use and sustainability."

"The workshop materials do not fit into an impact assessment or audit framework and are not designed to provide verifiable evidence of process, but more to elicit 'ethical thinking' from design teams, unlike the documentation tools which can provide evidence for audits."

Discussion

"Ex ante impact assessments are used at the early stages of use case development, and for procurement processes to provide a predictive decision-making tool for whether a proposed AI system should progress to development and/or be deployed or purchased and what are the possible impacts of its use."

"Technical tools do have an important role to play in addressing ethical issues in AI systems, but ultimately need to be part of a wider governance process."

"The documentation produced by these tools should form part of impact assessment and audit processes in order that all ethical aspects of a product can be captured (not just a focus on, e.g. metrics for fairness [23])."

"Clarifying the types of tools appropriate for which assessment and governance outcomes, and implementing well-regulated compliance regimes for producers of AI systems would be a great step towards effectively operationalising the ethical principles and concerns motivating the production of AI ethics tools."

Conclusion

"This work provides an analysis of the AI guidelines and frameworks that have practical tools to operationalise ethical concerns."

"By reviewing best practices from historical frameworks created to assess the effects of technology on the environment [24], information privacy [25], data protection [26] and human rights [27], we create a typology of concerns that previous generations of impact assessments and audits have found beneficial to consider."

"There is little participation in the assessment or audit process by certain stakeholder groups, particularly the voiceless, vested interests and users, who are not included in the process of applying the tools or interacting with the outputs as tools for transparency or decision-making."

"To missing large stakeholder groups, the current set of AI Guidelines and tools do not fully utilize the full range of techniques available, including: participation process, baseline study, life-cycle assessment, change measurement or expert committees."

AI Ethics: From Principles to Practice [8]

This is a machine-generated summary of:

Zhou, Jianlong; Chen, Fang AI ethics: from principles to practice [8]

Published in: AI & SOCIETY (2022)

Link to original: https://doi.org/10.1007/s00146-022-01602-z

If you want to cite the papers, please refer to the original.

For technical reasons we could not place the page where the original quote is coming from.

Abstract-Summary

"Much of the current work on AI ethics has lost its connection to the real-world impact by making AI ethics operable."

"This position paper presents challenges in making AI ethics operable and highlights key obstacles to AI ethics impact."

"We aim to inspire discussions on making AI ethics operable and focus on its impact on real-world applications."

Introduction

"Since diverse and ambitious claims of AI as well as its possible adverse effects to humans and society as mentioned above, it faces ethical challenges ranging from data governance, including consent, ownership, and privacy, to fairness and accountability and others."

"We are seeing increasing ethical concerns and debate about the principles and values that should guide AI's development and deployment, not just for individuals, but for humanity as a whole and for the future of humans and society [28–30]."

"The contributions of this work are: Identifying a fundamental problem in making AI ethics operable: a lack of collaboration among stakeholders and follow-through; suggesting stages towards solving the gaps; identifying challenges to direct efforts to make AI ethics operable for impact; highlighting a number of key obstacles to AI ethics impact, as an aid for focusing future efforts; providing a preliminary practice example to initiate practical implementations of AI ethics."

Ethical Principles for AI Uses

"Jobin and others [31] made an in-depth investigation in 2019 on ethical principles of AI and identified 84 documents related to ethical principles or guideline for AI."

"Various parties identified slightly different ethical principles of AI because of their background or other reasons."

"Organizations also identified mandatory ethical principles for the use of AI including community benefit, fairness, privacy and security, transparency, and accountability [32]."

"Despite the proliferation of ethical principles of AI, there is still an increasing trend of active discussion on ethical principles of AI and publishing guidelines or frameworks by various organizations."

"Does every organization need to show their positions and propose their own ethical principles of AI?"

"It is very hard to directly use those ethical principles by AI developers or users in the practical applications."

"Connecting active advances of ethical principles to real-world practices is part of the process of maturing of AI ethics."

Making Ethical Principles Operable

"What is needed is a fundamental change in or new definition on how we define metrics for validation of ethical principles, how we justify compliances of AI with ethical principles, how we consider differences among different sectors, how we educate the general public to get understanding with AI ethics, how we make AI ethics as a necessary component for each AI solution for impact, and who should monitor the adoption of ethical principles and police their impact as the development and use of AI increases?"

"An ethical AI committee can be set up to monitor the ethical principles in AI development and deployment."

"Both qualitative and quantitative metrics can be defined to validate ethical principles in AI."

"When various qualitative and quantitative metrics are available for the validation of ethical principles of AI, we need to decide whether the value of one metric meets the requirement of ethical principles."

Challenges for Making AI Ethics Operable

"Ambitious and meaningful challenges are helpful to direct efforts to make AI ethics operable."

"The following challenges are articulated as examples of making AI ethics operable that matters."

"Can we also quantify values imposed by ethics when we implement ethical principles of AI?"

"Balancing the economic value created by AI to be ethical or unethical."

"We have to confront the problem where economic value created by ethical AI and unethical AI conflict [33], raising the challenge of balancing ethical and unethical by considering economic values when developing AI technologies."

"Balancing the AI performance and ethical values."

"We have the challenge of balancing the AI performance and ethical values."

"These challenges seek to capture the key components in making AI ethics operable including the standardization, value quantification, and value balancing."

Obstacles to Making AI Ethics Actionable

"The smooth communication between AI research field and other disciplines such as ethics, philosophy, law and social science is significant for making AI ethics operable."

"AI ethics is related to different fields including engineering, law, science, economics, ethics, philosophy, politics, health, and others."

"Such subjectivity makes it difficult to have an objective justification of the compliance of AI with ethical principles."

"The design of more objective methods to validate the compliance of AI with ethical principles can erode this obstacle and make ethical principles of AI operable."

"We also need to associate risks caused by the violation of ethical principles with the validation of relevant ethical principles if we hope to infuse AI ethics into real-world applications."

"This is related to different fields at least including law, politics, AI, and ethics."

"These are effective attempts to overcome obstacles to making AI ethics operable."

Our Practices

"We propose to implement ethical principles of AI both qualitatively and quantitatively."

"Qualitative questionnaires aim to evaluate the compliance of AI with ethical principles by developing qualitative questions on ethical principles and collecting responses from AI developers."

"Quantitative questions aim to evaluate the compliance of AI with ethical principles by developing quantitative approaches to measure the compliance of AI with ethical principles."

"By considering the dynamics of investigations on ethical principles of AI, the platform is designed as an open platform so that new ethical principles and corresponding qualitative and quantitative questions can be added easily."

Conclusion

"This paper initiated discussions by providing example approaches to answer key questions on making ethical principles operable, such as setup of ethical AI committee, meaningful and operable validation metrics, standards for validation metrics, AI ethics for the whole AI lifecycle, and education of AI ethics."

"Key example challenges were articulated to inspire the field of AI ethics to take steps needed to mature into valuable contributions to making AI ethics operable besides the exploration of ethical principles."

"This position paper was not to provide specific solutions on making AI ethics operable, but to articulate key aspects to consider in making AI ethics operable and initiate discussions on steps needed to take in making AI ethics operable."

"Aiming for the real impact of AI ethics is not only to identify ethical principles, but also to build standards, implement them effectively, and deploy them easily in practical applications."

Ethical Principles for Artificial Intelligence in National Defence [34]

This is a machine-generated summary of:

Taddeo, Mariarosaria; McNeish, David; Blanchard, Alexander; Edgar, Elizabeth
Ethical Principles for Artificial Intelligence in National Defence [34]

Published in: Philosophy & Technology (2021)

Link to original: https://doi.org/10.1007/s13347-021-00482-3

If you want to cite the papers, please refer to the original.

For technical reasons we could not place the page where the original quote is coming from.

Abstract-Summary

"They remain unmatched by efforts to define ethical frameworks to guide the use of AI in the defence domain."

"It identifies five principles—justified and overridable uses, just and transparent systems and processes, human moral responsibility, meaningful human control and reliable AI systems—and related recommendations to foster ethically sound uses of AI for national defence purposes."

Introduction

"If these problems are left undressed, the use of AI for defence purposes risks undermining the fundamental values of democratic societies and international stability [35–37]."

"This article offers guidance to address these problems by identifying ethical principles to inform the design, development and use of AI for defence purposes."

"These principles should not be taken as an alternative to national and international laws; rather, they offer guidance to the use of AI in the defence domain in ways that are coherent with existing regulations."

"In offering these principles, the paper fills an important gap in the relevant academic and policy literature; while numerous ethical principles and frameworks have been published which focus on civilian applications of AI [31], very few so far address directly the problems inherent to the use of AI in the defence domain."

Methodology

"The choice of the method to identify the ethical problems posed by the use of AI for national defence is not a trivial one."

"Within the defence domain, these purposes can be clearly identified and are likely to shape both current and future uses of AI, and thus, ethical principles that focus on purposes of use, rather than on the specific function, of a given technology have a better-defined scope and their guidance is more likely to stand the test of time."

"The ethical principles for the use of AI in the defence domain that we provide in this article refer to sustainment and support uses and to adversarial and non-kinetic uses of AI."

"The ethical analysis of the use of AI for adversarial and kinetic purposes will be addressed in the second stage of our research."

Ethical Challenges of AI for Defence Purposes

"To be ethically sound, adversarial and non-kinetic uses of AI need to ensure some forms of meaningful control and measures to avoid escalation, while also respecting transparency and human autonomy, which appear in the sustainment and support category."

"While many countries have expressed their commitment not to develop or use fully autonomous weapon systems, it is still important to consider and address the ethical problems they pose in order to establish boundaries for the development and use of weapons which incorporate AI but are not fully autonomous in their operation or may not target human agents."

"A key challenge is to ensure that adversarial and kinetic uses of AI will be able to respect the tenets of the just war theory, for example necessity, proportionality and discrimination."

Ethical Guidelines for the Use of AI

"The principles defined by the US DIB [38] for the use of AI in defence are the only exception to this lack of focus."

"Human beings should exercise appropriate levels of judgment and remain responsible for the development, deployment, use, and outcomes of DoD AI systems" [38, p. 8]."

"When considering fairness with respect to AI, the DIB principles centre only on the unfair impact of the use of AI on the DoD personnel, disregarding the problems that the lack of fairness may pose when deploying AI on the cyber and kinetic battleground."

"The focus of the principle is not on the transparency of the technology but on the skills of the DoD personnel and their level of understanding of AI systems, insofar as these facilitate the traceability of the processes and decisions of AI systems at both development and deployment stages."

Five Ethical Principles for Sustainment and Support and Adversarial and Non-kinetic Uses of AI

"AI defence institutions should ensure that the deployed AI systems, and the processes in which they are embedded, remain transparent (and explicable) to facilitate the identification of the origin of any breach of the principles of the just war theory, of unintended and mistaken outcomes, the attribution of responsibilities, and guarantee the possibility of scrutinising and challenging processes and outcomes to ensure that they remain ethically sound."

"Three aspects are crucial: Establish processes for ethical auditing Ensure that developed and procured AI systems are deployed in ways that respect the principles of the just war theory Maintain traceability for the design, development or procurement and deployment of AI systems Ethical auditing should involve the entire decision-making process, and so, it should focus on both human and artificial agents, to ensure that both agents respect the relevant ethical principles [39]."

Conclusion

"As we mentioned at the beginning of this article, ethical principles for the use of AI in defence do not undermine international humanitarian laws."

"Rather, they offer guidance both with respect to what can be done post-compliance and with respect to those uses of AI in defence which international humanitarian laws do not address or do not address clearly."

"The principles need to be logically consistent with the broader ethical principles underpinning the wide set of uses of AI in our societies, like, for example, the OECD principles, and with the values shaping defence institutions and their role in democratic societies."

"This consistency is important, for it ensures that despite the domain-dependent differences, ethical principles shaping the uses of AI in defence remain coherent with fundamental principles of our societies."

From the Ground Truth Up: Doing AI Ethics from Practice to Principles [6]

This is a machine-generated summary of:

Brusseau, James From the ground truth up: doing AI ethics from practice to principles [6]

Published in: AI & SOCIETY (2022)

Link to original: https://doi.org/10.1007/s00146-021-01336-4

If you want to cite the papers, please refer to the original.

For technical reasons we could not place the page where the original quote is coming from.

Abstract-Summary

"Specific answers are less significant than the larger demonstration that AI ethics is currently unbalanced toward theoretical principles, and will benefit from increased exposure to grounded practices and dilemmas."

Introduction

"This distinction at—and as—the source of understanding itself means AI cannot be relied upon to obey human conventions of rationality."

"Initial work has been largely theoretical, with 84 sets of principles introduced in the last several years, and more on the way."

"Of descending from principles to practice, these explorations start from palpable human experiences and only subsequently climb to abstraction and the theoretical work of comparing and justifying principles."

"This report covers the initial phase of that grounded process, the birth of insight and ethical propositions from philosophers, engineers, and medical doctors laboring to make AI work for flesh and blood patients."

Cases

"The result is that the barrier to AI-fortified skin health is not technological advance so much as doctors' confidence."

"The other case starts from cardiac arrest in Denmark, and with a team lead by Stig Nikolaj Blomberg [40]."

"To save lives, Blomberg's group developed a machine learning tool to detect cardiac arrest and then alert Dispatchers with a light added to their console."

"True cardiac arrest was recognized more frequently and quickly by the artificial intelligence than by its human partner [41]."

"The machine was also less specific: the AI-returned many false positive alerts which were largely ignored by the dispatchers."

"Dejectedly, Blomberg concluded: "While a machine learning model recognized a significantly greater number of out-of-hospital cardiac arrests than dispatchers alone, this did not translate into improved cardiac arrest recognition by dispatchers" [40]."

Explainability or Performance?

"While it is true that an abundance of false positive alerts got logged along the way, the hard fact remained that true cardiac arrest was detected faster by algorithms and data than by human listening and experience."

"The model was partially open-sourced [42, 43], our group did not pursue a technical understanding of explaining how the system worked because we were convinced that winning human trust for the AI decisions would originate and remain within the parameters of performance defined as speed and accuracy."

"That will have to change, though, because no one has the responsibility to try the impossible, and the cardiac arrest case demonstrates that under time's pressure and on the edge splitting life from death the only functional source for trust in AI technology is power as demonstrated by performance."

"In which instances should trust be built on humanized knowledge about AI decisions?"

Trustworthy or Reliable?

"This is bare experience: trust is inseparable from betrayal."

"In lived experience, the fundamental distinction is not between trust on one side and betrayal on the other."

"All of this, finally, is inseparable from trustworthiness, it is the way the word and concept gain meaning."

"If machines are going to be trusted, if we are going to talk and write about them that way, there is a requirement—a condition of the possibility of being trustworthy—that they also betray."

"In our group's extensive work with two very different startups trying to promote trustworthy AI, not once did a single ethicist, engineer, lawyer, or doctor define false outputs as dishonesty, infidelity, deception, lies, betrayal."

"The problem with trustworthy AI—and the reason the idea should be abandoned for the neutral and inanimate term of reliability—is not that we cannot force ourselves as humans to trust the machines."

Protection or Performance?

"In AI ethics from the ground up, pure performance is a value because algorithmic designers find that high quality is worth having on its own."

"There is no end to the human catastrophes occasioned by exquisitely functioning machines, and advocating pure performance as an ethical value requires acknowledging this: even death-mechanisms like nuclear bombs can be majestic accomplishments, awesome, with all that word implies."

"As drawn from our working experience, the four traits of performance as a value in AI ethics are: Intrinsically valuable: The only justification required is engineering excellence."

"The central significance of performance as a value is that it transforms the role of AI ethics: it fundamentally reorients mainstream approaches as they are represented by the EC Ethics Guidelines."

"The proving will be easy and the addition of performance to AI ethics imperceptible."

"There are two conceptions of AI ethics, one without and the other with performance as a value."

Conclusion

"Of philosophy Plato taught that ethics was about purification: knowledge became truer as it increased in abstraction and decreased in humanity."

"This essay is an exercise in reversing the thinking: instead of learning about the world by escaping upward from it, knowledge is produced by diving down into the work of real AI developers as they crash into human dilemmas."

"Readers will draw varied conclusions about explainability and performance, and about trustworthiness and reliability, and about the intrinsic value of innovation, but the underlying assertion is that those conclusions will emerge stronger from the ground of lived human experiences than from cloistered philosophy."

Should Explainability Be a Fifth Ethical Principle in AI Ethics? [11]

This is a machine-generated summary of:

Cortese, João Figueiredo Nobre Brito; Cozman, Fabio Gagliardi; Lucca-Silveira, Marcos Paulo; Bechara, Adriano Figueiredo Should explainability be a fifth ethical principle in AI ethics? [11]

Published in: AI and Ethics (2022)

Link to original: https://doi.org/10.1007/s43681-022-00152-w

If you want to cite the papers, please refer to the original.

For technical reasons we could not place the page where the original quote is coming from.

Abstract-Summary

"It has been recently claimed that explainability should be added as a fifth principle to AI ethics, supplementing the four principles that are usually accepted in Bioethics: Autonomy, Beneficence, Nonmaleficence and Justice."

"We do agree that explainability is a key demand in AI Ethics, with practical importance for stakeholders to take into account; but we argue that it should not be considered as a fifth ethical principle, to maintain a philosophical consistency in the organization of AI ethical principles."

Introduction

"We wish to discuss some notions of Explainability in AI and address the relationship of Explainability to the four principles of Bioethics (Respect for Autonomy, Beneficence, Nonmaleficence and Justice, as proposed by Beauchamp and Childress [44]) in the context of AI Ethics."

"It is thus "conditionally" that we analyse the relation between explainability and the four other principles of Principlism, as other foundations for AI Ethics are surely possible."

"Another important contribution, by Ursin and others [45], argues that "explicability" is not a fifth principle in medical AI ethics, because the four principles of bioethics already encompass it."

"The discussion presented in this article is centred on the role of explainability in an ethical framework based on principles: in short, even if explainability is a desideratum in AI, it is not necessary that it should be considered for that reason as a fifth ethical principle."

The Many Concepts Around Explainability

"There has been a decades-long effort to define the kinds of explanations one can extract from statistical models known as Bayesian networks: sometimes the purpose is to explain the reasons why a Bayesian network is structured in a particular way, while in other cases the goal is to explain the probabilistic calculations that generate a result [46]."

"Another possibility is to build an interpreter that learns to explain decisions by examining the inputs and outputs of the opaque system; this is sometimes referred to as an agnostic strategy [47]."

"Most existing techniques in the literature focus on local explanations; that is, the goal is to explain a particular decision and not the global behaviour of an opaque system."

"While a local explanation may be relevant to an end user interested in a particular decision that affects her, a global explanation may be useful for instance to an auditing body interested in the behaviour of a system for automated credit analysis."

Explainability as a Fifth Principle for AI Ethics

"Despite the little consensus one can find around explainability and all interrelated concepts, Floridi and others [2] propose "explicability" as a fifth principle of AI Ethics."

"Explainability can be understood as a kind of requirement for ethical principles in AI."

"This requirement is necessary from an epistemic point of view, as it helps the other principles (in which sense we could agree with the choice of the verb "complements" by Floridi and others [2]); but even if there is a certain kind of dependence here, and an ethical demand derived from this, explainability does not become a principle in itself for that reason (in which sense we disagree with these authors)."

"We do not claim that all occurrences of principles in AI ethics claim for explainability as a requirement, such that it is not unconditional."

Explainability and Its Relationship with the Four Principles

"Requirements that come from principles of justice entail that AI is constrained by demands for explainability, so that algorithmic decision making would be just, unbiased and respecting the rights of people, especially those in disadvantaged groups."

"To know whether an algorithm respects this formal principle of justice, some degree of explainability is required."

"As we argued, this is not the case, since for each of the principles of autonomy, justice and nonmaleficence, we can find explainability as a requirement for, or derived from them."

"Also in this case, even if explainability has an ethical intrinsic value, it is not for that reason an ethical principle—as the authors say, in this case "explicability relates to the principles of justice and respect for autonomy"."

Conclusions

"Explainability is important in AI ethics, but we assert that it is not a fifth ethical "principle"."

"Explainability is required, from an ethical perspective, in several situations in AI Ethics."

"We do think that the use of AI algorithms do present new aspects of explainability questions with ethical implications."

"We think that even if this is so, explainability cannot be considered as a "fifth principle" in AI Ethics, for the reasons outlined above, namely that explainability (i) can be considered as an epistemic requirement for ethical principles; and (ii) it can be derived from other ethical principles."

Reconstructing AI Ethics Principles: Rawlsian Ethics of Artificial Intelligence [5]

This is a machine-generated summary of:

Westerstrand, Salla Reconstructing AI Ethics Principles: Rawlsian Ethics of Artificial Intelligence [5]

Published in: Science and Engineering Ethics (2024)
Link to original: https://doi.org/10.1007/s11948-024-00507-y

If you want to cite the papers, please refer to the original.

For technical reasons we could not place the page where the original quote is coming from.

Abstract-Summary

"This development has forced governmental organisations, NGOs, and private companies to react and draft ethics guidelines for future development of ethical AI systems."

"Rawls's theory of justice is applied to draft a set of guidelines for organisations and policy-makers to guide AI development towards a more ethical direction."

"The goal is to contribute to the broadening of the discussion on AI ethics by exploring the possibility of constructing AI ethics guidelines that are philosophically justified and take a broader perspective of societal justice."

"The paper discusses how Rawls's theory of justice as fairness and its key concepts relate to the ongoing developments in AI ethics and gives a proposition of how principles that offer a foundation for operationalising AI ethics in practice could look like if aligned with Rawls's theory of justice as fairness."

Introduction

"This development has pushed organisations to steer the development and application of AI systems towards a more ethical direction through principles and guidelines (see [3, 7, 31])."

"Whereas research around operationalising is essential in order for the principles to effectively guide AI development and deployment, I argue that the work around actionable ethics principles needs revisiting."

"This implies that to improve the state of AI systems and their alignment with collective values, it might be wise to inspect the larger ecosystem and the ethical foundations behind its guiding principles."

"Rawls intended his contractarian theory to build "the most appropriate moral basis for a democratic society" [48, p. viii], which makes it a theoretically interesting foundation for discussing the ethicality of AI development that comes with an increasing collective ethical and societal implications."

"The paper begins with an overview of Rawls's theory of justice in the context of AI, which serves as a theoretical starting point for revisiting AI ethics guidelines."

AI Ethics from a Rawlsian Perspective

"Characteristic of a contractarian, Rawls establishes an idea of a hypothetical original position to define the fairest conditions possible where the principles of justice would be agreed upon."

"In Rawls's original position, the principles of justice are defined by people behind a veil of ignorance: they know neither their position in the society, nor their personal attributes that might affect the distribution of rights and duties [49, p. 11]."

"The principles of justice defined by Rawls are justified by his arguments on the fairness of the original position."

"When Rawls first published his theory of justice, AI ethics as a field of study was in its infancy with only a couple of notable exceptions (see e.g., [50–52])."

"It seems that justice and fairness are values that people in modern democracies strive for AI technologies being no exception—which makes Rawls's theory of justice a theoretically interesting starting point for ethical AI principles."

Rawlsian Ethics Guidelines for Fair AI

"Drawing from liberties Rawls himself has listed [49, p. 53; 53, p. 335], the guideline is hereby extended with a set of requirements that aim to bring Rawls's basic liberties into the context of development and application of AI."

"These are examples of AI tools that violate the basic liberty of rule of law instead of supporting it, which demonstrates that more consideration is needed in institutions with a key role in ensuring the rule of law when applying AI systems in order for them to align their actions with Rawlsian principles of justice."

"From a Rawlsian perspective, the human decision-making should also aim at equality of opportunity, and thus the failure of, e.g., a recruiter to follow the principle should not justify any lesser principle for the use of AI systems."

Conclusions and Discussion

"The analysis shows that a number of conflicts still persist—the Rawlsian approach is not an off-the-shelf solution, or a silver bullet that would eradicate the need for contextualising the principles and exercising active ethical reflection while developing and deploying AI systems, which is, as e.g. Rességuier and Rodrigues [54] and Heilinger [55] note, is an essential part of effective application of ethics in the context of AI."

"Jobin and others [31] point out that the existing guidelines focused on negative characterisation of ethical values, and thus tended to neglect the possibility of promoting favorable values with AI, not just ensuring the principles are met despite of the use of AI in the context in question."

"Even though we need to keep bringing principles into practice, I argue that re-evaluating the moral-philosophical grounds of the existing principles and guidelines is still a vital part of practicing ethics in the dynamic, ever-changing context of AI development."

Actionable Principles for Artificial Intelligence Policy: Three Pathways [9]

This is a machine-generated summary of:

Stix, Charlotte Actionable Principles for Artificial Intelligence Policy: Three Pathways [9]

Published in: Science and Engineering Ethics (2021)

Link to original: https://doi.org/10.1007/s11948-020-00277-3

If you want to cite the papers, please refer to the original.

For technical reasons we could not place the page where the original quote is coming from.

Abstract-Summary

"These AI Ethics Principles often fail to be actioned in governmental policy."

"This paper proposes a novel framework for the development of 'Actionable Principles for AI'."

"The approach acknowledges the relevance of AI Ethics Principles and homes in on methodological elements to increase their practical implementability in policy processes."

"these elements are expanded on and evaluated in light of their ability to contribute to a prototype framework for the development of 'Actionable Principles for AI'."

Introduction

"This in turn led to critical debates over the usefulness and impact of such instruments, with a particular focus on what is often held as a lack of implementation of such AI Ethics Principles into actual policy-making."

"In response, this paper will propose a preliminary framework to support and improve the implementation of AI Ethics Principles in governmental policy at this critical time."

"It is important to recognize that while 'workable pragmatic outcomes' may rightly be perceived as suboptimal from a strict ethical perspective, they will often form the critical basis to moving AI Ethics Principles forwards into practical policy."

"This paper focuses on helping AI Ethics Principles strike such a balance, by complementing previous work (which focuses largely on identifying the ideals to be pursued) with a perspective that enables the achievement of 'workable pragmatic outcomes' in AI policy."

Actionable Principles

"To be clear, many AI Ethics Principles, such as those developed by industry actors or researchers for self-governance purposes, are not aimed at directly informing governmental policy-making, and therefore the challenge of bridging this gulf may not apply."

"This could mean, for example, concrete textual references reflecting a specific section of the AI Ethics Principle, or the establishment of (both enabling or preventative) policy actions building on relevant recommendations."

"A charitable interpretation could be that as governmental policy-making takes time, and given that the vast majority of AI Ethics Principles were published within the last 2 years, it may simply be premature to gauge (or dismiss) their impact."

"Another interpretation could be that the current versions of AI Ethics Principles have fallen short of their promise, and reached their limitation for impact in governmental policy-making (henceforth: policy)."

"Successful actionability in policy goes well beyond AI Ethics Principles acting as a reference point."

Case Study: The Ethics Guidelines for Trustworthy Artificial Intelligence

"The AI HLEG benefited from continuous engagement (including on earlier drafts of the Ethics Guidelines) with the European AI Alliance, a multi-stakeholder platform with over 4000 entities and various subject experts across Europe."

"Notwithstanding that, there is room for improvement in the establishment of groups developing Actionable Principles, especially in light of concerns over dominant representation of industry friendly voices [56] and a lack of sufficient representation of AI Ethicists [57] within the AI HLEG."

"In June 2019, 2 months post-publication of their final Ethics Guidelines, the European Commission opened a 'piloting phase' on behalf of the AI HLEG."

"The AI HLEG process highlighted the following procedural mechanisms: (i) involvement of diverse voices, both between the experts and through open public feedback; (ii) agile development process through interim and ex post feedback processes; and, (iii) mechanisms and methods to support actionability."

A Preliminary Framework for Actionable Principles

"To government departments comparing various policy options in order to decide on the best one to implement, or to conduct impact assessments prior to introducing new regulation, landscape assessments can support foresight and analysis in the drafting of Actionable Principles, making them more impactful and applicable."

"Landscape assessments are likely to concretise and strengthen an ethical principle such as 'an AI should not unduly influence human agency' which otherwise might be too broad (that is, not specific enough about its requirements), or too overarching in the scope of the AI applications it seeks to apply to in order for it to be actionable and functional in policy."

"Going forwards, stakeholder groups drafting Actionable Principles need to be able to ensure that the impact of their work is not minimised by a lack of, or, ability to conduct a landscape assessment."

Conclusion

"While their rise has been encouraging and needed, the majority of AI Ethics Principles today still suffer from a lack of actionability in policy-making."

"This paper has suggested that instead of abandoning the approach altogether, the community should iterate on and improve these tools in order to produce a form of 'Actionable Principles' on AI, which integrate actionability and ethical reasoning."

"In order to do so, this paper first briefly identified and examined a series of promising elements from the development process of the Ethics Guidelines by the AI HLEG."

"Excitement about AI Ethics Principles has waned as the reality has set in that significant work from all stakeholders needs to be undertaken to move them from paper to practice."

"Actionability is not and will not be the only hurdle AI Ethics Principles will face over the coming years."

Confucius, Cyberpunk and Mr. Science: Comparing AI Ethics Principles Between China and the EU [58]

This is a machine-generated summary of:

Fung, Pascale; Etienne, Hubert Confucius, cyberpunk and Mr. Science: comparing AI ethics principles between China and the EU [58]

Published in: AI and Ethics (2022)

Link to original: https://doi.org/10.1007/s43681-022-00180-6

If you want to cite the papers, please refer to the original.

For technical reasons we could not place the page where the original quote is coming from.

Abstract-Summary

"In highlighting such differences, we show that it is erroneous to believe that a similarity in concepts necessarily translates into a similarity in ethics as even the same words may have different meanings from a country to another—as exemplified by that of "privacy"."

"It would, therefore, be erroneous to believe that the world would have adopted a common set of ethical principles in only 3 years."

"China and the EU, however, share a common scientific method, inherited in the former from the "Chinese Enlightenment", which could contribute to better collaboration and understanding in the building of technical standards for the implementation of such ethics principles."

Introduction

"Stakeholders from different industries, international foundations, governmental organizations, and standards institutions quickly reacted in improvising codes of ethics for the purpose of establishing a first layer of control in the absence of existing State laws."

"They both noted a general convergence, which leads Fjeld and others to conclude that "the conversation around principled AI is beginning to converge" and that "these themes may represent the 'normative core' of a principle-based approach to AI ethics and governance"."

"Ethical pluralism is more about differences in which relevant questions to ask rather than different answers to a common question."

"To better understand the philosophical roots and cultural context underlying ethical principles in AI, we propose to analyze and compare the ethical principles endorsed by the Chinese National New Generation Artificial Intelligence Governance Professional Committee (CNNGAIGPC) and those elaborated by the European High-level Expert Group on AI (HLEGAI)."

Promotional Versus Prohibitive Approaches

"The European ethical principles, in contrast, emerge from a more individual-focused and rights-based approach."

"The individualist perspective reflected by the European approach to AI ethics should, however, not be mistaken for a form of selfish moral individualism, but rather as a result from the European history of individual reasoning."

"Its political elite, composed of civil servants mostly with backgrounds in science, technology, engineering, and mathematics (STEM), has adopted a pragmatic approach to AI ethics, grounded in existing applications and driven by society's needs."

"It explains the great pragmatism in the Chinese governmental approach to AI ethics, focusing on foreseeable harms that may derive from the use of AI in the near future."

"The EU principles aim to protect European citizens from vertical and horizontal abuses, conscient of the danger of nationalism."

A Utopian Versus a Dystopian Vision by Populations

"Other than roles of the governments, the two ethical sets of guidelines are informed by opposing views from the European and Chinese populations regarding AI."

"Such a practice would be shocking in Western countries; it is however readily accepted by Chinese citizens, accustomed to living in a protected society and have consistently shown high trust in their government [59]."

"This rapid ascend onto the world stage, together with the clear ambition to challenge the US leadership, has played a significant role in securing trust from the Chinese people in the actions of their government, including the strategic support given to AI."

"The gap in the cultural representation of AI, perceived as a force for good in China, and as a menacing force in the dystopian technological future in the Western world, could be rooted in the influence of popular culture."

A Scientific Common Ground

"Despite the seemingly different, though not contradictory, approaches on AI ethics from China and the EU, the presence of major commonalities between them points to a more promising and collaborative future in the implementation of these standards."

It results that "ISO data security standards have been widely adopted by cloud computing providers, e.g., Alibaba, Amazon, Apple, Google, Microsoft, and Tencent." [60] while the working group on IEEE Guidelines for Ethically Aligned Design keeps exploring "established ethics systems, including both philosophical traditions (utilitarianism, virtue ethics, and deontological ethics) and religious and culture-based ethical systems (Buddhism, Confucianism, African Ubuntu traditions, and Japanese Shinto) and their stance on human morality in the digital age."

"Chinese graduate students in AI have one time or another worked as interns in these companies in China."

"A significant number of Chinese AI researchers do not return to China within 5 years of completing their graduate studies abroad."

Conclusion

"The EU ethical framework is also built as a dialectic system between users on one side, and AI developers and service providers on the other side."

"Although the Chinese AI ethical principles seem similar to those of the EU in many ways, they however largely differ in the overall approach."

The EU principles mostly refer to deontologist normative rules—mainly negative obligations–, whereas the Chinese principles, stemming from Confucian values, tend to combine some strict deontologist normative rules (e.g., prohibiting evil uses and illegal activities) with softer constraints that could be satisfied on different levels (e.g., promote shared and inclusive development) and even some aspects of virtue ethics, referring to "vigilance" and "self-discipline."

"Whereas the Chinese principles tend to suggest directions to shape how AI should be developed and applied, the EU principles aim to precisely define what it should not be allowed to do."

In Defence of Principlism in AI Ethics and Governance [10]

This is a machine-generated summary of:

Seger, Elizabeth In Defence of Principlism in AI Ethics and Governance [10]
Published in: Philosophy & Technology (2022)
Link to original: https://doi.org/10.1007/s13347-022-00538-y

If you want to cite the papers, please refer to the original.

For technical reasons we could not place the page where the original quote is coming from.

Abstract-Summary

"It is widely acknowledged that high-level AI principles are difficult to translate into practices via explicit rules and design guidelines."

"There remains a question as to if and how high-level principles should be expected to influence the development of safe and beneficial AI."

"In this short commentary I discuss two roles high-level principles might play in AI ethics and governance."

Introduction

"According to these critics, ethics principles not demonstrably implemented into AI research and development practices serve as little more than smoke and mirrors that project an unwarranted image of trustworthiness to consumers, and which provide policymakers with reasons not to pursue enforceable regulation [61–63]."

"There remains a question as to if and how high-level principles should be expected to influence the development of safe and beneficial AI."

"I agree that the translation of high-level principles into practice poses a significant challenge; however, we should not be so quick to dismiss principles as a tool in the AI governance repertoire."

"In virtue of this second role of AI ethics principles, I argue for a dual approach to AI governance in which principlism is supplementary to external policy and recognized as instrumental to the successful implementation of extrinsic rules and regulations."

What Is the Point of a Principle?

"To understand the role of principles in AI governance, medical ethics is a good starting point."

"Brent Mittelstadt [62] explains that the translation of biomedical principles into medical practice has enjoyed some success because the medical profession benefits from a unified goal (to treat disease and alleviate patient suffering) in addition to a well-defined range of activities and established systems to facilitate in the deliberation and articulation of explicit rules and requirements (e.g. internal review boards)."

"A less discussed, though no less important role of AI ethics principles is in underpinning cultural norms and values."

"Rather, without being translated into explicit rules and requirements, high-level principles like nonmaleficence, beneficence, and respect for patient autonomy define a mindset that influences how practitioners construe the challenges they face and the solutions they entertain."

Why Care About Culture?

"Cultural norms and values go beyond explicit rules and requirements."

"Not every decision a physician or AI developer might face can be prescribed, and where formal rules do not dictate specific action, professional values and norms of conduct can provide overarching guidance to fill in the gaps."

"The alignment of cultural norms with policy goals is key to the uptake and efficacy of explicit rules and regulations."

"Extrinsic rules and regulations have greater efficacy if they appeal to the cultural norms and values held by the communities to which they are being applied."

"In the case of AI, we may similarly expect that any rules and requirements will be more effective and more willingly adhered to by AI researchers and developers if those extrinsic measures align with cultural norms internalized by the community."

Conclusion: A Dual Approach to AI Governance

"Principles still have a key role to play for AI ethics governance in their "cultural influence" function as catalysts for building cultures of responsibility and beneficence among AI developers."

"Encouraging AI developers to internalize new values and to alter their social norms to align with policy goals is not merely a matter of posting a set of principles on the wall."

"If the aim of AI governance is to ensure the responsible research, development, and deployment of safe and beneficial AI, then I posit that the most effective AI governance strategy is a dual approach; explicit rules and regulations should be buttressed by principle-based initiatives encouraging cultural change within AI research and development communities to deemphasize the cultural norms like optimization and scale that can be antagonistic to the goals of AI governance, and to promote values like beneficence and responsibility."

Beyond a Human Rights-Based Approach to AI Governance: Promise, Pitfalls, Plea [64]

This is a machine-generated summary of:

Smuha, Nathalie A. Beyond a Human Rights-Based Approach to AI Governance: Promise, Pitfalls, Plea [64]

Published in: Philosophy & Technology (2020)

Link to original: https://doi.org/10.1007/s13347-020-00403-w

If you want to cite the papers, please refer to the original.

For technical reasons we could not place the page where the original quote is coming from.

Abstract-Summary

"Asserting that human rights can provide such compass, this paper first examines what a human rights-based approach to AI governance entails, and sets out the promise it propagates."

"It examines the pitfalls associated with human rights, particularly focusing on the criticism that these rights may be too Western, too individualistic, too narrow in scope and too abstract to form the basis of sound AI governance."

"It is argued that, without elucidating the applicability and enforceability of human rights in the context of AI; adopting legal rules that concretise those rights where appropriate; enhancing existing enforcement mechanisms and securing an underlying societal infrastructure that enables human rights in the first place, any human rights-based governance framework for AI risks falling short of its purpose."

The Quest for "Good AI"

"Not much social good will be generated by an AI-system that was developed without considering ethical values in its design phase (for instance by foregoing to tackle its potential for biased decision-making or its vulnerability to harmful adversarial attacks)."

"Both nevertheless raise an important definitional question that needs to be addressed by those aspiring to work towards their achievement: what is this "good" that AI-systems should be steered towards or their design should be aligned with?"

"How should those in charge of creating governance policies decide which norms to consider when aspiring to steer AI-systems towards good designs and uses?"

"A diversity of views was aspired by appointing experts from different countries, backgrounds and interest groups, with the purpose to move beyond such diversity and reach—to the extent possible—some consensus on the ethical challenges raised by AI-systems [65]."

The Promise

"The Guidelines start by specifying human rights' dual role within the framework of "Trustworthy AI", which the Group characterised as AI-systems that are (1) legal, (2) ethical and (3) robust, and the foundational ambition to be striven towards."

"While not explicitly stated in the Guidelines, it could furthermore be argued that ensuring AI-systems' robustness also contributes to securing the physical and mental integrity of individuals interacting therewith (the right of which is enshrined in Article 3 of the EU Charter), and that human rights might hence also overlap with the third component of Trustworthy AI (robust AI)."

"Given the importance of human rights within the Guidelines' framework, it is no coincidence that the Assessment List's first requirement entails an evaluation of the AI-system's potential negative impact on human rights."

The Pitfalls

"Decades of institutionalised human rights enforcement resulted in a rich jurisprudence that can also guide enforcers when dealing with the impact of AI-systems on individuals and society and with the tensions stemming therefrom—be it in terms of conflicting rights, principles or interests."

"To the extent that many (if not most) AI-systems are developed and deployed by private companies rather than by the state, this might render the human rights framework less relevant, or even inapplicable, since a potentially harmed individual cannot directly rely thereon against an AI-system's private producer."

"Notwithstanding the above, even if a specific human right could not be directly invoked against a private party (or could not be invoked at all, for instance if it concerns a jurisdiction that lacks the legal enforceability thereof), this would still not diminish the role that it can play to secure an appropriate AI governance framework."

The Plea

"Although human rights are not bulletproof, they provide a sound normative framework to steer AI-systems towards the good."

"In one direction, those developing and deploying AI-systems need to gain an understanding of the values that human rights protect, the applicability—and potential legal enforceability—of those rights regarding their own actions, and the manner in which they can be practically implemented."

"In the other direction, it is equally crucial that those in charge of enforcing human rights gain an understanding of how AI-systems work, and the manner in which their particular design, training or deployment might breach human rights."

"None of the novel issues raised by AI-systems will make human rights obsolete."

"When working towards such governance framework for AI, it is therefore primordial to likewise consider the necessity to secure an underlying societal infrastructure that enables human rights in the first place."

Conclusion

"Besides setting out the promise that a human rights-based approach to AI governance entails and refuting its pitfalls, this article has made the plea to move beyond this debate and start taking the necessary steps to secure such governance framework in practice."

"It is clear that—beyond an increase in resources and skills for enforcers—this process will require (1) a translation exercise that illuminates the applicability and vulnerability of human rights in the context of AI, (2) the adoption of new legislation that concretises human rights wherever their interpretation is too abstract to provide sufficient protection or their legal enforceability is desired but lacking, (3) a thorough evaluation of the current enforcement mechanisms of these rights and (4) the realisation that all human rights, legal rules and governance frameworks—whichever their scope—are dependent on the underlying societal infrastructure of which they are part."

References

1. Floridi, L., & Cowls, J. (2021). A unified framework of five principles for AI in society. Ethics, governance, and policies. *Artificial Intelligence*. https://doi.org/10.1007/978-3-030-81907-1_2
2. Floridi, L., Cowls, J., Beltrametti, M., et al. (2018). AI4People—An ethical framework for a good AI society: Opportunities, risks, principles, and recommendations. *Minds and Machines, 28*, 689–707. https://doi.org/10.1007/s11023-018-9482-5
3. Hagendorff, T. (2020). The ethics of AI ethics: An evaluation of guidelines. *Minds and Machines, 30*(1), 99–120. https://doi.org/10.1007/s11023-020-09517-8
4. Murgia, M. (2024). Overcoming AI ethics, towards AI realism. *AI and Ethics, 5*. https://doi.org/10.1007/s43681-024-00552-0
5. Westerstrand, S. (2024). Reconstructing AI ethics principles: Rawlsian ethics of artificial intelligence. *Science and Engineering Ethics*. https://doi.org/10.1007/s11948-024-00507-y
6. Brusseau, J. (2022). From the ground truth up: Doing AI ethics from practice to principles. *AI & Society, 38*. https://doi.org/10.1007/s00146-021-01336-4
7. Ayling, J., & Chapman, A. (2022). Putting AI ethics to work: Are the tools fit for purpose? *AI and Ethics, 2*(3), 405–429. https://doi.org/10.1007/s43681-021-00084-x
8. Zhou, J., & Chen, F. (2022). *AI ethics: From principles to practice*. AI & Society. https://doi.org/10.1007/s00146-022-01602-z
9. Stix, C. (2021). Actionable principles for artificial intelligence policy: Three pathways. *Science and Engineering Ethics*. https://doi.org/10.1007/s11948-020-00277-3
10. Seger, E. (2022). *In defence of principlism in AI ethics and governance*. Philosophy & Technology. https://doi.org/10.1007/s13347-022-00538-y
11. Cortese, J. F. N. B., Cozman, F. G., Lucca-Silveira, M. P., & Bechara, A. F. (2022). Should explainability be a fifth ethical principle in AI ethics? *AI and Ethics, 3*. https://doi.org/10.1007/s43681-022-00152-w
12. McCarthy, J., Minsky, M. L., Rochester, N., & Shannon, C. E. (2006). A proposal for the Dartmouth summer research project on artificial intelligence, August 31, 1955. *AI Magazine, 27*(4), 12. https://doi.org/10.1609/aimag.v27i4.1904
13. Ding, J. (2018). *Deciphering China's AI dream*, March. https://www.fhi.ox.ac.uk/wp-content/uploads/Deciphering_Chinas_AI-Dream.pdf
14. Webster, G., Creemers, R., Triolo, P., & Kania, E. (2017). *China's plan to 'lead' in AI: Purpose, prospects, and problems*. New America, August, 1. https://www.newamerica.org/cybersecurity-initiative/blog/chinas-plan-lead-ai-purpose-prospects-and-problems/
15. Delcker, J. (2018). *Europe's silver bullet in global AI battle: Ethics*. Politico, March 3. https://www.politico.eu/article/europe-silver-bullet-global-ai-battle-ethics/
16. Cowls, J., Png, M.-T., & Au, Y. (n.d.). *Foundations for geographic representation in algorithmic ethics*. Unpublished.
17. Cowls, J., King, T. C., & Taddeo, M., & Floridi, L. (2019). *Designing AI for social good: Seven essential factors*. http://ssrn.com/abstract=3388669
18. Morley, J., L. Floridi, L. Kinsey, & Elhalal, A. (2019). *From what to how. An overview of AI ethics tools, methods and research to translate principles into practices*. ArXiv:1905.06876 [Cs]. Retrieved from http://arxiv.org/abs/1905.06876
19. Calo, R. (2017). Artificial intelligence policy: A primer and roadmap. *UC Davis Law Review*, 51, 399–435. Retrieved from https://digitalcommons.law.uw.edu/faculty-articles/640
20. Leonelli, S. (2016). Locating ethics in data science: Responsibility and accountability in global and distributed knowledge production systems. *Philosophical Transactions. Series A, Mathematical, Physical, and Engineering Sciences, 374*(2083), 1–12.
21. Williams, B. (2005). *In the beginning was the deed: Realism and moralism in political argument*. Princeton University Press.
22. Sleat, M. (2014). Legitimacy in realist thought. *Political Theory, 42*(3), 314–337. https://doi.org/10.1177/0090591714522250
23. Lee, M. S. A., & Singh, J. (2021). The landscape and gaps in open source fairness toolkits. In *Proceedings of the 2021 CHI Conference on Human Factors in Computing Systems, New York* (pp. 1–13). https://doi.org/10.1145/3411764.3445261

24. Morgan, R. K. (2012). Environmental impact assessment: The state of the art. *Impact Assessment and Project Appraisal, 30*(1), 5–14. https://doi.org/10.1080/14615517.2012.661557
25. Clarke, R. (2009). Privacy impact assessment: Its origins and development. *Computer Law and Security Review, 25*(2), 123–135. https://doi.org/10.1016/j.clsr.2009.02.002
26. Information Commissioner's Office. (2018). *Data protection impact assessments*. https://ico.org.uk/for-organisations/guide-to-the-general-data-protection-regulation-gdpr/accountability-and-governance/data-protection-impact-assessments/. Accessed 07 Jun 2018.
27. The Danish Institute for Human Rights. (2016). *Human rights impact assessment guidance and toolbox – road-testing version*. The Danish Institute for Human Rights. https://www.humanrights.dk/business/tools/human-rights-impact-assessment-guidance-and-toolbox. Accessed 03 Feb 2020.
28. Bird, E., Fox-Skelly, J., Jenner, N., et al. (2020). *The ethics of artificial intelligence: Issues and initiatives*. European Parliamentary Research Service.
29. Lo Piano, S. (2020). Ethical principles in machine learning and artificial intelligence: Cases from the field and possible ways forward. *Humanit Soc Sci Commun, 7*, 1–7.
30. Gupta, A., Lanteigne, C., Heath, V., et al. (2020). *The state of AI ethics report (June 2020)*. arXiv:2006.14662 [cs].
31. Jobin, A., Ienca, M., & Vayena, E. (2019). The global landscape of AI ethics guidelines. *Nature Machine Intelligence, 1*(9), 389–399. https://doi.org/10.1038/s42256-019-0088-2
32. NSW Government. (2020). Mandatory ethical principles for the use of AI. In *Artificial intelligence (AI) ethics policy*. https://www.digital.nsw.gov.au/policy/artificial-intelligence-ai/artificial-intelligence-ai-ethics-policy/mandatory-ethical. Accessed 20 Oct 2020.
33. Korinek, A. (2020). Integrating ethical values and economic value to steer progress in artificial intelligence. In M. D. Dubber, F. Pasquale, & S. Das (Eds.), *The Oxford handbook of ethics of AI*. Oxford University Press.
34. Taddeo, M., McNeish, D., Blanchard, A., & Edgar, E. (2021). *Ethical principles for artificial intelligence in national Defence*. Philosophy & Technology. https://doi.org/10.1007/s13347-021-00482-3
35. Taddeo, M. (2014). The struggle between liberties and authorities in the information age. *Science and Engineering Ethics, 21*, 1125–1138. https://doi.org/10.1007/s11948-014-9586-0
36. Taddeo, M. (2019). The challenges of cyber deterrence. In C. Öhman & D. Watson (Eds.), *The 2018 yearbook of the digital ethics lab* (pp. 85–103). Springer International Publishing. https://doi.org/10.1007/978-3-030-17152-0_7
37. Taddeo, M. (2019). Three ethical challenges of applications of artificial intelligence in cybersecurity. *Minds and Machines, 29*(2), 187–191. https://doi.org/10.1007/s11023-019-09504-8
38. DIB. (2020). *AI principles: Recommendations on the ethical use of artificial intelligence by the Department of Defense*. https://media.defense.gov/2019/Oct/31/2002204458/-1/-1/0/DIB_AI_PRINCIPLES_PRIMARY_DOCUMENT.PDF
39. Mökander, J., & Floridi, L. (2021). Ethics-based auditing to develop trustworthy AI. *Minds and Machines, 31*(2), 323–327. https://doi.org/10.1007/s11023-021-09557-8
40. Blomberg, S. N., Christensen, H. C., Lippert, F., Ersbøll, A. K., Torp-Petersen, C., Sayre, M. R., Kudenchuk, P. J., & Folke, F. (2021). Effect of machine learning on dispatcher recognition of out-of-hospital cardiac arrest during calls to emergency medical services: A randomized clinical trial. *JAMA Network Open, 4*(1), e2032320. https://doi.org/10.1001/jamanetworkopen.2020.32320
41. Zicari, R. V., et al. (2021). On assessing trustworthy AI in healthcare. Machine learning as a supportive tool to recognize cardiac arrest in emergency calls. *Frontiers in Human Dynamics*. https://doi.org/10.3389/fhumd.2021.673104
42. Havtorn, J. D., Latko, J., Edin, J., Borgholt, L., Maaløe, L., Belgrano, L., Jacobsen, N. F., Sdun, R., & Agi, Ž. (2020). *MultiQT: Multimodal learning for real-time question tracking in speech*. ArXiv:2005.00812. [Cs, Eess]. http://arxiv.org/abs/2005.00812

43. Maaløe, L., Fraccaro, M., Liévin, V., & Winther, O. (2019). BIVA: A very deep hierarchy of latent variables for generative modeling. *Advances in Neural Information Processing Systems, 32*, 6551–6562.
44. Beauchamp, T. L., & Childress, J. F. (2019). *Principles of biomedical ethics* (8th ed.). Oxford University Press.
45. Ursin, F., Timmermann, C., & Steger, F. (2022). Explicability of artificial intelligence in radiology: Is a fifth bioethical principle conceptually necessary? *Bioethics, 36*(2), 143–153.
46. Lacave, C., & Diez, F. J. (2002). A review of explanation methods for Bayesian networks. *Knowledge Engineering Review, 17*(2), 107–127.
47. Ribeiro, M. T., Singh, S., & Guestrin, C. (2016). Why should I trust you? Explaining the predictions of any classifier. In *Proceedings of the ACM International Conference on Knowledge Discovery and Data Mining* (pp. 1135–1144).
48. Rawls, J. (1971). *A theory of justice: Original edition*. Harvard University Press. https://doi.org/10.2307/j.ctvjf9z6v
49. Rawls, J. (1999). *A theory of justice: Revised edition*. Harvard University Press.
50. Wiener, N. (1954). *The human use of human beings: Cybernetics and society* ([2d ed. rev.]). Doubleday.
51. Weizenbaum, J. (1976). *Computer power and human reason: From judgment to calculation*. W. H. Freeman & Co..
52. Bynum, T. W. (2006). Flourishing ethics. *Ethics and Information Technology, 8*(4), 157–173. https://doi.org/10.1007/s10676-006-9107-1
53. Rawls, J. (2005). *Political liberalism*. Columbia University Press.
54. Rességuier, A., & Rodrigues, R. (2020). AI ethics should not remain toothless! A call to bring back the teeth of ethics. *Big Data & Society, 7*, 1–5.
55. Heilinger, J.-C. (2022). The ethics of AI ethics. A constructive critique. *Philosophy and Technology, 35*(3), 61. https://doi.org/10.1007/s13347-022-00557-9
56. Hidvegi, F., & Leufer, D. (2019). *Laying down the law on AI: Ethics done, now the EU must focus on human rights*. https://www.accessnow.org/laying-down-the-law-on-ai-ethics-done-now-the-eu-must-focus-on-human-rights/
57. Metzinger, T. (2019). *EU guidelines: Ethics washing made in Europe*. Der Tagesspiegel. Retrieved from https://www.tagesspiegel.de/politik/eu-guidelines-ethics-washing-made-in-europe/24195496.html
58. Fung, P., & Etienne, H. (2022). Confucius, cyberpunk and Mr. Science: Comparing AI ethics principles between China and the EU. *AI and Ethics*. https://doi.org/10.1007/s43681-022-00180-6
59. Cunningham, E., Saich, T., & Turiel, J. (2020). *Understanding CCP resilience: Surveying Chinese public opinion through time*. Ash Center for Democratic Governance and Innovation. https://ash.harvard.edu/publications/understanding-ccp-resilience-surveying-chinese-public-opinion-through-time
60. Cihon, P. (2019). *Standards for AI governance: International standards to enable global coordination in AI research & development*. Future of Humanity Institute's technical report
61. Calo, R. (2017). Artificial intelligence policy: A primer and roadmap. *UC Davis Law Review, 51*, 399–436.
62. Mittelstadt, B. (2019). Principles alone cannot guarantee ethical AI. *Nature Machine Intelligence, 1*, 501–507.
63. Whittlestone, J., Nyrup, R., Alexandrova, A., Dihal, K., & Cave, S. (2019). *Ethical and societal implications of algorithms, data, and artificial intelligence: A roadmap for research*. Nuffield Foundation.
64. Smuha, N. A. (2020). *Beyond a human rights-based approach to AI governance: Promise, pitfalls, plea*. Philosophy & Technology. https://doi.org/10.1007/s13347-020-00403-w
65. Smuha, N. (2019). The EU approach to ethics guidelines for trustworthy artificial intelligence. *Computer Law Review International, 20*(4), 97–106.

Chapter 3
AI Ethics Advisor's Guide to Trust: Why Perception Matters

Abstract The following discussion explores the critical role of trust in AI, arguing that perception significantly influences trustworthiness in AI systems. It addresses key factors contributing to trust, such as explainability, reliability, accountability, and socio-technical perceptions. The chapter analyses how misaligned perceptions can lead to misplaced trust in AI systems, potentially resulting in ethical breaches. It offers guidelines for AI ethics advisors on fostering trustworthy AI through transparent practices and effective communication, underscoring the importance of aligning stakeholder perceptions with actual system reliability.

Keywords Trust · Trustworthiness · Explainability · Reliability · Socio-technical perceptions

Introduction by the Editor

Whether—and how—people should trust AI systems is contested. Some scholars portray AI as a potential object of interpersonal trust, others treat the issue as one of measurable reliability, while a third group emphasises how users' perceptions of transparency, accountability, and control shape their behaviour. By setting these visions side by side, this chapter argues that the central challenge is not to declare AI trustworthy but to achieve a well-calibrated, context-sensitive reliance on it.

Trust as Interpersonal Analogy

The first perspective models human-AI relations on interpersonal trust, defining trust as "reliance plus an extra factor" such as goodwill or moral commitment [1]. Proponents insist that users need more than technical performance; they require assurances that the system—or those behind it—will act in their interests. Explainability, accountability, and external auditing therefore become prerequisites

A. Carnevale, *The AI Ethics Advisor*,
https://doi.org/10.1007/978-3-032-05526-2_3

for genuine trustworthiness [2, 3]. Critics reply that machines lack emotive or moral agency, so the analogy risks conceptual confusion: calling an artefact trustworthy may anthropomorphise it or shift responsibility away from human actors [4, 5].

Reliability Without Moral Trust

A second vision rejects any interpersonal analogy, asserting that machines should be relied on rather than trusted. Advocates argue that the phrase "trustworthy AI" misleads and that the relevant question is whether a system's performance can be measured, monitored, and communicated transparently [4, 6]. In this reframing, reliability metrics and confidence scores help users gauge how far to depend on a model. At the same time, moral responsibility remains squarely with the people and institutions that design and deploy it. Nevertheless, empirical studies demonstrate that users often follow algorithmic advice even when warned about flaws or given minimal information, suggesting that reliability signals alone do not prevent over-reliance [7].

The Explainability Dispute

Between these poles lies a debate about whether explainability is essential. One side claims that meaningful reliance is impossible without intelligible reasons for a system's output [2]; the other maintains that a strong empirical track record and independent validation can justify reliance even when the internal logic remains opaque [8]. At stake is an assessment of what users truly need to feel safe: semantic understanding, statistical assurance, or some combination of the two. The ethics advisor must steer developers through these expectations, recommending design or disclosure choices that reflect the context of use.

Modest Anthropocentrism

A moderating view, sometimes called "modest anthropocentrism", neither projects moral agency onto AI nor reduces evaluation to raw performance [9]. Instead, the obligations of an AI system are derived from the social role it occupies—diagnostic instrument, credit-scoring assistant, autonomous delivery drone—and the norms governing that role. Trust, on this account, is appropriate when the system fulfils its function in a way that aligns with those norms and adapts as practices evolve. Ethical appraisal becomes an ongoing process rather than a one-off certification.

Cross-Cutting Insights

Empirical evidence shows that users frequently over-trust opaque or demonstrably flawed systems, suggesting that the aim is to align perceived trust with actual risk [7]. Governance mechanisms such as ethics-based auditing and funding requirements can translate abstract principles into concrete discipline, making it harder for unreliable or unjust systems to reach deployment [3, 10]. Where full interpretability is unattainable, well-calibrated confidence indicators can still mitigate misuse if their status and limits are clearly explained [6].

Conclusion: The Ethics Advisor as Reliance Architect

Reframing trust as calibrated reliance places the ethics advisor at the centre of technical design, organisational governance, and user engagement. By translating competing theories of trust into coherent policy, the advisor prevents both conceptual conflation and ethics-washing. Through independent audits, scenario testing, and usability studies, the advisor can ensure that reliability signals are accurate, intelligible, and appropriate for the context. By tracing accountability back to identifiable human or institutional actors, the advisor has to clarify where moral responsibility resides and how redress mechanisms operate. Finally, by instituting regular "reliance reviews" that revisit risk, transparency, and user expectations, the advisor can maintain a dynamic equilibrium in which dependence on AI remains informed rather than blind. Only through such stewardship can AI serve societal interests while respecting the nuanced contours of human vulnerability.

Machine Generated Summaries

Trust and Trustworthiness in AI [1]

This is a machine-generated summary of:

Durán, Juan Manuel; Pozzi, Giorgia Trust and Trustworthiness in AI [1]

Published in: Philosophy & Technology (2025)

Link to original: https://doi.org/10.1007/s13347-025-00843-2

If you want to cite the papers, please refer to the original.

For technical reasons we could not place the page where the original quote is coming from.

Abstract-Summary

"Achieving trustworthy AI is increasingly considered an essential desideratum to integrate AI systems into sensitive societal fields, such as criminal justice, finance, medicine, and healthcare, among others."

"This article is the first survey in the specialized literature that maps out the philosophical landscape surrounding trust and trustworthiness in AI."

"We start by discussing philosophical positions on trust and trustworthiness, focusing on interpersonal accounts of trust."

"This allows us to explain why trust, in its most general terms, is to be understood as reliance plus some "extra factor"."

"We then turn to the first part of the definition provided, i.e., reliance, and analyze two opposing approaches to establishing AI systems' reliability."

"We consider viewpoints that most actively resist the possibility and desirability of trusting AI systems before turning to the analysis of the most prominent advocates of it."

Introduction

"Many technical solutions are available today that aim to fortify our trust in AI and ensure their trustworthiness (e.g., [11])."

"While the example above may apply to interpersonal trust between two humans (a trustor and a trustee, a physician and a patient), its relevance to AI systems is less clear."

"This article aims to analyze the complexity of this issue by first distinguishing trust from trustworthiness, and then discussing the former as a two-part concept: reliance and the "extra factor.""

"A key takeaway from this section is that studies on trust in AI can be analytically divided into two categories: reliance, which examines the conditions for scientifically valid outputs, and an "extra factor," which explores the moral motivations underlying trust [12]."

"This should contribute to the analysis of different positions regarding the "extra factor" concerning both the conceptual and normative possibility of genuinely trusting (and not merely relying on) AI systems."

The Multiple Dimensions of Trust and Trustworthiness

"We express our present and future trust in our physicians and friends because they have shown to be trustworthy."

"Philosophical inquiries into trust and trustworthiness focus on understanding the practical commitment between a trustor and a trustee."

"We label the physician as trustworthy because they have demonstrated that they are deserving of our trust."

"Understood, trust and trustworthiness are distinct but related concepts, allowing for the possibility of trusting an untrustworthy person or entity and, vice versa, withholding trust even when the trustee is, in fact, trustworthy."

"Instances in which trust is withheld, even though the trustee is trustworthy, often arise when the trustor holds biases that deflate the perceived trustworthiness of the trustee."

"Trust, on the other hand, is a more complex issue for a comprehensive understanding of trustworthy AI."

"Solving the issue of trust in AI is at the root of any comprehensive understanding of trustworthy AI."

Reliance

"Transparency means the cognitive ability to comprehensively survey and account for variables, system relations, and other elements within the algorithm with the purpose of having reasons to believe in the scientific validity of the output."

"According to CR, three token reliability indicators can be identified: RI_1Technical performance of algorithms: it focuses on the design, coding, execution, and other technical aspects of artificial intelligence systems that make the system robust, including the collection, curation, storage, and analysis of data; RI_2Computer-based scientific practice: focuses on the practices incumbent to ML-based scientific research and which results from the implementation of scientific theories, principles, and hypotheses, as well as the interactions, debates, and other ways of engaging in standard scientific research; and finally, RI_3 Social construction of scientific beliefs: focuses on the broader goals of accepting the AI and its outputs in diverse communities (e.g., scientific, academic, general public, etc) through debates and other forms of intellectual exchange."

The "Extra Factor"

"Authors who hold a skeptical position regarding trustworthy AI take that AI systems cannot be seen as genuinely trustworthy because (1) it is either impossible to trust AI systems without anthropomorphizing them (see the critique to the affective and normative accounts), or (2) an account of trust that does not require AI systems' anthropomorphization fails to maintain the conceptual distinction between morally-loaded trust and mere reliance, thus rendering the debate about trust in AI obsolete (see the critique to the rational-choice account of trust)."

"This brings us to the second main position on trust in AI, which does not require any form of agency for AI systems but rather focuses on advancing a non-normative and non-affective account."

"Key to these authors' account is that trust in AI comes in degrees, and we do not need to consider AI systems as suitable bearers of affective or normative expectations in order to meaningfully say that we trust them."

Concluding Remarks

"With this distinction in mind, we considered two opposing views on how to secure the reliance of AI algorithms, namely transparency and computational reliabilism."

"Despite these, computational reliabilism still proves to be a suitable method to account for the reliance condition needed to secure trust in AI systems."

"We showed that scholars holding a skeptical view regarding the very possibility and desirability of trust in AI systems advance convincing arguments that need to be accounted for."

"We sketched some approaches that try to exclude the normative dimension of trust from the picture, while others attribute to AI systems either some form of minimal agency or require to trace trust back to the human beings behind its development."

"It is unclear whether the agency attributed to AI systems accounts for the 'extra factor' or whether it is legitimate to exclude the normativity of trust and thus blur the line between (mere) reliance and genuine (morally robust) trust."

In AI We Trust: Ethics, Artificial Intelligence, and Reliability [4]

This is a machine-generated summary of:

Ryan, Mark In AI We Trust: Ethics, Artificial Intelligence, and Reliability [4]
Published in: Science and Engineering Ethics (2020)
Link to original: https://doi.org/10.1007/s11948-020-00228-y

If you want to cite the papers, please refer to the original.

For technical reasons we could not place the page where the original quote is coming from.

Abstract-Summary

"Trust is one of the most important and defining activities in human relationships, so proposing that AI should be trusted, is a very serious claim."

"This paper will show that AI cannot be something that has the capacity to be trusted according to the most prevalent definitions of trust because it does not possess emotive states or can be held responsible for their actions—requirements of the affective and normative accounts of trust."

"While AI meets all of the requirements of the rational account of trust, it will be shown that this is not actually a type of trust at all, but is instead, a form of reliance."

"Even complex machines such as AI should not be viewed as trustworthy as this undermines the value of interpersonal trust, anthropomorphises AI, and diverts responsibility from those developing and using them."

Introduction

"This paper will show that AI cannot be something that has the capacity to be trusted according to the most prevalent definitions of trust because it does not possess emotive states or be held responsible for its actions—requirements of the affective and normative accounts of trust."

"For AI to be classified as something that we can trust, it would require an explicit capacity to be morally responsible for its actions, in particular, the act that it is entrusted to carry out."

"Regardless of the level of autonomy of the decision-making process of AI at eBay, its user-base places a trust in the company, and individuals working in the company, to ensure that they meet their normative commitments or are acting in the best interests of trustors when they trust them."

Conclusion

"One needs to either change 'trustworthy AI' to 'reliable AI' or remove it altogether."

"The rational account of reliability does not require AI to have emotion towards the trustor (affective account) or be responsible for its actions (normative account)."

"This is the main reason why human-made objects, such as AI, can be reliable, but not trustworthy, according to the affective account."

"Whereas, reliable AI places the burden of responsibility on those developing, deploying, and using these technologies."

"Proponents of AI ethics should abandon the 'trustworthy AI' paradigm as it is too fraught with problems, replacing it with the reliable AI approach, instead."

Trust and Trustworthiness in AI Ethics [13]

This is a machine-generated summary of:

Reinhardt, Karoline Trust and trustworthiness in AI ethics [13]

Published in: AI and Ethics (2022)

Link to original: https://doi.org/10.1007/s43681-022-00200-5

If you want to cite the papers, please refer to the original.

For technical reasons we could not place the page where the original quote is coming from.

Abstract-Summary

"Due to the extensive progress of research in artificial intelligence (AI) as well as its deployment and application, the public debate on AI systems has also gained momentum in recent years."

"With the publication of the Ethics Guidelines for Trustworthy AI (2019), notions of trust and trustworthiness gained particular attention within AI ethics-debates; despite an apparent consensus that AI should be trustworthy, it is less clear what trust and trustworthiness entail in the field of AI."

"I give a detailed overview on the notion of trust employed in AI Ethics Guidelines thus far."

"I argue that, currently, AI ethics tends to overload the notion of trustworthiness."

Introduction

"With the publication of the Ethics Guidelines for Trustworthy AI by the Independent High-Level Expert Group on Artificial Intelligence (2019), the notions of trust and trustworthiness gained particular attention within AI ethics-debates with regard to AI governance; the term trustworthy AI (TAI) has since been widely adopted by the AI research community [14–27], public sector organizations, and political bodies issuing AI ethics guidelines."

"Despite an apparent consensus that AI should be trustworthy, it is less clear what trust and trustworthiness entail in the field of AI and what ethical standards, technical requirements and practices are needed for the realization of TAI."

"I give a detailed overview on the notion of trust employed in AI Ethics Guidelines."

"I argue that currently AI ethics overloads the notion of trust and trustworthiness and turns it into an umbrella term for an inconclusive list of things deemed "good"."

Trust and Trustworthiness in AI Ethics: An Evaluation of Guidelines

"Different from the other overviews that cover with one exception [18] the entire landscape of AI ethics, I focus on the notions of trust and trustworthiness and key concepts associated with these two notions in the guidelines."

"Most guidelines refer to trust, however, as something to be advanced [28], built [29–39], created, [40] cultivated, [41] earned [34, 37, 42], elevated [29], enabled [43], established [30, 41, 44], gained [44–46], fostered [30, 35, 38, 47–49], improved [32], increased [29, 44, 49, 50], inspired [35], maintained [33, 39, 46, 51], promoted [30, 35, 36, 47, 49], reinforced [36], and upheld [47]."

"In the guidelines, trustworthiness is linked to a whole range of different principles; transparency does play a major role and is linked to trust and trustworthiness in a number of guidelines [28–30, 34–37, 40, 42, 44, 47–50, 52–62]."

"Rarely it is mentioned that accreditation, approval and certification schemes and the formulation of guidelines can help establish trust [30, 33, 44]."

"The connection between trust and a variety of ethical principles is made in the guidelines, no single principle is linked to trust as making AI trustworthy throughout the entire corpus of documents."

Assessing AI Ethics Guidelines

"One almost gets the impression that everything that is considered "good" is also supposed to inspire trust and on top of that regarded as a necessary precondition for AI systems to be trustworthy."

"Related to this point is, fifthly, that possible trade-offs and conflicts between these various values and principles that are supposed to generate trust are rarely reflected and how they would play out with regard to an AI system's trustworthiness [52]."

"The last apparent omission I want to mention here is of a less conceptual, but a more practical nature; although it is occasionally mentioned in the guidelines that TAI systems should benefit the environment and the economy, or at least not harm them, surprisingly, even in those guidelines that focus on customer and user trust, the conditions under which AI products are created hardly plays a role and they are rarely mentioned as a factor for increasing or decreasing people's trust in AI."

Closing the Gaps: Future Research on the T in TAI

"I will focus on three aspects: the overlooked ambivalence of trust, the problematic conflation of trust and trustworthiness, and the problem of conflict of principles in the guidelines: Ambivalence of trust As mentioned above, trust is a highly ambivalent concept; trust "is important, but it is also dangerous" [63]."

"Much effort might be put in designing trustworthy AI and people might still not trust it, let alone adopt it."

"They might ultimately not lead to a wider adoption of AI systems, simply because trustworthiness does not automatically lead to trust in the way that many of the guidelines seem to assume."

"This is not to say that we should not care about the principles that AI systems endorse or violate, we just might need to provide a different reasoning, or different incentives from gaining trust."

Conclusions

"Notions of trust and trustworthiness have gained significant attention in AI research especially after the publication of Europe's High-Level Expert Group's Ethics guidelines for trustworthy AI, ethics guidelines referring to trust with regard to AI diverge substantively in no less than four main areas: (1) why trust is important or of value, (2) who or what the envisioned trustors and trustees are, (3) what trustworthiness is and entails, and (4) how it should be implemented technically."

"Philosophy can help to conceptualize trust and trustworthiness."

"We need to discuss possible conflicts between the various principles associated with trustworthiness in more detail."

"In further research, it might turn out that in the end what we need is not more trust in AI but rather institutionalized forms of distrust."

Explainability Is Necessary for AI's Trustworthiness [2]

This is a machine-generated summary of:

Fan, Ning Explainability Is Necessary for AI's Trustworthiness [2]

Published in: Philosophy & Technology (2025)

Link to original: https://doi.org/10.1007/s13347-025-00847-y

If you want to cite the papers, please refer to the original.

For technical reasons we could not place the page where the original quote is coming from.

Abstract-Summary

"In a recent article in this journal, Baron [8] argues that we can appropriately trust unexplainable artificial intelligence (AI) systems, so explainability is not necessary for AI's trustworthiness."

"I first offer a positive argument for the claim that explainability is necessary for trustworthiness."

Introduction

"In a recent article in this journal, Baron [8] argues that while many artificial intelligence (AI) systems used for decision-making are unexplainable, they are still trustworthy."

"Unexplainable AI systems, according to Baron, are such that "no-one can explain why those systems provide the outputs that they do, either in specific cases or in general" [8 , p. 1]."

"Drawing on this argument, I then show that Baron's argument that explainability is not necessary for AI's trustworthiness fails."

Trust and Trustworthiness

"In light of this remark, the relation between trust and trustworthiness, at least in the present discussion, should be understood as follows: X is trustworthy for a person S if and only if it is fitting for S to trust X. Baron does not specify the notion of fittingness, so this needs to be clarified."

"Account, we can then understand trustworthiness as the property of having some feature that calls for trust."

"To having features that merit trust, an object, in order to be trustworthy, must not have other features that call for questioning attitudes."

"I take this to be equivalent to asking whether an object is trustworthy, for we can appropriately trust an object just in case that object is trustworthy for us."

"Appropriate trust just is fitting trust, and only trustworthy objects can be the targets of this type of trust."

Why Explainability Is Necessary for Trustworthiness

"The second premise is this: (2) If X has some feature that calls for questioning attitudes regarding whether X will P, then X is not trustworthy regarding whether X will P. The underlying idea of premise (2) is that properties can be incompatible with one other."

"Pulling the two premises together, I formulate the argument as follows: (1) If X is unexplainable regarding why X can P, then X has some feature that calls for questioning attitudes regarding whether X will P. (2) If X has some feature that calls for questioning attitudes regarding whether X will P, then X is not trustworthy regarding whether X will P. (3) If X is unexplainable regarding why X can P, then X is not trustworthy regarding whether X will P. (From (1) and (2)) (C) Conclusion: If X is trustworthy regarding whether X will P, X is explainable regarding why X can P. (From (3)) The conclusion entails that an object's explainability is necessary for its trustworthiness."

Rejecting Baron's Argument

"I don't really understand how my laptop works and yet I am unquestioningly relying on it right now. [8, p. 12] The examples of car and laptop, however, do not show that we can appropriately trust something that is unexplainable."

"Since cars and laptops are not unexplainable in the relevant sense, they cannot be used to show that unexplainable objects can be appropriately trusted."

"Baron may reply that an object, despite unexplainable, can still be appropriately trusted for doing a certain task if that object has past success in that task."

"He says, "one can appropriately adopt an unquestioning attitude [i.e., trust] based just on an induction over the past success of an object to function as desired" ([8 , p. 12], my emphasis)."

"Baron's remark entails that an object's past success in a task by itself makes it the case that the object can be appropriately trusted, i.e., trustworthy."

Trust, Explainability and AI [8]

This is a machine-generated summary of:

Baron, Sam Trust, Explainability and AI [8]

Published in: Philosophy & Technology (2025)

Link to original: https://doi.org/10.1007/s13347-024-00837-6

If you want to cite the papers, please refer to the original.

For technical reasons we could not place the page where the original quote is coming from.

Abstract-Summary

"It is commonly claimed that explainability is necessary for trust in AI, and that this is why we need it."

"For notions of trust that are appropriate for AI, explainability is not a necessary condition."

"I thus conclude that explainability is not necessary for trust in AI that matters."

Introduction

"For if an AI system is not explainable, then it is thought it cannot be trusted."

"Explainability is necessary for trust in AI."

"For notions of trust that are appropriate for AI, explainability is not a necessary condition."

"I therefore conclude that explainability is not after all necessary for appropriate trust in AI."

"For the kind of trust in AI that matters, there is no need for explainability."

"I then consider notions of trust for which explainability is plausibly necessary, and argue that they are not appropriate for AI. §"

"Ryan [4] and Frieman [64] argue that some notions of trust are inappropriate for AI, but do not consider how this relates to explainability."

"The paper draws these strands on trust and explainability together, by providing the first general argument against the idea that explainability is needed for trust in AI that matters."

Types of Trust

"According to this account, trust is a matter of relying on the performance P of someone or something where (i) it is worth relying on P and (ii) we are entitled to rely on P. Note that the 'entitlement' is a normative expectation, specifically a normative expectation about performance P. For instance, suppose once again that Ping trusts her computer to save her document, where this is sufficiently valuable that it is worth relying on her computer to do that."

"On a simple account of normative trust, x trusts y when x relies on y and x believes that y will act out of a normative commitment toward x. Thus, Cathy trusts Ping to look after Simon when she relies on Ping to do so and believes that Ping will look after Simon because she is motivated to do the right thing, morally speaking, by Cathy."

Trust and Explainability

"We are interested in whether explainability is necessary for appropriate trust in AI."

"I will thus argue that appropriate reliance on AI does not require explainability."

"The question we need to answer is whether explainability is necessary for appropriate reliance on AI in the relevant sense."

"The claim I have been arguing for is this: T1: Explainability is not necessary for appropriate reliance on AI, in cases where good information indicating the reliability of an AI system is available."

"The question, then, is whether explainability is necessary for appropriate trust in AI in Nyugen's sense."

"On this picture trust in x is a matter of relying on x without monitoring x. Trust as reliance plus monitoring is clearly appropriate for AI."

"The question, then, is whether explainability is necessary for appropriate trust in AI in this sense."

Objections

"The argument: while moderate notions of trust are appropriate for AI, it is plausible that explainability is not a necessary condition on those notions."

"For strong notions of trust, by contrast, explainability likely is a necessary condition, but such notions are not appropriate for AI."

"One can appropriately trust a doctor to use an AI system for diagnosis, where this involves an appropriate belief that the doctor uses the tool with goodwill toward the patient."

"We really should be able to trust doctors to use AI tools with the right motivations, and with the patient's interests weighing on them in their deliberations."

"I have argued that explainability is not necessary for trust in AI that matters."

"This is because, roughly, AI systems don't have the right kinds of mental properties or mental states for any strong notion of trust to be appropriate."

Final Thoughts

"The argument that I have presented focuses on local explainability."

"That being so, it is likely the arguments will indeed generalise, and thus that neither local nor global explainability are necessary for trust in AI that matters."

"It is thus likely that explainability is important for the ethical legitimacy and long-term public acceptance of AI systems, as well as for regulatory compliance, even if it is not necessary for trust."

"Explainability can also be important in cases where one is using AI as a tool for scientific discovery (see, e.g., [65]), in part because it can be helpful for uncovering mechanisms or causal processes (for discussion, see [66])."

"Rather, what the arguments may recommend is a reorientation of the discussion of trust and explainability."

"That's because, as noted above, explainability plays a number of important roles for AI."

Trustworthy AI: A Plea for Modest Anthropocentrism [9]

This is a machine-generated summary of:

Nyrup, Rune Trustworthy AI: a plea for modest anthropocentrism [9]

Published in: Asian Journal of Philosophy (2023)

Link to original: https://doi.org/10.1007/s44204-023-00096-w

If you want to cite the papers, please refer to the original.

For technical reasons we could not place the page where the original quote is coming from.

Abstract-Summary

"Simion and Kelp defend a non-anthropocentric account of trustworthy AI, based on the idea that the obligations of AI systems should be sourced in purely functional norms."

"I outline an alternative account, based on the idea that AI systems should not be considered primarily as tools but as technological participants in social practices."

"I propose to source the obligations of an AI system in the norms that should govern the role it plays within the social practices it participates in, taking into account any changes to the social practices that its participation may bring about."

AI Anthropomorphism or Trustworthiness Anthropocentrism?

"Some question whether it makes sense to ascribe trustworthiness to AI systems."

"Since AI systems lack these capacities, they should not be described as trustworthy."

"Doing so, argues Ryan, would either inappropriately anthropomorphise AI systems (since it misleadingly suggests they have capacities they in fact lack) or deflate the concept of trustworthiness to the extent that it undermines the value of interpersonal trust."

"They presuppose that it does make sense to call AI systems trustworthy, aiming instead to develop an account of trustworthiness capable of making sense of such ascriptions."

"They are of course well aware that the classical accounts of trustworthiness would entail ascribing contentious anthropomorphic capacities to AI systems."

"They regard this as a problem for the classical accounts, rather than a reason to reject the emerging practice of ascribing trustworthiness to AI systems."

Simion and Kelp's Account

"While persons are typically obligated to take responsibility for the consequences of their actions, artefacts are usually only obligated to reliably carry out their proper functions."

"Their answer is that artefacts acquire obligations based on their functions."

"Simion and Kelp distinguish two ways that artefacts acquire functions."

"The first is based on the designers' intentions (d-functions): an artefact d-functions properly when it (reliably enough under normal circumstances) is able to do what the designers intended it to do."

"Artefacts can also acquire functions etiologically (e-functions), based on the history of that type of artefact."

"An artefact acquires an e-function when past tokens of that artefact type had a certain ability, and this fact contributes to explaining the continuous existence of artefacts of that type."

"According to Simion and Kelp, this is because cancer-diagnostic AIs have the e-function to reliably recognise such tumours, since this ability contributes to explaining their continuous existence."

Untrustworthy but Properly Functioning AI

"The problem for Simion and Kelp's account is that there are cases of untrustworthy AI systems that nonetheless reliably fulfil their d-function and e-function."

"Suppose they argued that they are d-functions, since many designers do want to ensure their AI systems avoid these problems."

"Suppose, instead, they argued that they are e-functions, since people are more likely to use and accept unbiased and non-polarising AI systems, and this contributes to explaining their continuous existence."

"It also seems normatively problematic: if a type of AI continues to exist because of its ability to convince users that it is unbiased, regardless of the actual behaviour of the system, would that count towards its trustworthiness?"

"Technologies can be deliberately designed with functions that are contrary to the interests of those who would trust them; in fact, many artefacts are designed, and continue to exist, exactly because they serve interests antagonistic to the user and other potential trustors."

A Modestly Anthropocentric Proposal

"My proposal is, roughly, that because AI systems take up human-like roles within important social practices, they inherit some of the same obligations that would apply to humans occupying those roles."

"To cash out these ideas, I propose the following: Modest anthropocentrism: an AI system's obligations to phi are sourced in the norms that should govern the role it plays within the social practices it participates in, taking into account any changes to the social practices that its participation may bring about."

"An AI system participates in a social practice, P, if and only if it performs one or more tasks that either (i) play the same functional role as a meaningful action in P or (ii) contribute to the actions of agents participating in P. Thus, a fully automated cancer-diagnostic AI and a medical decision-support system would both count as participating in the practice of medical diagnosis."

Conclusion

"To close, a final remark: I suggested that the norms governing AI systems should be determined by the overall social function of the practices they participate in."

"This seems to be in the spirit of Simion and Kelp's general framework, especially since they (briefly) outline an etiological account of the functions of social practices."

"The reason for my hesitation is as follows: like Haslanger, I worry that many social practices, in their current formation, in part function to serve unjust ends—e.g. to facilitate and reinforce the exploitation of marginalised populations and scarce natural resources for the benefit of the already well off."

"For those who share this worry, calling AI systems that merely preserve the current functions of social practices 'trustworthy' will be deeply unsatisfactory (to put it mildly)."

"Quasi-Metacognitive Machines: Why We Don't Need Morally Trustworthy AI and Communicating Reliability Is Enough" [6]

This is a machine-generated summary of:

Dorsch, John; Deroy, Ophelia "Quasi-Metacognitive Machines: Why We Don't Need Morally Trustworthy AI and Communicating Reliability is Enough" [6]

Published in: Philosophy & Technology (2024)

Link to original: https://doi.org/10.1007/s13347-024-00752-w

If you want to cite the papers, please refer to the original.

For technical reasons we could not place the page where the original quote is coming from.

Abstract-Summary

"We argue that developing morally trustworthy AI is not only unethical, as it promotes trust in an entity that cannot be trustworthy, but it is also unnecessary for optimal calibration."

"We show that reliability, exclusive of moral trust, entails the appropriate normative constraints that enable optimal calibration and mitigate the vulnerability that arises in high-stakes hybrid decision-making environments, without also demanding, as moral trust would, the anthropomorphization of AI and thus epistemically dubious behavior."

"Drawing on recent empirical findings that suggest providing reliability scores (e.g., F1-scores) to human decision-makers improves calibration in the AI system, we argue that reliability scores provide a good index of competence and enable humans to determine how much they wish to rely on the system."

Introduction

"Since the emergence of automated systems (AS) and, more recently, systems of artificial intelligence (AI) as integral parts to the decision-making process, questions concerning trust in AS/AI have been at the forefront of research (for a review, see [67])."

"If the goal is to develop ethical policies for the development and implementation of such systems, we ought to question whether this assumption is justified and ask whether moral trust ought to be employed in our relationship to machines or whether a related, but ultimately distinct concept, such as reliability (exclusive of moral trust), ought to modulate behavior toward automation."

"For our criticism, we are solely concerned with autonomous systems, whose purpose is to facilitate human decision-making by taking autonomous action that assists the human in reaching her goal, which, in virtue of its automation, places the human (and potentially other people) in a position of vulnerability, wherein concerns of trustworthiness and reliability become central to her use of the application."

Reliability, Trustworthiness, and Vulnerability

"An agent's reliability thus serves as a pro tanto reason for trusting her, since knowing her to be reliable will justify, as far as it goes, making oneself vulnerable to her (for a discussion of the importance of vulnerability in trust-based relationships, see [21])."

"This is because vulnerability to AI can never be justified since its actions only ever support a pro tanto reason to trust (namely, reliability), which is inevitably defeated by knowledge that AI's intentions cannot be grounded in a recognition of rational constraints, so that vulnerability is a necessary consequence of hybrid decision-making situations."

"We discuss this problem in more detail (particularly, how to mitigate it by developing machine learning applications to meet the normative conditions of reliability), but for now, we need to expose why designing systems to manifest moral trustworthiness would not actually mitigate the vulnerability that arises in high-stakes decision-making environments."

Why Morally Trustworthy AI Is Unnecessary

"The specific issue that our discussion aims to shed light on is how it is deeply unclear whether designing AI to be morally rational, such that they possess either (i) the emotional system or (ii) the conceptual system and so would be deserving of the appellation "trustworthy AI", would mitigate vulnerability arising in high-stakes hybrid decision-making environments."

"While this might be helpful in determining whether the score should be relied upon, and so might assist in mitigating the vulnerability for all stakeholders, the AI can be designed to yield this information without thereby having the capacity to base its decision on moral norms as such."

"Moving on to (ii) the emotional system, which enables agents to be motivated by norms, we might likewise ask whether designing an AI to be morally rational in this manner would help alleviate the problem of vulnerability in high-stakes hybrid decision-making environments."

Quasi-Metacognitive Machines and Alleviating the Problem of Vulnerability

"While products of a fundamentally different mechanism, reliability scores can be the machine analogue to metacognitive sensitivity, with specific scores being analogues to calibrated confidence."

"Zhang and others [68] found that providing reliability scores not only led to the collective benefit of higher accuracy in discrimination and classification tasks, but it also facilitated human decision-makers in calibrating their reliance on the AI (i.e., mitigating the problem of vulnerability)."

"This result is also supported by Rechkemmer and Yin [69] that showed that providing reliability scores positively influences whether people believe an AI's predictions, so long as these scores are well-calibrated with performance (i.e., so long as the model exhibits consistent competence)."

"In combination with the capacity to report reliability scores (i.e., the machine analogue to confidence), the AI should also be designed to provide explanations for the reliability scores."

Conclusion and Future Directions

"What trustworthy AI ultimately amounts to is morally rational AI, which, feasibility aside, is unnecessary for promoting optimal calibration of the human decision-maker on AI assistance."

"Reliability, exclusive of trust, ought to be the appropriate goal of ethical AI, as it entails the normative constraints that, when met, are effective in mitigating the vulnerability created by having AI make meaningful contributions in high-stakes decision-making environments."

"Crucially, the AI ought to be designed to report reliability scores to the human decision-makers due to how such scores enable the human to calibrate her reliance on the AI's advice."

"By highlighting the importance of such explanations in promoting optimal calibration, without any need for moral trust, we have pointed the way to developing more ethical applications by way of developing quasi-metacognitive machines."

Zombies in the Loop? Humans Trust Untrustworthy AI-Advisors for Ethical Decisions [7]

This is a machine-generated summary of:

Krügel, Sebastian; Ostermaier, Andreas; Uhl, Matthias Zombies in the Loop? Humans Trust Untrustworthy AI-Advisors for Ethical Decisions [7]

Published in: Philosophy & Technology (2022)

Link to original: https://doi.org/10.1007/s13347-022-00511-9

If you want to cite the papers, please refer to the original.

For technical reasons we could not place the page where the original quote is coming from.

Abstract-Summary

"Departing from the claim that AI needs to be trustworthy, we find that ethical advice from an AI-powered algorithm is trusted even when its users know nothing about its training data and when they learn information about it that warrants distrust."

"We conducted online experiments where the subjects took the role of decision-makers who received advice from an algorithm on how to deal with an ethical dilemma."

"Our findings suggest that AI is overtrusted rather than distrusted."

Introduction

"The algorithm can serve as a moral advisor to its human user, who still makes the decision and accounts for it."

"This argument assumes that the human user does not naïvely trust the algorithm regardless of how trustworthy it is but carefully checks its advice and makes his or her own decision if a red flag rises."

"We explore, first, whether users trust the moral advice of an algorithm if they know nothing about how it generates advice."

"An algorithm is more transparent to its users if they know it was trained on judgments of impartial human advisors than if they know nothing about how it generates moral advice."

"We study whether users trust the algorithm's advice when the integrity of its training data is dubious."

Procedure

"CloudResearch is an online platform to recruit subjects and conduct studies [70]."

"Prime Panels members must pass default screening questions to take part in a study, and they are more diverse and more representative of the US population than MTurk participants in terms of age, family background, religion, education, and political attitudes [71]."

"We used Qualtrics to randomly assign the subjects each to one condition, and CloudResearch to preclude repeated participation."

"We posed a question to probe the subjects' understanding and attention (screen #4)."

"We determined that the analyses would be restricted to subjects who answered the comprehension question correctly, and we set the number of subjects per condition to 50."

"Anticipating that some would fail to prove their comprehension, we recruited more subjects; we attained the planned number of subjects after excluding about 20%, who had answered the comprehension question incorrectly."

Study 1

"To explore how decision-makers respond to advice by an human-trained AI-powered algorithm, we designed an experiment which required the subjects to make a decision that would benefit either a friend or a stranger."

"Our experiment employs a 2 × 2 × 3 factorial design with either a human advisor or the algorithm, who advises that it is acceptable or unacceptable for the decision-maker to favor her friend in one of three scenarios."

"They show that advice to favor the friend, both when the advisor is human and when it is an algorithm, reduces decision-makers' inclination to decide in favor of the stranger, or makes them tend to decide in favor of the friend, across the three scenarios."

"Our decision-makers do not slavishly follow the algorithm's or the human advice, but the change in their inclination to favor the stranger or the friend depending on the nature of advice shows that they are influenced by it."

Study 2

"While transparency is seen as a means to make algorithms more trustworthy, there is considerable variation in what ethics guidelines claim should be made transparent, including how AI is used in decision-making, the source code, the training data, the legal regulations, the limitations, or the potential impact [72]."

"To complete the picture, the effect of the algorithm's advice needs to be benchmarked against that of human advice—i.e., the response of decision-makers who were told that they were advised by an impartial human advisor in our first study."

"We recall that the percentages are similar in our first study, where 23 or 43% of the advisees would decide in favor of the friend, depending on what the human advice says, and 20 and 34%, depending on the transparent algorithm's advice."

"Decision-makers trust moral advice from more and less transparent algorithms alike."

Study 3

"Along the lines of our first study, we ran another experiment on CloudResearch, where the algorithm's advice was described as based on the ethical judgments of convicted criminals rather than impartial human advisors."

"To benchmark the impact of advice by the criminals-trained algorithm against that of a human advisor, we ran another condition where a human convicted criminal replaced the impartial human advisor from our first study."

"The decision-makers who were advised by the human advisor (i.e., a convicted criminal) showed a similar inclination to decide in favor of the friend, regardless of whether the advice said that it was acceptable or unacceptable to favor the friend."

"Like the convicted criminal, the impartial human advisor from our first study is, again, a meaningful benchmark for the influence of the convicts-trained algorithm's advice."

Further Results

"To address this question, we posed a post-experimental question to ask our subjects, first, whether they would make the same judgment if there were no moral advice."

"To examine the influence of advice on moral judgements and decisions, we intentionally raised the ethical question of whether to favor a friend over a stranger."

"While this question allows for a role of moral advice, the answer might also hinge on the decision-maker's personal morality."

"To consider the potential effect of personal morality, we included a post-experimental question about ethical self-assessment, which asked the subjects how moral they considered themselves relative to other subjects."

"We added moral self-assessment as a covariate to our regressions to test whether it is associated with the inclination to favor the stranger over the friend and to isolate the influence of ethical advice."

Conclusion

"We found, first, that the algorithm's advice influences users' decisions like advice from an impartial human advisor."

"Our data suggest that people follow AI-generated as much as much as human advice; that they do not bother about untransparency; that they follow AI-generated advice even in the presence of suspicous information; that they (over)confidently believe others are more susceptible to the algorithm's influence than themselves."

"The results of our experiment suggest that the impact of AI-generated and human moral advice are very similar. (Technically, we see appreciation of the algorithm that mimics convicts relative to the human convict, but not the impartial human advisor.) As evidence keeps accumulating on both sides, along with evidence like ours, which argues for neither side, it seems that neither algorithm appreciation nor algorithm aversion generally prevails, but that multiple factors matter."

Ethics-Based Auditing to Develop Trustworthy AI [3]

This is a machine-generated summary of:

Mökander, Jakob; Floridi, Luciano Ethics-Based Auditing to Develop Trustworthy AI [3]

Published in: Minds and Machines (2021)

Link to original: https://doi.org/10.1007/s11023-021-09557-8

If you want to cite the papers, please refer to the original.

For technical reasons we could not place the page where the original quote is coming from.

Abstract-Summary

"Building on ongoing discussions concerning ethics-based auditing, we offer three contributions."

"We identify and discuss the constraints associated with ethics-based auditing."

"Only by understanding and accounting for these constraints can ethics-based auditing facilitate ethical alignment of AI, while enabling society to reap the full economic and social benefits of automation."

Towards Trustworthy AI

"New mechanisms are thus needed to ensure ethical alignment of the AI systems that increasingly permeate society."

"Leading institutions across the political, commercial, and academic strata of society have responded to the urgency of this task by creating ethics guidelines for trustworthy AI [73]."

"The industry lacks useful tools and incentives to translate high-level ethics principles to verifiable and actionable criteria for designing and deploying AI [74]."

"A series of recent developments points towards ethics-based auditing as a promising mechanism to bridge the gap between principles and practice in AI ethics."

"It is important to remain realistic about what ethics-based auditing of AI can and cannot be reasonably expected to achieve."

Ethics-Based Auditing of AI—What It Is and How It Works

"Ethics-based auditing is a governance mechanism that can be used by organisations that design and deploy AI systems to control or influence the behaviour of AI systems."

"Operationally, ethics-based auditing is characterised by a structured process by which an entity's behaviour is assessed for consistency with relevant principles or norms."

"Rather than attempting to codify ethics, ethics-based auditing helps identify, visualise, and communicate whichever normative values are embedded in a system."

"Although standards have yet to emerge, a range of different approaches to ethics-based auditing of AI already exists: Functionality audits focus on the rationale behind the decision, code audits entail reviewing the source code, and impact audits investigate the effects of an algorithm's outputs."

"Ethics-based auditing contributes to good governance."

"By promoting procedural regularity and strengthening institutional trust, ethics-based auditing can help: 1."

Getting It Right

"As a gold standard, we propose that the process of ethics-based auditing should be continuous, holistic, dialectic, strategic and design-driven."

"Ethics-based auditing is a process, not a destination."

"A holistic approach to ethics-based auditing takes knowledge of available alternatives into account when evaluating AI-based systems."

"Ethics-based auditing should thus be viewed as a dialectical process wherein the auditor exists to ensure that the right questions have been asked."

"Ethics-based auditing support this aim by providing active feedback to the continuous (re-)design process."

A Roadmap for Future Research

"As a governance mechanism, it is subject to a range of conceptual, technical, economic, social, organisational, and institutional constraints."

"One function of ethics-based auditing would be to arrive at resolutions that, even when imperfect, are at least publicly defensible."

"Because ethics-based auditing imposes costs, financial and otherwise, care must be taken to not unduly burden particular sectors or groups in society."

"Even in cases where audits reveal flaws in AI-based systems, asymmetries of power may prevent corrective steps from being taken."

"Ethics-based auditing is only as good as the institutions backing it."

"The effectiveness of ethics-based auditing remains constrained by a tension between national jurisdictions, on the one hand, and the global nature of technology, on the other."

Outlook

"Policymakers are encouraged to consider ethics-based auditing as an integral component of holistic approaches to managing the ethical risks posed by AI."

"The solution here is that governments retain supreme sanctioning power by authorising independent agencies who, in turn, conduct ethics-based audits of AI systems."

"Only if these constraints are understood and accounted for will ethics-based auditing help address the ethical risks posed by AI."

"Ethics-based auditing of AI affords good governance by strengthening the ethical infrastructure of mature information societies."

Making Sense of the Conceptual Nonsense 'Trustworthy AI' [5]

This is a machine-generated summary of:

Freiman, Ori Making sense of the conceptual nonsense 'trustworthy AI' [5]

Published in: AI and Ethics (2022)

Link to original: https://doi.org/10.1007/s43681-022-00241-w

If you want to cite the papers, please refer to the original.

For technical reasons we could not place the page where the original quote is coming from.

Abstract-Summary

"Several AI ethicists argue against using this concept, often backing their arguments with decades of conceptual analyses made by scholars who studied the concept of trust."

"Despite suggestions to shift the paradigm from 'Trustworthy AI' to 'Reliable AI', I argue that, realistically, this concept will be kept being used."

"I end by arguing that, ultimately, AI ethics is also about power, social justice, and scholarly activism."

"I propose that community driven and social justice-oriented ethicists of AI and trust scholars further focus on (a) democratic aspects of trust formation; and (b) draw attention to critical social aspects highlighted by phenomena of distrust."

Introduction

"AI policy documents that include ethical principles and guidelines have mushroomed in recent years and many of these documents include the concept of 'Trustworthy AI' [72, 75–81]."

"The HLEG's document, Ethics Guidelines for Trustworthy AI [56], sparked interest in this term."

"If, in the future, an untrustworthy corporation or government behaves unethically and possesses good, robust AI technology, this will enable more effective unethical behaviour. (2019, emphasis added) The introduction mentioned a few criticisms of Trustworthy AI, such as ethics washing, the HLEG's narrative, and the 'Trustworthy AI' as conceptual nonsense."

"Despite agreeing with some of the existing criticisms about the concept of trustworthy AI and its unsuitability for ethical analysis or regulatory frameworks, I argue that advocating to stop using it is useless, since it is already widespread."

Anthropocentric View of Trust

"Such a definition does not limit the concept of trust only to relations between humans."

"It enables researchers to consider trust in a technological context, including AI [82], cited in: [67]."

"As could be expected, scholars in the field of AI/ML use different definitions of trust, too."

"Within social epistemology, the standard view on trust is that trust relations are based on a human quality such as goodwill [83–91]."

"This view describes several different approaches to trust, all commonly share two features: (a) not ascribing human agency to technologies; and (b) referring to humans behind the technologies in matters regarding trust and responsibility."

"Weydner-Volkmann & Feiten [92] defend the concept of 'trust in technology' to make sense of the concept of 'Trustworthy AI'."

"They defend the notion that AI can be considered trustworthy by opposing the traditional philosophical view of trust."

Criticizing the Concept of 'Trustworthy AI'

"Her second argument is that if accountability can be traced back to humans, there is no reason to trust AIs."

"He argues that the objects of trust must be held responsible for their actions, thus distancing himself from the view that trust in AI is possible when it refers to trust in the humans and institutions behind the AI."

"They identify four epistemic and moral difficulties for attaining 'Trustworthy AI': the AI system must be (i) capable of fulfilling the trustor's expectation by being reliable; (ii) self-assess and monitor the system's limitations and promises to those who trust it; (iii) account for the interests and values of those who trust it (focusing on the most vulnerable groups of users); and (iv) require information disclosure about the inner working of the system and its goals, including financial interests."

"The moral requirements of their account of trust can only be met by cultivating a 'trustworthy AI culture'."

Trust Scholars and AI Ethicists: What's Next?

"The latter represents primarily philosophers and ethicists of AI, who are aware of the anthropocentricity of the concept of 'trustworthy' and hold an anthropocentric view of trust."

"The reason is to ensure that we focus on the important domains of trust: Overall, proponents of AI ethics should abandon the 'trustworthy AI' paradigm as it is too fraught with problems, replacing it with the reliable AI approach, instead [4]: p. 17) Ryan's call to replace the terminology is directed at proponents of AI ethics."

"Within the scholarly field of AI ethics, there are normative expectations to subscribe to the anthropocentric view of trust and therefore use the reliable AI approach."

"If the criticisms expressed by trust scholars were to be summarized into a practical suggestion, it would be ensuring that individuals and institutions that regard AIs are trustworthy."

Conclusion

"This paper explained why trust scholars and AI ethicists criticize the concept of 'Trustworthy AI'."

"I pointed to the anthropocentric view of trust within social epistemology, which argues that only human agents can be objects of trust, and therefore trust in AI is reduced to issues of trust in the institutions and people behind the technology."

"The scholarly fields of trust and AI ethics are about power, social justice, and activism."

"The concepts of 'trust' and 'distrust' in democratic institutions are about power."

"If community driven and social justice-oriented ethicists of AI and trust scholars wish to stay relevant, they must become scholarly activists, who uncover power relations, challenge unfair status quo, and suggest democratic ways to form trust relations."

Adaptable Robots, Ethics, and Trust: A Qualitative and Philosophical Exploration of the Individual Experience of Trustworthy AI [93]

This is a machine-generated summary of:

Sheir, Stephanie; Manzini, Arianna; Smith, Helen; Ives, Jonathan Adaptable robots, ethics, and trust: a qualitative and philosophical exploration of the individual experience of trustworthy AI [93]

Published in: AI & SOCIETY (2024)

Link to original: https://doi.org/10.1007/s00146-024-01938-8

If you want to cite the papers, please refer to the original.

For technical reasons we could not place the page where the original quote is coming from.

Abstract-Summary

"It is not always clear whether individuals are speaking of a technology's trustworthiness, a developer's trustworthiness, or simply of gaining the trust of users by any means."

"In sociotechnical circles, trustworthiness is often used as a proxy for 'the good', illustrating the moral heights to which technologies and developers ought to aspire, at times with a multitude of diverse requirements; or at other times, no specification at all."

"This qualitative study employed an empirical ethics methodology to address how developers and users define and construct requirements for trust throughout development and use, through a series of interviews."

"The most significant requirement for user trust and assessment of trustworthiness was the accountability of AI developers for the outputs of AI systems, hinging on the identification of accountable moral agents and perceived value alignment between the user and developer's interests."

Introduction

"Trust' and 'trustworthy' are often used interchangeably, particularly by political and corporate actors, with varying meanings and implications for action."

"The drive for trustworthy AI can mean a technology which possesses attributes that are deserving of trust, which implies the need for safe, well-functioning systems; or it can mean a sociotechnical system possessing these attributes, implying also the existence of accountable, beneficent human creators and operators [94, p. 88]."

"There is a need to seek conceptual clarity about trust and trustworthiness in the context of ASEFs."

"How and why do other stakeholders (including end users) place trust in autonomous systems and what are their requirements for trustworthiness?"

"How should an ASEF be developed and deployed to be not only trusted, but also trustworthy?"

Methods

"Interview data were gathered from three types of participants: 'developers', 'end users', and 'other stakeholders' from August 2021 to November 2022."

"Purposive sampling was used to recruit developers with relevant knowledge about the development of swarm robots, soft robots, and UAVs."

"Snowball sampling was then used to recruit colleagues of these initial contacts to discover potential participants who have relevant knowledge of autonomous systems."

"To guide participants' reasoning, three use cases of ASEFs were chosen: swarm robots (used for tasks such as storing and retrieving objects); soft robots (used for gripping and manipulating objects of varying shapes and tolerances); and UAVs (used for parcel delivery)."

"End users and other stakeholders were also given the choice of watching one of the three videos depicting a sample scenario of an ASEF: either swarm robots, soft robots, or UAVs."

Findings

"A few participants reflected on how the lack of an identifiable and accountable moral agent, responsible for the behavior and particularly failure of technology, engenders suspicion and distrust, which is to be distinguished from any assessment of the technology's reliability. "[…] with the drone element […] I'm not sure whether it's the technology that I don't trust or the person controlling the technology […] So for about a week last summer somebody kept flying a drone over the fields around the back of our house and coming very close to our house and there's an element of suspicion there about, what is that drone, what it is doing, what is it capable of doing […] you can't see the operator and it doesn't feel right." (EU3) "I suppose my concern […] is that I'm handing over a lot of data for which I've got no idea who that data is going to. […] it's the facelessness of where that data is going, and the lack of accountability for it." (EU8) Without engaging in debate about moral agency for non-human or artificial agents, it was generally acknowledged by participants that moral responsibility and agency is only held by human beings, and not by even the most highly complex and autonomous systems."

Limitations

"Our study is limited by the ethnic and gender homogeneity of the sample, which likely reflects the self-selected nature of the participants (recruited through snowball sampling and networks), as well as the demographic characteristics of the robotics profession in the UK."

"The generalizability of some of our findings may be somewhat limited."

"We issue two caveats; first, we do not suggest that the views expressed by our participants on trustworthiness are universal or representative of the general population."

"We also intend for these findings to inform thinking on trustworthy AI and to connect with existing debate in the philosophical literature, as opposed to perfectly representing the views of the public."

Discussion

"Simion and Kelp [95] argue that conceptualizing trust as incurring and fulfilling appropriate commitments can be applied to AI, which is considered trustworthy if it fulfills its design functions, as specified by a developer, and its etiological functions, which are expectations of its functioning based on historical norms of the use context."

"In response to Simion and Kelp, Nyrup constructs a 'modest anthropocentric' account of trust, refusing to grant that AI is automatically trustworthy if it fulfills design and etiological functions, as these may not be sufficient to align with a user's fundamental interests [95]."

"Speaking, the precise details of these mechanisms were not significant to participants in the abstract but formed a central part of their assessment of trustworthiness by presenting a clear signal of value alignment, with the additional potential for punitive action against agents who betray consumer trust."

Conclusion

"Despite ongoing debates on machine agency or even questions about their potential consciousness [96–98], it is not appropriate, given current technological capacities, to ascribe moral responsibility to AI systems."

"It is clear that individuals will continue to intuitively reason about trusting AI, regardless of their ultimate capacities, just as they do about other machines, animals, and young children, whose moral responsibilities and capacity to act autonomously on par with human adults may also be in question."

"Our interview study has provided further evidence that both lay users and developers use the language of trust rather reflexively in reference to machines and their functional reliability, but that they also use trust in a fundamentally relational manner which centers human beings as the ultimate holders and arbiters of moral responsibility."

"It would be impractical to proscribe the use of trust language in the context of AI."

Ethical Funding for Trustworthy AI: Proposals to Address the Responsibilities of Funders to Ensure that Projects Adhere to Trustworthy AI Practice [10]

This is a machine-generated summary of:

Gardner, Allison; Smith, Adam Leon; Steventon, Adam; Coughlan, Ellen; Oldfield, Marie Ethical funding for trustworthy AI: proposals to address the responsibilities of funders to ensure that projects adhere to trustworthy AI practice [10]

Published in: AI and Ethics (2021)

Link to original: https://doi.org/10.1007/s43681-021-00069-w

If you want to cite the papers, please refer to the original.

For technical reasons we could not place the page where the original quote is coming from.

Abstract-Summary

"Such reports beg the question as to why such systems continue to be funded, developed and deployed despite the many published ethical AI principles."

"We highlight the responsibilities of funding bodies to ensure investment is channelled towards trustworthy and safe AI systems and provides case studies as to how other ethical funding principles are managed."

"The first proposal is for the inclusion of a Trustworthy AI Statement' section in the grant application form and offers an example of the associated guidance."

"The second proposal outlines the wider management requirements of a funding body for the ethical review and monitoring of funded projects to ensure adherence to the proposed ethical strategies in the applicants Trustworthy AI Statement."

"The anticipated outcome for such proposals being employed would be to create a 'stop and think' section during the project planning and application procedure requiring applicants to implement the methods for the ethically aligned design of AI."

Introduction

"The result of this myriad of issues is the obvious human cost, that we have outlined thus far, plus the significant financial loss to public funds and reputational damage due to the withdrawal of expensive and harmful AI solutions."

"One way in which we can encourage and ensure the development and deployment of Trustworthy AI systems is to influence public and charitable funding."

"Addressing the funding of AI systems may act as a significant nudge to require applicants to educate themselves in and apply Ethical/Trustworthy AI principles and design frameworks."

"In response to these issues we propose that grant funding and public tendering of AI systems should require a Trustworthy AI Statement within the grant proposal or tendering document."

"We acknowledge that this solution is not enough on its own to address the issue of untrustworthy public sector algorithms and that it should be embedded within a wider AI governance and regulatory framework."

Frameworks for Ethical Governance of AI

"Did you put in place measures to ensure that the data (including training data) used to develop the AI system is up-to-date, of high quality, complete and representative of the environment the system will be deployed in?"

"The Data governance section includes questions regarding the production of a data Privacy Impact Assessment, measures to achieve privacy-by-design, data minimisation and: Did you align the AI system with relevant standards (e.g. ISO, IEEE) or widely adopted protocols for (daily) data management and governance?"

"For Humanity have devised the Independent Audit of AI systems, a framework for auditing AI systems (products, services and corporations) by examining the downside risks focussing on Privacy, Bias, Ethics, Trust and Cybersecurity [99]."

"This guidance was developed post the 2013 MacPherson Review [100] to ensure fit for purpose modelling and could easily be updated and developed for AI, particularly for those in high risk scenarios such as healthcare, along with recommendations from ethics committees and, in particular, the House of Lords Committee on AI."

The Role of Funders in Promoting and Ensuring Trustworthy AI

"There are many examples of AI systems being funded, developed and deployed that are not fit for purpose, unethical, unfair, unsafe and further embedding discrimination in society."

"It may be reasonable to predict that at some point, given the increasing number of challenged AI systems, that questions will be asked of those funding questionable projects."

"One of the solutions we propose in this paper is a simple adjustment to the application procedure which requires a Trustworthy AI Statement, in which applicants must outline their plans to ensure they follow an ethically aligned design approach."

"Many of the problems with AI systems can be traced to unconscious bias at all stages of the AI lifecycle it would therefore seem reasonable to suggest that developers undergo unconscious bias or implicit bias training."

"It is worth considering similar operational and system changes that can be introduced in the funding requirements that could begin to address the problems experienced regarding AI development."

Case Studies

"An example of a simple approach to addressing ethical issues is the Gender Equality Statement required by the £1.5 billion Global Challenges Research Fund (GCRF) and the £735 million Newton Fund managed in the UK by BEIS and with a number of delivery partners including the UKRI and British Council."

"As this grant is a broad-based grant it also has a section for applicants to outline the Research Governance and Ethics for the project."

"ERPIC is a council of seven experts who advise on policy relating to a wide range of issues including ethics, legislation and regulation and matters relating to research involving animals or human participation (including personal information)."

"The onus is placed on the applicant to perform the research and find the expertise required to be informed of the specific ethical or governance requirements, such as gender equality issues in case study 1."

Proposals

"The team includes a researcher with experience of grant-writing and grant review panels, industry standards and AI ethics experts and representatives of a grant funding body."

"This would take the form of describing how the proposal will address a stated ethical AI framework (either as required by the funding body or chosen by the applicants if not previously specified) and including details of their intended methods."

"This could be implemented by a simple change to current application forms and guidance (proposal 1), the presence of an AI ethicist on review panels, and/or the constitution of Ethical AI Boards, that could nudge the AI field effectively towards ethical development."

"Requiring applicants to outline the ethical considerations relevant to their project proposal will provide the opportunity for funding bodies, researchers and developers a point of reflection and the opportunity to identify and mitigate potential problems or harms at the outset."

Discussion

"The expectation is that the funding body will provide call specific guidance regarding the expected requirements for ethical design of the proposed AI systems."

"This concern led to the development of proposal 2 which includes the utilisation of AI ethics experts as advisors in design of grant calls and on review panels."

"In the medium term we feel the impact could be that more calls would enact the proposals and the process begins to become an accepted norm and a backbone of ethical support is provided for both funding bodies and researchers."

"In the longer term, whilst we accept this is not a singular cure-all we will see more responsible development and, as the flow of money is affected by these proposals, greater investment directed to the ethical design for trustworthy AI projects."

Future Work

"The proposals will be open for review in a stakeholder workshop with participants from funding bodies and academics."

"Should a funding body choose to introduce the Trustworthy Statement (or a version of it) then it is proposed that the impact should be evaluated."

"Future research would entail a meta-analysis of the funding of AI projects prior to implementation of the statement and afterwards."

"This would determine if there were any substantive changes in the types of projects funded, the make-up of the research teams and styles of application."

Conclusion

"We propose that funding bodies incorporate the requirement for trustworthy AI statements in their application procedure."

"This process will have a twofold aim of educating funding applicants as to the importance and processes for developing Trustworthy AI systems and hopefully ensuring only those systems that have addressed issues such as bias for example are funded."

"Not only would this prevent harms to individuals, groups and communities caused by poorly developed and biased AI systems but also prevents large amounts of funding to be wasted on projects that eventually need to be withdrawn."

References

1. Durán, J. M., & Pozzi, G. (2025). *Trust and trustworthiness in AI*. Philosophy & Technology. https://doi.org/10.1007/s13347-025-00843-2
2. Fan, N. (2025). *Explainability is necessary for AI's trustworthiness*. Philosophy & Technology. https://doi.org/10.1007/s13347-025-00847-y

3. Mökander, J., & Floridi, L. (2021). Ethics-based auditing to develop trustworthy AI. *Minds and Machines, 31*. https://doi.org/10.1007/s11023-021-09557-8
4. Ryan, M. (2020). In AI we trust: Ethics, artificial intelligence, and reliability. *Science and Engineering Ethics, 26*, 2749–2767. https://doi.org/10.1007/s11948-020-00228-y
5. Freiman, O. (2022). Making sense of the conceptual nonsense 'trustworthy AI'. *AI and Ethics, 3*. https://doi.org/10.1007/s43681-022-00241-w
6. Dorsch, J., & Deroy, O. (2024). Quasi-metacognitive machines: Why we don't need morally trustworthy AI and communicating reliability is enough. *Philosophy & Technology*. https://doi.org/10.1007/s13347-024-00752-w
7. Krügel, S., Ostermaier, A., & Uhl, M. (2022). *Zombies in the loop? Humans trust untrustworthy AI-advisors for ethical decisions*. Philosophy & Technology. https://doi.org/10.1007/s13347-022-00511-9
8. Baron, S. (2025). Trust, explainability and AI. *Philosophy & Technology, 38*(1), 1–23. https://doi.org/10.1007/s13347-024-00837-6
9. Nyrup, R. (2023). Trustworthy AI: A plea for modest anthropocentrism. Asian. *Journal of Philosophy, 2*. https://doi.org/10.1007/s44204-023-00096-w
10. Gardner, A., Smith, A. L., Steventon, A., Coughlan, E., & Oldfield, M. (2021). Ethical funding for trustworthy AI: Proposals to address the responsibilities of funders to ensure that projects adhere to trustworthy AI practice. *AI and Ethics*. https://doi.org/10.1007/s43681-021-00069-w
11. Cho, J. H. (2019). StRAM: Measuring the trustworthiness of computer-based systems. *ACM Computing Surveys, 51*, 6. issn: 15577341. https://doi.org/10.1145/3277666
12. Hawley, K. (2019). *How to be trustworthy*. Oxford University Press.
13. Reinhardt, K. (2022). Trust and trustworthiness in AI ethics. *AI and Ethics*. https://doi.org/10.1007/s43681-022-00200-5
14. Floridi, L. (2019). Translating principles into practices of digital ethics: Five risks of being unethical. *Philosophy and Technology, 32*, 185–193.
15. Varshney, K. R. (2019). Trustworthy machine learning and artificial intelligence. *XRDS Crossroads The ACM Magazine for Students, 25*, 26–29.
16. Harrison, T. M., & Luna-Reyes, L. F. (2020). Cultivating trustworthy artificial intelligence in digital government. *Social Science Computer Review, 40*. https://doi.org/10.1177/0894439320980122
17. Janssen, M., et al. (2020). Data governance: Organizing data for trustworthy artificial intelligence. *Government Information Quarterly, 37*, 101493.
18. Thiebes, S., Lins, S., & Sunyaev, A. (2020). Trustworthy artificial intelligence. *Electronic Markets, 31*. https://doi.org/10.1007/s12525-020-00441-4
19. Shneiderman, B. (2020). Human-centered artificial intelligence: Reliable, safe & trustworthy. *International Journal of Human–Computer Interaction, 36*, 495–504.
20. OECD. (2020). *Trustworthy artificial intelligence (AI) in education: Promises and challenges*. https://www.oecd.org/education/trustworthy-artificial-intelligence-in-education.pdf
21. Baier, A. (1986). Trust and antitrust. *Ethics, 96*(2), 231–260.
22. Gambetta, D. (1988). *Trust*. B. Blackwell.
23. Holton, R. (1994). Deciding to trust, coming to believe. *Australasian Journal of Philosophy, 72*, 63–76.
24. Jones, K. (1996). Trust as an affective attitude. *Ethics, 107*, 4–25.
25. Lahno, B. (2001). On the emotional character of trust. *Ethical Theory and Moral Practice, 4*, 171–189.
26. Uslaner, E. M. (2002). *The moral foundations of trust*. Cambridge University Press.
27. Hawley, K. (2014). Trust, distrust and commitment. *Noûs, 48*, 1–20.
28. National Science and Technology Council. (2016). *The National Artificial Intelligence*. Research and Development Strategic Plan. https://www.nitrd.gov/PUBS/national_ai_rd_strategic_plan.pdf

29. IEEE. (2016). *Ethically aligned design*. IEEE Standards v1. https://standards.ieee.org/content/dam/ieee-standards/standards/web/documents/other/ead1e.pdf
30. Information Commissioner's Office. (2017). *Big data, artificial intelligence, machine learning and data protection*. https://ico.org.uk/media/for-organisations/documents/2013559/big-data-ai-ml-and-data-protection.pdf
31. NITI: National Strategy for artificial intelligence. (2018). http://niti.gov.in/sites/default/files/2019-01/NationalStrategy-for-AI-Discussion-Paper.pdf
32. Institute of Business Ethics. (2018). *Business ethics and artificial intelligence*. https://www.ibe.org.uk/uploads/assets/5f167681-e05f-4fae-ae1bef7699625a0d/ibebriefing58businessethicsandartificialintelligence.pdf
33. Department of Health and Social Care. (2018). *Initial code of conduct for data-driven health and care technology*. http://allcatsrgrey.org.uk/wp/download/informatics/www_gov_uk_government_publications_code_of_conduct_for_data_.pdf
34. Dawson, D., Schleiger, E., Horton, J., McLaughlin, J., Robinson, C., Quezada, G., Scowcroft, J., & Hajkowicz, S. (2019). *Artificial intelligence: Australia's ethics framework*. Data 61 CSIRO. https://consult.industry.gov.au/strategic-policy/artificial-intelligence-ethics-framework/supporting_documents/ArtificialIntelligenceethicsframeworkdiscussionpaper.pdf
35. PDPC – Personal Data Protection Commission Singapore. (2018). *Discussion paper on artificial intelligence (AI) and personal data*. https://www.pdpc.gov.sg/-/media/Files/PDPC/PDF-Files/Resource-for-Organisation/AI/Discussion-Paper-on-AI-and-PD%2D%2D-050618.pdf
36. Intel: Intel's AI Privacy Policy White Paper. (2018). *Protecting individuals privacy and data in the artificial intelligence world*. Intel. https://blogs.intel.com/policy/files/2018/10/Intels-AI-Privacy-Policy-White-Paper-2018.pdf
37. Microsoft. (2018). *Responsible bots: 10 guidelines for developers of conversational AI*. https://www.microsoft.com/en-us/research/publication/responsible-bots/.
38. Floridi, L., et al. (2018). Ai4people – an ethical framework for a good ai society: Opportunities, risks, principles, and recommendations. *Minds and Machines, 28*, 689–707.
39. UK House of Lords. (2018). *AI in the UK: Ready, willing and able?* https://publications.parliament.uk/pa/ld201719/ldselect/ldai/100/100.pdf
40. IBM. (2019). *Everyday ethics for artificial intelligence*. https://www.ibm.com/watson/assets/duo/pdf/everydayethics.pdf
41. Report Montréal Declaration. (2018). *For a responsible development of artificial intelligence*. https://monoskop.org/images/b/b2/Report_Montreal_Declaration_for_a_Responsible_Development_of_Artificial_Intelligence_2018.pdf
42. IBM. (2018). *IBM's principles for trust and transparency*. https://www.ibm.com/blogs/policy/wp-content/uploads/2018/06/IBM_Principles_SHORT.V4.3.pdf
43. ITI – Information Technology Industry Council. (2017). *Information technology industry AI policy principles*. https://www.itic.org/public-policy/ITIAIPolicyPrinciplesFINAL.pdf
44. Future Advocacy. (2018). *Ethical, social, and political challenges of artificial intelligence in health*. https://wellcome.org/sites/default/files/ai-in-health-ethical-social-political-challenges.pdf
45. EPSRC. (2011). *Principles of robotics*. https://epsrc.ukri.org/research/ourportfolio/themes/engineering/activities/principlesofrobotics/
46. Conference toward AI Network Society. (2017). *Draft AI R&D guidelines for international discussions*. https://www.soumu.go.jp/main_content/000507517.pdf
47. OECD. (2021). *Recommendation of the council on artificial intelligence*. https://legalinstruments.oecd.org/en/instruments/OECD-LEGAL-0449
48. UNESCO. (2021). *Recommendation on the ethics of artificial intelligence*. https://unesdoc.unesco.org/ark:/48223/pf0000379920#page=14
49. Executive Office of the President, USA. (2020). *Guidance for regulation of artificial intelligence applications*. https://www.whitehouse.gov/wp-content/uploads/2020/01/Draft-OMB-Memo-on-Regulation-of-AI-1-7-19.pdf?utm_source=morning_brew

50. Rathenau Instituut. (2017). *Human rights in the robot age*. https://www.rathenau.nl/sites/default/files/2018-02/Human%20Rights%20in%20the%20Robot%20Age-Rathenau%20Instituut-2017.pdf
51. Sony. (2018). *AI engagement within Sony Group*. https://www.sony.net/SonyInfo/csr_report/humanrights/AI_Engagement_within_Sony_Group.pdf
52. Fraunhofer IAIS. (2021). *Leitfaden zur Gestaltung vertrauenswürdiger Künstlicher Intelligenz*. https://www.iais.fraunhofer.de/content/dam/iais/fb/Kuenstliche_intelligenz/ki-pruefkatalog/202107_KI-Pruefkatalog.pdf
53. Deutsche Telekom. (2018). *Guidelines for artificial intelligence*. https://www.telekom.com/en/company/digital-responsibility/details/artificial-intelligence-ai-guideline-524366
54. Accenture. (2018). *Responsible AI: A framework for building trust in your AI solutions*. https://www.accenture.com/_acnmedia/PDF-92/Accenture-AFSResponsible-AI.pdf
55. Beijing AI Principles. (2019). *AI principles*. https://www.baai.ac.cn/news/beijing-ai-principles-en.html
56. HLEG – High-Level Expert Group on AI. (2019). *Ethics guidelines for trustworthy AI*. https://digital-strategy.ec.europa.eu/en/library/ethics-guidelines-trustworthy-ai
57. Special Interest Group on Artificial Intelligence. (2018). *Dutch artificial intelligence manifesto*. http://ii.tudelft.nl/bnvki/wp-content/uploads/2018/09/Dutch-AI-Manifesto.pdf
58. IBM. (2017). *Transparency and trust in the cognitive era*. https://www.ibm.com/blogs/think/2017/01/ibm-cognitive-principles/
59. Internet Society. (2017). *Artificial intelligence and machine learning: Policy paper*. https://www.internetsociety.org/wp-content/uploads/2017/08/ISOC-AI-Policy-Paper_2017-04-27_0.pdf
60. UNI Global. (2017). *Top 10 principles for ethical AI*. http://www.thefutureworldofwork.org/media/35420/uni_ethical_ai.pdf
61. RCP. (2018). *Artificial Intelligence (AI) in health*. https://www.rcplondon.ac.uk/projects/outputs/artificial-intelligence-ai-health
62. Unity Technologies (2018). *Introducing unity's guiding principles for ethical AI*. https://blog.unity.com/technology/introducing-unitys-guiding-principles-for-ethical-ai
63. McLeod, C. (2020) "Trust." *The Stanford encyclopedia of philosophy*. Edward N. Zalta (Ed.) https://plato.stanford.edu/archives/fall2020/entries/trust/
64. Frieman, O. (2023). Making sense of the conceptual nonsense 'trustworthy AI'. *AI and Ethics, 3*, 1351–1360.
65. Wu, Z., Chen, J., Li, Y., Yafeng, D., Zhao, H., Chang-Yu, H., & Hou, T. (2023). From black boxes to actionable insights: A perspective on explainable artificial intelligence for scientific discovery. *Journal of Chemical Information and Modeling, 63*(24), 7617–7627.
66. Sullivan, E. (2022). Understanding from machine learning models. *British Journal for the Philosophy of Science, 73*(1), 109–133.
67. Glikson, E., & Woolley, A. W. (2020). Human Trust in Artificial Intelligence: Review of empirical research. *Academy of Management Annals, 14*(2), 627–660. https://doi.org/10.5465/annals.2018.0057
68. Zhang, Y., Liao, Q. V., & Bellamy, R. K. E. (2020). Effect of confidence and explanation on accuracy and trust calibration in AI-assisted decision making. In *Proceedings of the 2020 Conference on fairness, Accountability, and Transparency, Barcelona, Spain*. https://doi.org/10.1145/3351095.3372852.
69. Rechkemmer, A., & Yin, M. (2022). When confidence meets accuracy: Exploring the effects of multiple performance indicators on trust in machine learning models. In *Proceedings of the 2022 CHI Conference on Human Factors in Computing Systems, New Orleans, LA, USA*. https://doi.org/10.1145/3491102.3501967
70. Litman, L., Robinson, J., & Abberbock, T. (2017). TurkPrime.com: A versatile crowdsourcing data acquisition platform for the behavioral sciences. *Behavior Research Methods, 49*(2), 433–442.

71. Chandler, J., Rosenzweig, C., Moss, A. J., Robinson, J., & Litman, L. (2019). Online panels in social science research: Expanding sampling methods beyond mechanical turk. *Behavior Research Methods, 51*(5), 2022–2038.
72. Jobin, A., Ienca, M., & Vayena, E. (2019). The global landscape of AI ethics guidelines. *Nature Machine Intelligence, 1*(9), 389–399. https://doi.org/10.1038/s42256-019-0088-2
73. Floridi, L., & Cowls, J. (2019). A unified framework of five principles for AI in society. *Harvard Data Science Review*. https://doi.org/10.1162/99608f92.8cd550d1
74. Raji, I. D., Smart, A., White, R. N., Mitchell, M., Gebru, T., Hutchinson, B., Smith-Loud, J., Theron, D., & Barnes, P. (2020). Closing the AI accountability gap: Defining an end-to-end framework for internal algorithmic auditing. In *Proceedings of the 2020 Conference on Fairness, Accountability, and Transparency* (pp. 33–44). FAT* '20. Association for Computing Machinery. https://doi.org/10.1145/3351095.3372873
75. Dotan, R. (2021). *The proliferation of AI ethics principles: What's next?* MAIEI. https://montrealethics.ai/the-proliferation-of-ai-ethics-principles-whats-next/
76. Fjeld, J., Achten, N., Hilligoss, H., Nagy, A., & Srikumar, M. (2020). *Principled artificial intelligence: Mapping consensus in ethical and rights-based approaches to principles for AI*. Berkman Klein Center Research Publication.
77. Floridi, L., & Cowls, J. (2021). A unified framework of five principles for AI in society. In *Ethics governance and policies in artificial intelligence* (pp. 5–17). Springer. https://doi.org/10.1007/978-3-030-81907-1_2
78. Hagendorff, T. (2020). The ethics of AI ethics: An evaluation of guidelines. *Minds and Machines, 30*(1), 99–120. https://doi.org/10.1007/s11023-020-09517-8
79. Mittelstadt, B. (2019). Principles alone cannot guarantee ethical AI. *Nature Machine Intelligence, 1*, 501–507.
80. Renda, A. (2020). Europe: Toward a policy framework for trustworthy AI. In *The Oxford handbook of ethics of AI* (pp. 649–666). Oxford University Press. https://doi.org/10.1093/oxfordhb/9780190067397.013.41
81. Schiff, D., Borenstein, J., Biddle, J., & Laas, K. (2021). AI ethics in the public, private, and NGO sectors: A review of a global document collection. *IEEE Transactions on Technology and Society, 2*. https://doi.org/10.1109/TTS.2021.3052127
82. Wang, W., Qiu, L., Kim, D., & Benbasat, I. (2016). Effects of rational and social appeals of online recommendation agents on cognition- and affect-based trust. *Decision Support Systems, 86*, 48–60. https://doi.org/10.1016/j.dss.2016.03.007
83. Freiman, O. (2021). *The role of knowledge in the formation of trust in technologies*. [Ph.D. Dissertation, Bar-Ilan University]
84. McLeod, C. (2002). *Self-trust and reproductive autonomy*. MIT Press.
85. Miller, B., & Freiman, O. (2020). Trust and distributed epistemic labor. In J. Simon (Ed.), *The Routledge handbook on trust and philosophy*. Routledge.
86. Nguyen, T. C. (2022). Trust as an unquestioning attitude. In *Oxford studies in epistemology*. Oxford University Press.
87. Nickel, P. (2013). Trust in technological systems. In M. de Vries, S. Hansson, & A. Meijers (Eds.), *Norms in technology* (pp. 223–237). Springer.
88. Nickel, P. J. (2017). Being pragmatic about trust. In P. Faulkner & T. Simpson (Eds.), *The philosophy of trust* (pp. 195–213). Oxford University Press. https://doi.org/10.1093/acprof:oso/9780198732549.003.0012
89. Nickel, P. J., Franssen, M., & Kroes, P. (2010). Can we make sense of the notion of trustworthy technology? *Knowledge Technology & Policy, 23*(3), 429–444.
90. Simon, J. (2010). The entanglement of trust and knowledge on the web. *Ethics and Information Technology, 12*(4), 343–355. https://doi.org/10.1007/s10676-010-9243-5
91. Simpson, T. (2012). What is trust? *Pacific Philosophical Quarterly, 93*(4), 550–569.
92. Weydner-Volkmann, S., & Feiten, L. (2021). Trust in technology: Interlocking trust concepts for privacy respecting video surveillance. *Journal of Information, Communication and Ethics in Society, 19*(4), 506–520. https://doi.org/10.1108/jices-12-2020-0128

93. Sheir, S., Manzini, A., Smith, H., & Ives, J. (2024). Adaptable robots, ethics, and trust: A qualitative and philosophical exploration of the individual experience of trustworthy AI. *AI & SOCIETY, 40*. https://doi.org/10.1007/s00146-024-01938-8
94. Smith, D. H., et al. (2023a). Ethics of trust/worthiness in autonomous systems: a scoping review. In *Proceedings of the First International Symposium on Trustworthy Autonomous Systems. TAS '23: First International Symposium on Trustworthy Autonomous Systems, Edinburgh United Kingdom: ACM* (pp. 1–15). https://doi.org/10.1145/3597512.3600207
95. Simion, M., & Kelp, C. (2023). Trustworthy artificial intelligence. *Asian Journal of Philosophy, 2*, 8. https://doi.org/10.1007/s44204-023-00063-5
96. Dennett, D. (2006). Cognitive wheels: The frame problem of AI. In *Philosophy of psychology: Contemporary readings*. Taylor and Francis Group/Routledge.
97. Torrance, S. (2008). Ethics and consciousness in artificial agents. *AI & Society, 22*(4), 495–521. https://doi.org/10.1007/s00146-007-0091-8
98. O'Grady, K. L., et al. (2022). Trust, ethics, consciousness, and artificial intelligence. In *2022 IEEE/AIAA 41st Digital Avionics Systems Conference (DASC). 2022 IEEE/AIAA 41st Digital Avionics Systems Conference (DASC)* (pp. 1–9). IEEE. https://doi.org/10.1109/DASC55683.2022.9925874
99. Carrier, R. (2019). *Independent audit of AI systems—FAQ*. ForHumanity. https://www.forhumanity.center/blog-posts/2019/8/8/independent-audit-of-ai-systems-faq. Accessed 8 Aug 2019.
100. HM Treasury. (2013). *Review of quality assurance of government analytical models*. https://assets.publishing.service.gov.uk/government/uploads/system/uploads/attachment_data/file/206946/review_of_qa_of_govt_analytical_models_final_report_040313.pdf

Chapter 4
AI Ethicist in Action: Strategies for Operationalising AI Ethics

Abstract A comprehensive overview is provided of pragmatic approaches and methodologies for operationalising AI ethics within organisations. It provides a comparative overview of existing tools, methods, and frameworks that translate ethical principles into actionable practices. The discussion highlights successful strategies, including ethics as a service, ethics-based auditing, and integrating ethical considerations into agile development processes. Case studies from various sectors illustrate how organisations can effectively bridge the gap between ethical theory and practical implementation, offering actionable insights for AI ethics advisors tasked with embedding ethical principles into organisational workflows.

Keywords Operationalisation · Ethics tools · Ethics auditing · Agile ethics · Organisational practices

Introduction by the Editor

Translating ethical principles into concrete AI practices has become a central challenge in both academic discourse and industry settings. Despite the proliferation of AI ethics guidelines, a persistent gap remains between normative aspirations and technical implementation. Many toolkits designed to support ethical AI are themselves shaped by a reductive, technosolutionist logic [1], often reducing ethics to checklist compliance rather than fostering a dynamic, relational practice.

This chapter critically reconsiders the role of such tools, proposing that ethics should function as scaffolding for reflection rather than procedural endpoints. Recognising the ethico-political implications of design choices—including indirect social and environmental consequences—requires rethinking how responsibility, power, and value are distributed across AI system development. In this context, the chapter explores emerging strategies to embed ethics meaningfully within AI governance and practice, highlighting both industry efforts and conceptual innovations. It also considers the conditions under which ethical oversight can be genuinely transformative.

A. Carnevale, *The AI Ethics Advisor*,
https://doi.org/10.1007/978-3-032-05526-2_4

From Principles to Practice: Bridging the Governance Gap

The operationalisation of AI ethics is frequently framed as a shift from abstract principles to practical implementation. Various approaches attempt to mediate this transition. The "Ethics as a Service" model, for instance, embeds ethical oversight directly into development teams, supporting iterative guidance throughout the AI lifecycle [2]. Meanwhile, a teleological methodology offers a goal-oriented approach that connects ethical principles to functional outcomes in high-risk domains such as defence [3].

Nevertheless, many governance frameworks still lack clear pathways for integrating ethics into data science and machine learning workflows [4]. Tools such as ethics committees and formal auditing systems [5, 6] have gained traction, yet tensions persist between internal accountability and independent oversight. Should ethical reflection be embedded within design processes, or should it be maintained as a separate, external function?

What is needed are hybrid models that balance technical autonomy with external legitimacy. This shift requires not only procedural mechanisms but cultural transformation—embedding ethical deliberation as a core part of innovation, not an afterthought.

Trust, Toolkits, and the Agile Lifecycle

As seen in the previous Chapter, trust remains a vital dimension of ethically-aligned AI, particularly regarding public perception and system adoption. One promising strategy involves embedding ethics into the agile software development lifecycle, aligning moral reflection with the iterative nature of software engineering [7]. This integration allows ethical considerations to evolve alongside technological development, supporting flexibility over fixed compliance models.

Responsible AI capabilities—such as governance structures, bias mitigation tools, and transparency mechanisms—contribute to building trust [8]. Yet these tools often rest on assumptions about the neutrality and completeness of existing frameworks. As noted in [1], many toolkits prioritise measurable or procedural concerns while overlooking systemic harm or power asymmetries. Reducing ethics to a set of compliance tasks risks obscuring its normative depth.

The implication is clear: the tools we use to promote ethical AI must themselves be subjected to critical scrutiny. What is required is not just a broader set of tools, but an expanded logic—one that is participatory, reflexive, and sensitive to context.

Cross-Cutting Insights

Ethical conduct in AI does not arise solely from individual intention or adherence to high-level principles. It is shaped by the socio-technical infrastructures within which decisions are made [6, 7]. When toolkits are applied uncritically, they can reify narrow conceptions of responsibility and reduce ethics to a form of reputational risk management [1]. A shift is needed—from a logic of control to one of care: care for values embedded in technologies, for affected communities, and for the epistemic conditions under which ethical judgements are formed [2, 8].

Ethical initiatives—whether in the form of internal consultancy, independent audits, or agile methodologies—should be assessed not just for procedural soundness but for their transformative capacity [3, 5]. Genuine ethical operationalisation fosters reflexive spaces that embrace contestation, uncertainty, and plural values as essential to responsible innovation [9].

Developing such an approach requires cultivating ethical capabilities across organisations: combining technical fluency with critical reflection, and procedural integration with normative imagination [8]. From this perspective, the role of the Ethics Advisor is not to enforce conformity but to enable institutional learning and moral experimentation. Bridging the gap between principle and practice thus involves reshaping the very cultures and infrastructures of AI design.

Conclusion: The Ethics Advisor and the Future of Operationalisation

In this evolving landscape, the Ethics Advisor plays a pivotal role. As a translator of values, a guide for moral reasoning, and a facilitator of ethical reflection, the Advisor is uniquely positioned to navigate the complexities of AI practice.

Operationalising ethics is not about converting values into technical specifications. It requires institutional frameworks that support deliberation, accountability, and learning. Ethical tools and procedures must avoid becoming vehicles of symbolic compliance. Instead, they should support the surfacing of value conflicts, encourage critical questioning, and ensure that decisions are justified not only technically, but normatively.

As [1] cautions, toolkits can either enable genuine ethical engagement or obscure its absence. The Ethics Advisor must therefore help organisations move beyond toolkittification and foster a culture where ethics is practised, not merely performed.

In this way, the Ethics Advisor becomes not a gatekeeper, but a steward of ethical possibility—ensuring that AI ethics remains grounded in care, reflection, and the pursuit of the public good.

Machine Generated Summaries

From What to How: An Initial Review of Publicly Available AI Ethics Tools, Methods and Research to Translate Principles into Practices [10]

This is a machine-generated summary of:

Morley, Jessica; Floridi, Luciano; Kinsey, Libby; Elhalal, Anat From What to How: An Initial Review of Publicly Available AI Ethics Tools, Methods and Research to Translate Principles into Practices [10]

Published in: Science and Engineering Ethics (2019)

Link to original: https://doi.org/10.1007/s11948-019-00165-5

If you want to cite the papers, please refer to the original.

For technical reasons we could not place the page where the original quote is coming from.

Abstract-Summary

"In recent years symbolic AI has been complemented and sometimes replaced by (Deep) Neural Networks and Machine Learning (ML) techniques."

"This has vastly increased its potential utility and impact on society, with the consequence that the ethical debate has gone mainstream."

"Such a debate has primarily focused on principles—the 'what' of AI ethics (beneficence, non-maleficence, autonomy, justice and explicability)—rather than on practices, the 'how.'"

"Our intention in presenting this research is to contribute to closing the gap between principles and practices by constructing a typology that may help practically-minded developers apply ethics at each stage of the Machine Learning development pipeline, and to signal to researchers where further work is needed."

"The focus is exclusively on Machine Learning, but it is hoped that the results of this research may be easily applicable to other branches of AI."

Introduction

"Rising to the challenge of designing 'ethical ML' is both essential and possible."

"It is possible to design an algorithmically-enhanced society pro-ethically [11], so that it protects the values, principles, and ethics that society thinks are fundamental [12]."

"Section 'Moving from Principles to Practice' discusses how efforts to data have been too focused on the 'what' of ethical AI (i.e. debates about principles and codes of conduct) and not enough on the 'how' of applied ethics."

"The 'Methodology' section outlines the research planned to contribute to closing this gap between principles and practice, through the creation of an 'applied ethical AI typology,' and the methodology for its creation."

"The section on 'A way forward' argues that there is a need for a more coordinated effort, from multi-disciplinary researchers, innovators, policymakers, citizens, developers and designers, to create and evaluate new tools and methodologies, in order to ensure that there is a 'how' for every 'what' at each stage of the Machine Learning pipeline."

Moving from Principles to Practices

"A review of 84 ethical AI documents by Jobin and others [13] found that although no single principle featured in all of them, the themes of transparency, justice and fairness, non-maleficence, responsibility and privacy appeared in over half."

"As argued by, taken together these themes 'define' ethically-aligned ML as that which is (a) beneficial to, and respectful of, people and the environment (beneficence); (b) robust and secure (non-maleficence); (c)respectful of human values (autonomy); (d) fair (justice); and (e) explainable, accountable and understandable (explicability)."

"Such risks, associated with a lack of practical guidance on how to produce ethical ML, make it clear that the ethical ML community needs to embark on the second phase of AI ethics: translating between the 'what' and the 'how.'"

"The aim of this research project is to identify the methods and tools already available to help developers, engineers, and designers of ML reflect on and apply 'ethics' [14] so that they may know not only what to do or not to do, but also how to do it, or avoid doing it [15]."

Methodology

"Vakkuri and others [16] sought to answer the question 'what practices, tools or methods, if any, do industry professionals utilise to implement ethics into AI design and development?'"

"Whilst analysis of the interviews revealed that the developers were aware of the potential importance of ethics in AI, the companies seemed to provide them with no tools or methods for implementing ethics."

"Based on a hypothesis that these findings did not imply the non-existence of applied-ethics tools and methods, but rather a lack of progress in the translation of available tools and methods from academic literature or early-stage development and research, to real-life use, this study used the traditional approach of providing an overarching assessment of a research topic, namely a literature review [17]."

"They provide a practical or theoretical contribution to the answer of the question: 'how to develop an ethical algorithmic system."

Framing the Results

"The purpose of presenting it is not to imply that it is 'complete,' nor that the tools and methodologies highlighted are the best, or indeed the only, means of 'solving' each of the individual ethical problems."

"The typology is intended to eventually be an online searchable database so that developers can look for the appropriate tools and methodologies for their given context, and use them to enable a shift from a prescriptive 'ethics-by-design' approach to a dialogic, pro-ethical design approach [18, 19]."

"In the present scenario of developers rationalising ML design decisions to ensure that they are ethically-optimised, the tools and methods in the typology replace the role of language and act as the medium for identifying, checking, creating and re-examining ideas and giving fair consideration to differing interests, values and norms [20, 21]."

Discussion of Initial Results

"Temporarily that this is indeed the case, and that by dint of being explicable an ML system can more easily meet the principles of beneficence, non-maleficence, autonomy and justice, then the fact that the ethical ML community has focused so extensively on developing tools for explanations may not seem problematic."

"Available of tools and methods in a variety of typology areas is also important in the context of culturally and contextually specific ML ethics."

"The tools and methods included in the typology are positioned as discourse aids, designed to facilitate and document rational decisions about trade-offs in the design process that may make an ML system more or less ethically-aligned."

"There is no clear problem statement (and therefore no clear business case) that the ML community can use to justify time and financial investment in developing much-needed tools and techniques that truly enable pro-ethical design."

A Way Forward

"Bridging together multi-disciplinary researchers into the development process of pro-ethical design tools and methodologies will be essential."

"The resulting collaborations are likely to be highly beneficial for the development of applied ethical tools and methodologies for at least three reasons."

"It would also mitigate a significant risk—posed by the current sporadic application of ethical-design tools and/or methods during different development stages—of the ethical principles having been written into the business and use-case, but coded out by the time a system gets to deployment."

"This approach to applied ML ethics of regular reflection and application will heavily rely on (i) the creation of more tools—especially to fill the white spaces of the typology (for the reasons discussed in the previous section) and (ii) acceleration of tools' maturity level from research labs into production environments."

Limitations

"The first is that the research question 'what tools and methods are available for ML developers to 'apply' ethics to each stage of the ML system design' is very broad."

"Building on this, it is again, very likely that there are a number of proprietary applied ethics tools and methods being developed by private companies for internal or consulting purposes that we will have missed, for example the 'suite of customisable frameworks, tools and processes' that make up consulting firm PWC's "Responsible AI Toolkit" [22]."

"Governments are increasingly setting standards and system requirements for ethical ML, but delegating the means for meeting these to the developers themselves [23]—the tools and methods of the typology can be seen as the means of providing evidence of compliance."

"The typology (and the tools and methods it contains within) help developers take responsibility for embedding ethics in the part of the development, deployment, and use of ML solutions that they control [24]."

Conclusion

"This makes it difficult to assess the scope of their use (resulting in Arvan's [25] 'moral-semantic trilemma') and consequently hard to encourage their adoption by the practically-minded ML developers, especially when the competitive advantage of more ethically-aligned AI is not yet clear."

"Unless a longer-term and sector-wide perspective in terms of return on investment can be encouraged—so that mechanisms are developed to close the gap between what and how—the lack of guidance may (a) result in the costs of ethical mistakes outweighing the benefits of ethical successes; (b) undermine public acceptance of algorithmic systems, even to the point of a backlash [26]; and (c) reduce adoption of algorithmic systems."

"The need for 'AI Ethics' has arisen from the fact that poorly designed AI systems can cause very significant harm."

"The potential benefits of pro-ethically designed AI systems are considerable."

Beyond Principlism: Practical Strategies for Ethical AI Use in Research Practices [9]

This is a machine-generated summary of:

Lin, Zhicheng Beyond principlism: practical strategies for ethical AI use in research practices [9]

Published in: AI and Ethics (2024)

Link to original: https://doi.org/10.1007/s43681-024-00585-5

If you want to cite the papers, please refer to the original.

For technical reasons we could not place the page where the original quote is coming from.

Abstract-Summary

"The rapid adoption of generative artificial intelligence (AI) in scientific research, particularly large language models (LLMs), has outpaced the development of ethical guidelines, leading to a "Triple-Too" problem: too many high-level ethical initiatives, too abstract principles lacking contextual and practical relevance, and too much focus on restrictions and risks over benefits and utilities."

"Existing approaches—principlism (reliance on abstract ethical principles), formalism (rigid application of rules), and technological solutionism (overemphasis on technological fixes)—offer little practical guidance for addressing ethical challenges of AI in scientific research practices."

"It outlines five specific goals for ethical AI use: (1) understanding model training and output, including bias mitigation strategies; (2) respecting privacy, confidentiality, and copyright; (3) avoiding plagiarism and policy violations; (4) applying

AI beneficially compared to alternatives; and (5) using AI transparently and reproducibly."

"I propose documentation guidelines to enhance transparency and reproducibility in AI-assisted research."

"By refining these ethical guidelines and adapting them to emerging AI capabilities, we can accelerate scientific progress without compromising research integrity."

The "Triple-Too" Problem of AI Ethics

"As it stands, the current discourse on AI ethics faces what we term the "Triple-Too" problem: too many initiatives, frameworks, and documents on high-level ethical directives, which can be overwhelming and difficult to navigate; too abstract concepts and principles that lack contextualization and practical relevance, making them hard to implement and follow; and too negative a focus on restrictions and risks rather than on benefits and utilities."

"To wit, existing AI ethics initiatives primarily focus on establishing general principles for the development, deployment, and governance of AI, addressing developers, consumers, policymakers, and healthcare practitioners [27, 28]."

"Historical lessons from medical ethics teach us that high-level principles must be translated into practices by embedding them into specific norms and cultures."

"AI ethics lacks corresponding norms and cultures to develop best practices for implementing principles and policies."

A Shift to User-Centered Realism in Scientific Contexts

"One is to clarify the nature of generative AI systems in scientific research: are they best conceptualized as tools or as automatic agents (i.e., systems that can perceive their environment, make decisions, and act to achieve predetermined goals)?"

"The second issue then is: in the AI ecosystem, what is the ethical role of practicing scientists?"

"What, then, should a thoughtful scientist do to use AI tools ethically in research practices?"

"If we think of AI as a method of discovery, the pressing issue becomes how to ethically use this method in day-to-day scientific practices."

"This approach is grounded in five specific goals and actionable strategies for the ethical AI implementation in scientific research and training."

"Developed by researchers for researchers, they aim to bridge the gap between abstract ethical principles and practical application, facilitating responsible AI use that supports the adoption of generative AI tools and empowers researchers [29]."

Five Specific Goals and Action-Guiding Strategies for Ethical AI Use in Research Practices

"These techniques include: reweighting (e.g., assigning higher weights to data points from underrepresented or domain-specific subgroups to compensate for their scarcity in the training dataset, thereby helping the model generalize better across domains); adversarial learning (e.g., training the model alongside a competitive model, or adversary, that aims to detect and maximize the loss associated with biases or domain-specific features, thereby forcing the primary model to learn representations that are invariant to domain-specific variations); and style transfer (e.g., applying transformations to data from different domains to make them more similar in appearance or feature distribution, which helps the model learn from a more consistent and unified dataset, even if the original data came from different sources)."

"The key takeaway is that, when integrating generative AI such as LLMs into scientific practices, users must develop a conceptual understanding of how these models work—their probabilistic nature, issues related to truthfulness, the array of biases (sources, types, measures, mitigation strategies, and potential consequences), and their inherent opacity (e.g., challenges with interpretability and explainability, differences between open-source and closed-source models)."

Concluding Remarks

"Looking ahead, two critical areas emerge for immediate action: professional development and training, and the enforcement of ethical standards."

"Training should cover both the operational aspects of AI tools and the ethical implications of AI systems—both benefits and risks."

"The establishment of guidelines and training programs is effective only if accompanied by reasonable enforcement mechanisms [30]."

"By focusing on continually refining these ethical guidelines, adapting training programs to emerging AI advancements, and ensuring that enforcement mechanisms are both reasonable and effective, the emergent capabilities of AI could markedly accelerate human understanding without eroding the integrity of science."

Glossary

"Domain Adaptation: Techniques that adjust a model trained in one domain (data type or environment) to perform well in a different but related domain, addressing distribution shifts or domainspecificbiases."

"Federated Learning: A privacy-preserving technique that allows machine learning models to be trained across decentralized data sources, improving data security by keeping the data local."

"Out-of-Distribution (OOD) Data: Data that substantially differ from the data used to train an AI model, often leading to poor model performance in real-world applications."

"Reweighting: A bias mitigation technique that assigns higher importance to underrepresented data points during training to improve the model?s fairness and accuracy across different groups."

"Targeted Data Collection: A technique for deliberately gathering additional data from underrepresented groups or specific domains to improve model performance and reduce bias, ensuring that AI models generalize better to diverse populations."

Ethics as a Service: A Pragmatic Operationalisation of AI Ethics [2]

This is a machine-generated summary of:

Morley, Jessica; Elhalal, Anat; Garcia, Francesca; Kinsey, Libby; Mökander, Jakob; Floridi, Luciano Ethics as a Service: A Pragmatic Operationalisation of AI Ethics [2]

Published in: Minds and Machines (2021)

Link to original: https://doi.org/10.1007/s11023-021-09563-w

If you want to cite the papers, please refer to the original.

For technical reasons we could not place the page where the original quote is coming from.

Abstract-Summary

"As the range of potential uses for Artificial Intelligence (AI), in particular machine learning (ML), has increased, so has awareness of the associated ethical issues."

"It has become increasingly clear that a significant gap exists between the theory of AI ethics principles and the practical design of AI systems."

"We analysed whether it is possible to close this gap between the 'what' and the 'how' of AI ethics through the use of tools and methods designed to help AI developers, engineers, and designers translate principles into practice."

"If no, then how can AI ethics be made useful for AI practitioners?"

"This is the question we seek to address here by exploring why principles and technical translational tools are still needed even if they are limited, and how these limitations can be potentially overcome by providing theoretical grounding of a concept that has been termed 'Ethics as a Service.'"

Introduction

"It has become increasingly clear that highly abstract principles provide little protection from potential harms related to AI when AI practitioners have no guidance on how to design and deploy algorithms within these ethical boundaries [23, 31]."

"The development of these translational tools and methods may have been useful for enabling individual groups of researchers/companies to raise internal awareness of AI ethics and to examine different interpretations of ethical principles."

"We concluded that the existing translational tools and methods fail to operationalise AI ethics effectively."

"Pages, we seek to answer these questions by exploring why principles and technical translational tools are still needed even if they are limited, and how these limitations can be potentially overcome by providing theoretical grounding of a concept that has been termed 'Ethics as a Service'."

Lowering the Level of Abstraction

"AI ethical guidance documents have been produced by a range of stakeholders, from technology companies, professional bodies and standards-setting bodies to governments and research organisations [32]."

"Many of the ethical harms that the principles in these documents purport to protect against are poorly understood because they are described too vaguely [23]."

"Ethical principles have been accused of being too flexible (or too undefined) to be of practical use to AI practitioners [32, 33]."

"The accusation is mistaken insofar as the ethical principles should be seen as providing the foundation and not the details of ethical practices, in a way comparable to what a Constitution does when compared to specific legislation."

"This is why a promising and reasonable approach to the problem of not-yet actionable AI ethical principles is to bring ethical guidance down to the Design level, by providing tools and methods that translate the 'what' of AI ethics into the 'how' of technical specifications."

Limits of Principlism and Translational Tools

"When the parameters for the 'diagnosis' of fairness, transparency or accountability are set by the AI practitioners themselves, the potential for objective critique is easily lost and so the aim of the translational tool or method ceases to 'ensure the algorithmic system meets the criteria of social preferability' [34] (and therefore ethical justifiability)."

"This critique of AI ethics principlism and translational tools and methods raises the question whether the entire pro-ethical design endeavour is futile, if even with technical guidance, AI ethics is difficult or impossible to embed in the process of algorithmic design, development, deployment, and use."

"Companies using the DCEF to translate high-level ethical principles into practice are encouraged to consult it at validation, verification and evaluation stages of their product development pipeline, to ensure that at each stage time is dedicated to thinking through the ethical implications of all decisions made."

A Series of Compromises

"If AI ethics is to be operationalised in a way that is useful to AI practitioners and simultaneously protective of individuals, groups, society and the environment, then the operationalisation must: (a) happen at the appropriate Level of Abstraction (where translational tools are neither too flexible, nor too strict); and (b) must not consist solely of a one-off tick-box exercise completed only at the beginning of the Design process."

"An operationalisation of AI ethics focused on procedural regularity and public reason would commit a company producing algorithmic systems to: (a) justifying all design decisions to a set of common principles agreed through an inclusive and discursive process that involves all individuals, groups and environmental representatives likely to be directly or indirectly affected by the AI products of a specific company or research group."

"It is clear, therefore, that external ethical auditing will be a key component of any form of operationalised AI ethics."

Outlining Ethics as a Service

"We would encourage others to develop partial or complete pilots of the concept, so that answers to the following questions might be developed: how should members of the independent ethics board be selected; should members of the board be paid for their time or would this introduce conflicts of interest; should the independent ethics board be the same group who conducts the audit, or would this introduce problematic incentives to make their work appear more successful than it is in reality; where does the responsibility sit for deciding to stop development of an AI solution if it is found to be harmful; how does the implementation of Ethics as a Service vary between companies of different sizes (e.g., start-up vs. large established company) and working in different sectors; how do the benefits/drawbacks vary in these different contexts?"

Conclusion

"It seems reasonable to hypothesise that AI ethics would benefit from an equally customisable approach, and that if this balance can be achieved then the pro-ethical Design endeavour may succeed."

"Encouraging a procedural approach can, for example, help make the parallels between AI ethics and other quality assurance processes, such as safety testing, clearer and thus make it more obvious why careful consideration needs to be given to each Design decision."

"Whilst these opportunities for moving forward the conversation about AI ethics and the role that Ethics as a Service may play in this, should be celebrated, it must be acknowledged that the impacts of AI systems cannot be entirely controlled through technical design [31]."

"Regular re-evaluation of all aspects of algorithm systems, and the extent to which they achieve their goals, including pro-ethical Design approaches, will be crucial."

From AI Ethics Principles to Practices: A Teleological Methodology to Apply AI Ethics Principles in the Defence Domain [3]

This is a machine-generated summary of:

Taddeo, Mariarosaria; Blanchard, Alexander; Thomas, Christopher From AI Ethics Principles to Practices: A Teleological Methodology to Apply AI Ethics Principles in The Defence Domain [3]

Published in: Philosophy & Technology (2024)

Link to original: https://doi.org/10.1007/s13347-024-00710-6

If you want to cite the papers, please refer to the original.

For technical reasons we could not place the page where the original quote is coming from.

Abstract-Summary

"This article provides a methodology for the interpretation of AI ethics principles to specify ethical criteria for the development and deployment of AI systems in high-risk domains."

"The methodology presented in this article is designed to be agile, adaptable, and replicable, and when used as part of a pro-ethical institutional culture, will help to foster the ethical design, development, and deployment of AI systems."

Introduction

"We set out a methodology to interpret and apply AI ethics principles into practices with a specific focus on the defence domain."

"To be effective, AI ethics principles need to be coupled with appropriate methodologies to offer domain-specific guidance as to how to apply them [35], to answer the question 'what do I (provider/designer/developer/user) have to do to ensure that this step of the AI lifecycle respects the AI ethics principles?'"

"There is a midway step between AI ethics principles and AI ethics tools which concerns the specification of a methodology for the interpretation and application of these principles into practices."

"To do so, we describe a new, three-step methodology for the interpretation and application of AI ethics principles in the defence domain."

"To illustrate the application of the methodology we use the ethics principles for AI provided by the UK MoD [36]."

A Three-Step Methodology to Extract Guidelines from Ethical AI Principles in Defence

"The EB has three tasks: identifying the LoA to model the AI lifecycle; interpreting the principles to extract specific requirements to be met at each step of the AI lifecycle; and defining criteria to inform purpose- and context-specific balancing of the principles."

"When interpreting the principle of 'justified and overridable uses', the EB could specify the following requirements for an AI system to move from the procurement to the design step: There has to be an analysis mapping ethical risks related to the use of the envisaged AI system for a specified goal and detailing mitigation strategies for such risks; There has to be a cost–benefit analysis showing the military (or organizational) value of the proposed solution which demonstrates beneficial outcomes and proportionality of possible breaches of rights and values; The conceptualization of the AI solution should specify procedures to ensure human overridability of the system."

The Application of the Method to the Principles: Applying the Human-Centric AI Principles in Procurement

"We offer an example of the requirements that an EB may elicit when considering specific ethics principles for AI in defence."

"The impact of AI-enabled systems on humans must be assessed and considered, for a full range of effects both positive and negative across the entire system lifecycle."

"This means assessing and carefully considering the effects on humans of AI-enabled systems, taking full account of human diversity, and ensuring those effects are as positive as possible."

"The interpretation of the principle with respect to step-specific ethical risks, as identified by the EB on the basis of the model of the AI lifecycle adopted, will lead the board to define the requirements as necessary steps for a project to move from the procurement stage to the next one."

Conclusion

"We have focused on the need to develop a methodology to interpret and apply AI ethics principle to specific practices, in this case those of the defence domain."

"We shall submit that the proposed methodology has great potential to be practical and agile, because following it an EB can identify ethical risks and requirements focusing on types of AI systems and for purposes of use."

"It has to be noted that the methodology is a necessary but insufficient element to foster ethical design, development and deployment of AI systems."

"We leave these topics to further steps in our research; but it is crucial to mention them here to outline, albeit briefly, that a methodology without institutional support would not be more useful to achieve ethical outcomes than the AI ethics principles alone."

From AI Ethics Principles to Data Science Practice: A Reflection and a Gap Analysis Based on Recent Frameworks and Practical Experience [4]

This is a machine-generated summary of:

Georgieva, Ilina; Lazo, Claudio; Timan, Tjerk; van Veenstra, Anne Fleur From AI ethics principles to data science practice: a reflection and a gap analysis based on recent frameworks and practical experience [4]

Published in: AI and Ethics (2022)

Link to original: https://doi.org/10.1007/s43681-021-00127-3

If you want to cite the papers, please refer to the original.

For technical reasons we could not place the page where the original quote is coming from.

Abstract-Summary

"Operationalisation is required, since ethics frameworks are often not suited to be used by data scientists in the development of AI-based services or products."

"In this paper, we aim to contribute to this third wave by mapping AI ethical principles onto the lifecycle of an AI-based digital service or product and combining it with an explicit governance model to clarify responsibilities in operationalisation."

Introduction

"This paper contributes to the third wave of scholarship on ethical AI by mapping AI ethical principles onto the lifecycle of an AI-based digital service or product to investigate their applicability for the practice of data science."

"It is challenging for data scientists and organizations aiming to develop digital services to adhere to principles of AI ethics as a result of a lack of actionable guidelines and governance."

"Focusing on the development of actional guidelines for data science, our paper highlights which phases of the AI lifecycle require more attention in the implementation of ethical principles, and more importantly by whom."

"By combining the results from visualizing the ethical principles on an AI system's continuum and Shneiderman's structures model, we identity conceptual and organizational gaps in the current conversation on trustworthy AI and draw conclusions for effective principles translation and human-centric governance of AI."

Dealing with High-Level AI Principles: The HLEG Ethics Guidelines for Trustworthy AI

"Even though the ethics principles formulated by the AI HLEG have not been left uncriticized, stakeholders of all shapes and sizes have been dedicating time and resources to embed them in their operations."

"While aware of AI ethics and checklists on national level, public bodies struggle to single-handedly align them with EU-level guidance and would often opt for an 'AI requirements mix'."

"Organizations are reported to focus only on a limited set of issues and mitigation measures, maintaining that a number of ethical concerns lie beyond the scope of their expertise and remit, and suggesting the need for a broader stakeholder framework to ensure a comprehensive engagement and coverage of AI ethics [37]."

"As most actors that look into the use of AI to optimise their processes, public authorities are struggling to understand which principles apply to which applications, when and how to structure their oversight, and how to fit both principles and oversight in their organizational culture."

Methodology

"The HLEG requirements for trustworthy AI are mapped onto the general AI-lifecycle stages, for which we use the AI-lifecycle typology of Morley [10] that guides machine learning (ML)—a specific type of AI—developers through the phases of algorithmic development."

"Under 'Explainability', the ALTAI checklist poses the question 'Do you continuously survey the users if they understand the decision(s) of the AI system?' (p. 15), which relates process explainability to the continuous surveying of users [38]; thus, the requirement is also meant to apply in the monitoring phase."

"Upon investigating the corresponding ALTAI checklist [38], we find that for both sub-requirements, the focus is widened across the AI lifecycle."

"We see in general that questions of bias and fairness also reside in several steps in the AI-lifecycle process, with similar challenges both in AI technology itself as in the requirements and context around the AI-based system or service that is being developed."

Results and Discussion

"The heatmap contains the requirements—vertically grouped per high-level requirement (e.g., 'Transparency'), and the AI lifecycle (in the horizontal direction), containing the phases of Business/use-case development, Design, Training and test data procurement, Building, Testing, Deployment, and Monitoring."

"On theoretical level, the requirements are designed to raise questions of the explainability of the business model for review purposes, but requirements expected to have a more direct regulatory impact on AI effects such as human agency (including human dignity and autonomy), accountability, and oversight remain outside of the scope of the business model stage."

"Operationalizing AI ethical guidelines is something that is currently taking place in pilots and experiments (often after something has gone wrong); we are also contributing to this process through an action-research approach [39], in which the aim is to connect ethics and politics of local governmental organization with their data science departments and industry standards on questions of transparency, accountability, and explicability of AI-based public services."

Conclusion

"This contribution consists of analysing current work in defining guidelines on what European and human-centric AI could look like, most notably the AI HLEG, the work by Morley and others and Shneiderman, and connecting these through a current case study in which the authors work with a local Dutch municipality that aims to develop an AI-based public service based on ethical guidelines."

"The practical implications evolve around translation work from principles into software engineering standards and requirements, which at the moment are lacking in AI engineering."

"Connecting the latter point to the political or normative implications, the development of ethical AI is also highly dependent on the political and institutional landscape."

"The analysis offered in this paper shows that we will need an entire landscape of methods, standards and procedures if we want to develop AI-based services for 'good'."

Operationalising AI Ethics: How Are Companies Bridging the Gap Between Practice and Principles? An Exploratory Study [5]

This is a machine-generated summary of:

Ibáñez, Javier Camacho; Olmeda, Mónica Villas Operationalising AI ethics: how are companies bridging the gap between practice and principles? An exploratory study [5]

Published in: AI & SOCIETY (2021)

Link to original: https://doi.org/10.1007/s00146-021-01267-0

If you want to cite the papers, please refer to the original.

For technical reasons we could not place the page where the original quote is coming from.

Abstract-Summary

"Despite the increase in the research field of ethics in artificial intelligence, most efforts have focused on the debate about principles and guidelines for responsible AI, but not enough attention has been given to the "how" of applied ethics."

"This paper aims to advance the research exploring the gap between practice and principles in AI ethics by identifying how companies are applying those guidelines and principles in practice."

"Through a qualitative methodology based on 22 semi-structured interviews and two focus groups, the goal of the current study is to understand how companies approach ethical issues related to AI systems."

"Despite some obvious limitations, such as the type and number of companies interviewed, this work identifies real examples and direct priorities to advance the research exploring the gap between practice and principles in AI ethics, with a specific focus on Spanish companies."

Introduction

"Most of the countries and companies worldwide that are developing AI technologies have established and published ethical principles and guidelines to be followed by organisations in the development of AI systems."

"Through a detailed review of the existing literature on principles and a review of similar studies, the goal of the current study is to understand how the interviewed companies approach ethical issues related to AI systems and apply guidelines and principles, with particular attention to the topics of privacy, explainability, and fairness."

"The focus of this research is on four main questions regarding how companies apply AI ethics principles in practice, their perceptions about privacy, explainability and fairness issues, and how they try to approach them."

"Despite some obvious limitations, such as the type and number of companies interviewed, the paper provides real examples and identifies direct priorities to advance understanding with regard to the gap between practice and principles in AI ethics."

Objective and Justification: From Principles to Practice

"Companies need to face the ethical consequences of AI development."

"One of the most recent developments is the responsible AI toolkit by PwC. It consists of different frameworks and tools to facilitate the understanding of AI ethics maturity in a company."

"To the need for different tools and frameworks, AI ethics requires legal enforceability, an issue that remains unresolved in the majority of countries around the world [40]."

"The study concludes with recommendations that might be helpful such as following a systematic approach to prevent AI ethics issues or improving transparency."

"Stahl and others [37] develop 10 case studies with 42 interviews and note that companies are aware of the issue but have typically developed limited mitigation strategies focusing only on organisational awareness, analysis of privacy, ethics training and human oversight."

Theoretical Framework and Research Questions

"Through research from the private sector, government, civil society and other stakeholders, those studies have selected AI principles documents from relevant sources, regions and sectors."

"Research, we have chosen three main principles: privacy, explainability and fairness."

"AI systems should respect individuals' privacy, both in the use of data to develop technological systems and to provide people with control over their data and the decisions they make with it."

"How do companies try to apply the existing guidelines or principles for responsible AI?"

"How do companies consider privacy, and what specific measures (if any) do they take with regard to this issue?"

"How do companies consider explainability, and what specific measures (if any) do they take with regard to this issue?"

"How do companies consider potential biases and fairness, and what specific measures (if any) do they take with regard to this issue?"

Methods

"A qualitative methodology based on interviews and focus groups was developed for this study's exploratory purpose."

"Interview results can provide helpful information for developing focus group guidance; similarly, focus groups can enrich interview results by facilitating discussion and interaction on shortlisted topics [41]."

"Based on the theoretical framework described above, an interview script was developed grouping the topics around the main research questions."

"The main goal of a focus group is to help interpret and contrast interview results by facilitating debate and interaction on the selected topics, furthered by the creation of an adequate trustworthy climate [42]."

"The script for the focus groups was developed after the interviews were completed and analysed, and a short introduction document was shared with the participants."

"Once the interviews were analysed and the first draft for discussion was elaborated, two focus groups were held with ten interviewed participants to contrast the findings and gather further feedback."

Results and Discussion

"Quote #11 There is no perceived ethical concern, yes for regulatory concern [...] I have not found any RFP case that says, "this algorithm has to be explainable or has to avoid some type X of bias, for example, gender bias" I have not found it."

"Quote #11 But in the end, biases are often a topic of the data themselves, without the algorithm."

"Quote #7 Those of us working at ML are pretty aware, in general, of the risk that either the model or the data will be biased."

"Quote #10 We from the design only use controlled data, and we can explain what sources have been used, in case there were biases, or there were behaviours that I could not avoid or detect [...] So from the design, we assure you what the data sources are."

Conclusions

"We could distinguish two main perspectives: a bottom-up approach, whereby companies first develop AI systems and then try to understand how to generate ethical principles and standardise best practices, and a top–bottom approach, whereby companies receive high-level guidelines and principles and try to find a way to land them into their day-to-day operations."

"This needs to be accounted for when addressing the gap between practices and principles since bridging the gap is different if we depart from practices to principles (as most companies seem to be doing) or from principles to practices (as most guidelines seem to suggest)."

"Regarding the concepts explored: privacy, explainability and fairness, one of the research's main findings has been the relevance of considering the ethical issues related to these concepts throughout the life cycle of the project, system, or product."

"There are two different meanings for companies regarding privacy: one is related to data protection relative to the users (as stated in the GDPR and most principles)."

Limitations and Further Research

"Given the nature of qualitative research, some apparent limitations must be considered such as the need to limit the number of companies interviewed."

"Research, the study could be extended to other regions and more companies or more deeply into specific sectors or applications."

"It would also be interesting to build a maturity level survey to assess how companies address the identified issues."

Operationalising AI Governance Through Ethics-Based Auditing: An Industry Case Study [6]

This is a machine-generated summary of:

Mökander, Jakob; Floridi, Luciano Operationalising AI governance through ethics-based auditing: an industry case study [6]

Published in: AI and Ethics (2022)

Link to original: https://doi.org/10.1007/s43681-022-00171-7

If you want to cite the papers, please refer to the original.

For technical reasons we could not place the page where the original quote is coming from.

Abstract-Summary

"Ethics-based auditing (EBA) is a structured process whereby an entity's past or present behaviour is assessed for consistency with moral principles or norms."

"EBA has attracted much attention as a governance mechanism that may help to bridge the gap between principles and practice in AI ethics."

"Over 12 months, we observed and analysed the internal activities of AstraZeneca, a biopharmaceutical company, as it prepared for and underwent an ethics-based AI audit."

"The case study presented in this article contributes to the existing literature by providing a detailed description of the organisational context in which EBA procedures must be integrated to be feasible and effective."

Introduction

"Recent publications have identified ethics-based auditing (EBA) as a governance mechanism with the potential to help bridge the gap between principles and practice in AI ethics [43–48]."

"The literature on EBA contains few case studies: Buolamwini and Gebru [49] assessed the efficacy of external audits to address biases in facial recognition systems; Mahajan and others [50] outlined a procedure to audit AI systems that replicate cognitive tasks in radiology workflows; and Kazim and others [51] applied a systematic audit to algorithmic recruitment systems."

"By outlining the challenges and tensions involved in conducting a real-world AI audit, it identifies transferable best practices for how to develop EBA procedures."

"Our findings suggest that the main difficulties organisations face when conducting AI audits mirror corporate governance challenges."

"Efforts to operationalise AI governance are interdisciplinary in nature and the transfer of knowledge from different fields of study will be a key success factor to design and implement EBA procedures."

"This paper is thus aimed at computer scientists, ethicists, and auditors that develop EBA procedures as well as managers tasked with the implementation of corporate AI ethics principles."

The Need to Operationalise AI Governance

"Using AI systems in the healthcare sector may allow humans to live more healthy lives while enabling societies to manage the rising costs associated with ageing populations [52]."

"The use of AI systems in the healthcare sector is coupled with ethical challenges [53, 54]."

"While the adoption of AI systems have outpaced the development of governance mechanisms designed to address the associated ethical concerns [55], abstaining from using AI systems in sensitive areas of application is not the way forward [26]."

"No purely technical solution will thus be able to ensure that AI systems operate in ways that are ethically-sound [56, 57]."

"It is essential that public and private actors seeking to benefit from AI systems understand and address the varied ethical challenges associated with their use."

"Responding to this need, numerous governments and NGOs have proposed ethical principles that provide normative guidance to organisations designing and deploying AI systems [13, 58]."

"Principles alone cannot guarantee that AI systems are designed and used in ethically-sound ways."

AstraZeneca and AI Governance

"Examples of use cases of AI systems within AstraZeneca are abundant."

"In November 2020, AstraZeneca's board moved towards addressing these risks by publishing a set of Principles for Ethical Data and AI (henceforth, ethics principles."

"Taking those considerations into account, AstraZeneca allowed each business area to develop their own AI governance structures to reflect local variations in objectives, digital maturity, and ways of working—as long as these align with the externally published ethics principles."

"A Responsible AI Playbook was developed to provide more detailed, end-to-end guidance on developing, testing, and deploying AI systems within AstraZeneca."

"An AI resolution board was created to review 'high-risk' AI use cases and an internal Responsible AI Consultancy Service was launched to facilitate the sharing of best practices and to educate staff about the risks of using AI systems in different contexts."

An 'Ethics-Based' AI Audit

"In Q4 2021, AstraZeneca underwent an AI audit."

"The AI audit conducted within AstraZeneca was an ethics-based, process-oriented audit conducted in collaboration with an independent third party."

"The AI audit conducted within AstraZeneca corresponds to (ii) since it was directed towards demonstrating adherence to voluntary codes of conduct."

"The audit was coordinated by AstraZeneca's internal audit function and conducted by an external service provider."

"Operationally, the audit conducted within AstraZeneca consisted of two types of activities: a high-level governance audit of organisational structures and processes and in-depth audits of specific projects that either develop or use AI systems."

"AstraZeneca's AI audit focussed on processes and people, i.e., on assessing (i) the soundness and completeness of organisational processes and (ii) the extent to which different organisational entities adhered to these processes."

"No technical audits of individual AI systems were conducted during AstraZeneca's AI audit."

Methodology: An Industry Case Study

"We observed and analysed AstraZeneca's internal activities as it prepared for and underwent an AI audit."

"With respect to these RQs, AstraZeneca's AI audit constituted what Merton [59] calls 'strategic research material' for at least two reasons."

"Methodologically, the present study leveraged two qualitative research methods: participant observation and semi-structured interviews."

"Participant observation meant embedding ourselves in the organisation to observe the activities associated with preparing for and conducting the AI audit."

"We observed two types of meetings: internal meetings, in which AstraZeneca employees prepared for (or evaluated the results from) the AI audit, and audit meetings, in which external auditors asked questions to, and reviewed documentation provided by, AstraZeneca employees."

"We conducted semi-structured interviews [60] with different stakeholders involved in the audit."

"A parallel research design [61] was used, in which the participant observation and the semi-structured interviews were conducted simultaneously."

Lessons Learned from AstraZeneca's 2021 AI Audit

"As one of the external auditors put it: "The really rich information comes not from asking a pre-curated list of questions, but from listening to the answers and asking relevant follow-up questions." (P9) Taken together, our observations before, during, and after AstraZeneca's AI audit suggest that the primary purpose of metrics in the process of operationalising AI governance is not to decide whether a specific system is 'ethical' or not, but rather to spark ethical deliberation, inform design choices, and help visualise the normative values embedded in that system."

"In AstraZeneca's case, the process of drafting and agreeing on the ethics principles included multiple consultations with executive leaders on strategy, with senior developers to understand AI-related risks, with heads of different business areas to compare the agreed-upon principles with existing codes of conduct, as well as with academic researchers and industry experts to receive external feedback."

Limitations

"We discuss important limitations with regards to the validity, independence, and generalisability of our findings."

"Since our study relied on descriptive methods, it is most relevant to consider construct validity, i.e., the ability to link research observations to their intended theoretical constructs [62]."

A further risk related to validity concerns the possibility of replicating findings from previous research, which may be affected by confirmation bias [63].

"While difficult to eliminate, this risk was managed through an iterative process, with findings from the literature and the case study continuously informing each other."

"Including longitudinal case studies helps strengthen the validity of nonexperimental research designs [64]." (see also [65])

"Another limitation concerns the independence of the research."

"When such dependencies exist, researchers may feel pressured to produce 'positive' results, i.e., findings that the industry partner wants to hear [66]."

"A final set of limitations concerns the generalisability of the case study's findings."

Conclusions

"In such a fast-moving and high-stakes environment, it is of increasing importance for both regulators and business executives to understand the conditions under which EBA is a feasible and effective mechanism for operationalising AI governance."

"EBA procedures that do not include any technical elements are fundamentally unable to produce verifiable claims about the effects autonomous and self-learning AI systems may have over time."

"Efforts to operationalise AI governance through EBA are most effective when internal communication is centred around how this would help employees with their daily tasks."

"Large multinational organisations attempting to operationalise AI governance through EBA will inevitably face at least three critical challenges."

"It will remain difficult for any EBA procedure to produce verifiable claims until the material scope of AI governance is accepted throughout an organisation."

"To successfully operationalise AI governance, EBA procedures must treat AI systems developed in-house and those procured from third-party vendors equally."

Operationalising AI Ethics Through the Agile Software Development Lifecycle: A Case Study of AI-Enabled Mobile Health Applications [7]

This is a machine-generated summary of:

Amugongo, Lameck Mbangula; Kriebitz, Alexander; Boch, Auxane; Lütge, Christoph Operationalising AI ethics through the agile software development lifecycle: a case study of AI-enabled mobile health applications [7]

Published in: AI and Ethics (2023)

Link to original: https://doi.org/10.1007/s43681-023-00331-3

If you want to cite the papers, please refer to the original.

For technical reasons we could not place the page where the original quote is coming from.

Abstract-Summary

"Although numerous ethical principles and guidelines have been proposed to guide the development of artificial intelligence (AI) systems, it has proven difficult to translate these principles into actionable practices beyond mere adherence to ethical ideas."

"To address this challenge, we propose a shift from one-size-fits-all ethical principles to contextualized case-based ethical frameworks."

"Our framework is built on existing ethical guidelines and principles, including the AI4People framework, the EU High-Level Expert Group on trustworthy AI, and wider human rights considerations."

"Our approach is based on "ethics by design," where ethical principles are integrated throughout the entire AI development pipeline, ensuring that ethical considerations are not an afterthought but implemented from the beginning."

"For our case study, we identified 7 ethical principles: fairness, agility, precision, safeguarding humanity, respect for others, trust and accountability, and robustness and reproducibility."

"We believe that the best way to mitigate and address ethical consequences is by implementing ethical principles in the software development processes that developers commonly use."

Introduction

"The growing application of machine learning (ML) techniques in healthcare has increased awareness of the ethical issues that arise in the design, deployment and use of AI systems."

"A consensus guidance framework outlining six principles for the ethical use of AI in healthcare [67]."

"Hagendorff [68] proposed recommendations to translate AI ethics from mere discussions into concrete actions that developers and users of AI for healthcare can utilize throughout the AI development life cycle."

"A universal ethical framework cannot adequately address all the ethical concerns arising from the use of AI in healthcare across all use cases."

"To address these concerns, we identify ethical issues that arise when AI systems are applied to AI-enabled mobile health (mHealth) applications for healthcare."

"We provide practical examples of how these ethical principles can be operationalized throughout the development lifecycle using AI-enabled mHealth application examples."

Review of AI-Enabled mHealth Applications

"We examine the latest AI-based methodologies that have been employed for dietary assessment, patient monitoring, mental health management, and healthcare administration, with a specific focus on frameworks accessible on mobile devices."

"In the field of mental health, mHealth applications that incorporate AI have shown to be promising tools to support individuals dealing with anxiety and depression [69, 70]."

"AI-powered applications provide a cost-effective and scalable way to enable access to mental health support [71]."

"These applications demonstrate the versatility and adaptability of AI agents in addressing various mental health needs, providing evidence-based interventions for users."

"A major concern is safety, which necessitates the need for well-designed and closely monitored AI systems to prevent potential harm, particularly for users who may require specialized professional mental health interventions rather than general support."

Methodology

"The relational ethics will ensure that the predictions made by the AI solution are grounded in prioritizing the contextual understanding of patients, existing socioeconomic inequalities and historical biases."

"Our framework is conceived and applied using the "ethics by design" approach, where ethical principles are incorporated iterative throughout the entire AI development pipeline (from requirements elicitation to deployment and maintenance) in the agile SDLC."

"Our approach ensures that ethical considerations are not just an afterthought but practically integrated into the development of AI solutions."

"We posit the best way to mitigate and address ethical consequences is by applying ethical principles in the SDLC that developers commonly use."

Ethical Principles and Values for AI-Enabled mHealth Applications

"In the context of AI applications, the complexity is wider involving the teams that make decisions on the data and algorithms to be used."

"Fairness has been associated with the ethical principle of justice, which is concerned with ensuring that AI systems treat all individuals equally and do not advantage the privileged few."

"The ethical principle of justice emphasizes the importance of equality to prevent any form of discrimination against vulnerable groups and to uphold an individual's right to challenge decisions made by AI systems [13]."

"The design, development and use of AI applications in healthcare should comply with existing legal regulations, such as the General Data Privacy Regulation (GDPR) [72] and alike that aim to safeguard the well-being of society."

"For an AI algorithm to personalize prediction to each individual, personal data is required."

Framework for Operationalising AI Ethics

"We recommend that development teams consider techniques to assess how the developed mHealth application aligns with the 12 principles of agile software development, which include (1) user satisfaction; (2) accommodating requirements changes; (3) frequent delivery of working software; (4) collaboration with stakeholders; (5) support, trust and motivation; (6) Effective communication; (7) Measure progress through functional delivery of system; (8) Consistency in development and maintenance; (9) Attention to technical detail and improve design agility; (10) Simplicity; (11) Self-organising teams; (12) Regular reflections on how to improve effectiveness in the team [73]."

"In terms of fairness, developers of AI-enabled mHealth solutions should ensure that AI systems treat all patients equally, by considering both the current privilege and potential empowerment of individuals."

"After the development, different versions of the AI-driven mHealth applications should go through various testing phases with real users."

Discussion

"By operationalizing AI ethics in a familiar process, developers can better reason for trade-offs between performance and ethical principles throughout the development lifecycle."

"Addressing ethical implications through an iterative and continuous process from the start of development could effectively integrate ethical considerations into the practical development of mobile medical AI solutions."

"We propose integrating ethical principles within the SDLC will enable developers of mobile AI systems in healthcare better address its ethical concerns whilst accounting for the technical capabilities of the solution."

"We propose a shift from one-size-fits-all ethical frameworks to contextualized case-based principles to assist AI developers in values-conscious development, the aim is to identify specific ethical values that can be operationalized."

"Incorporating ethical principles into the agile development process will increase the sensitivity of AI developers to the ethical dimensions of the technology."

Conclusion

"AI ethics has garnered significant attention to ensure the ethical development, deployment, and usage of AI systems."

"Existing frameworks and principles primarily concentrate on adhering to ethical principles and do not provide practical approaches to operationalizing AI ethics."

"This paper proposes a contextualized case-based framework that empowers developers to operationalize ethical principles within the agile SDLC using practical examples of AI-enabled mHealth applications."

"We emphasize the crucial role of community involvement in the development of human-centred AI systems for healthcare, advocating for co-designing AI systems with the local community and expert clinicians."

"We offer examples to operationalise ethical principles throughout the entire development lifecycle, ensuring that mHealth AI systems are ethically grounded and aligned with the needs and values of the communities they intend to serve."

Operationalizing Responsible AI Principles Through Responsible AI Capabilities [8]

This is a machine-generated summary of:

Akbarighatar, Pouria Operationalizing responsible AI principles through responsible AI capabilities [8]

Published in: AI and Ethics (2024)

Link to original: https://doi.org/10.1007/s43681-024-00524-4

If you want to cite the papers, please refer to the original.

For technical reasons we could not place the page where the original quote is coming from.

Abstract-Summary

"This study, grounded in recent RAI literature in organizational contexts and dynamic capability theory, and informed by literature on RAI principles and expert interviews in organizations deploying AI systems, (1) problematizes the high-level principles and low-level requirements and underscores the need for mid-level norms by adopting dynamic capability as a theoretical lens, and (2) develops five themes to capture firms' RAI capability, including (i) understandable AI model, (ii) bias remediation, (iii) responsiveness, (iv) harmless, and vi) common good."

"As our contribution to the field of information systems (IS), this study extends the emerging literature on operationalizing RAI and dynamic capabilities, empirically elucidating the capabilities needed by firms."

"For IS practice, we provide organizations deploying AI with novel insights to aid in the responsible implementation of AI."

The Emergent of Responsible AI

"AI can be defined as the field of study aimed at developing technologies that exhibit intelligent behavior, as Nils J. Nilsson explained in stating that "Artificial Intelligence is actively devoted to making machines intelligent, and intelligence is that which enables an entity to function appropriately, and with foresight in its environment [74].""

"Addressing these responsibilities requires understanding how to balance the needs of diverse stakeholders and govern AI development responsibly [75]."

"Organizations implementing AI must navigate these complex dynamics by developing responsible practices for engaging with data [76], overseeing algorithmic performance, and collaborating on AI governance."

"Achieving this balance is crucial for realizing AI's potential while minimizing risks, especially given recent legislative developments like the approval of the AI Act by parliament."

"By cultivating these competencies and implementing responsible practices, firms can leverage AI's benefits safely and foster responsible AI."

Responsible AI Principles

"These guidelines, such as those proposed by AI4People and the European Commission, emphasize key principles like autonomy, beneficence, and fairness, while also stressing the significance of transparency and explainability in AI systems [77, 78]."

"Barredo Arrieta and others (2020) categorized these principles into two groups: AI-specific principles, which concentrate on aspects unique to AI, and end-to-end principles, covering all facets involved in AI development and implementation [79]."

"The insights gathered from diverse sources contribute to a comprehensive understanding of these pivotal principles, underlining the importance of ethical considerations in AI initiatives and projects worldwide."

Problem Statement

"Applying the Resource-Based View (RBV) theory to integrate responsible AI principles into their strategic framework enables organizations to enhance their capacity to leverage AI effectively while ensuring adherence to ethical principles and minimizing risks (responsibility in/of)."

"In the realm of responsible AI, RBV theory assists organizations in identifying and developing specific competencies and repeatable activities—referred to as capabilities in this research—to effectively implement responsible AI principles."

"Through this lens, I define Responsible AI (RAI) capability as "the ability of a firm to strategically select, orchestrate, and effectively implement responsible AI throughout the AI lifecycle, with a commitment to continuous adherence to RAI principles and readiness to act responsibly at any critical decision point.""

"The interview guide included 25 questions organized into four themes: Demographics, AI projects and RAI implementation, RAI practices and actions, and reasons for operationalizing RAI principles in organizations."

"This approach helped organize our understanding of how capabilities related to responsible AI development may emerge based on insights from experts' industry experiences implementing relevant principles."

Results

"Some recommendations for achieving this capability from the literature include providing training to the team engaged in AI initiatives within the organization on recognizing potential biases in datasets and implementing strategies to evaluate them, examining historical data to recognize potential biases, ongoing monitoring and auditing of AI model outputs, and analyzing and identifying minority groups that could be impacted by AI initiatives to ensure unbiased outputs [80, 81]."

"Examining AI through the lens of dynamic capability emphasizes the importance for organizations using AI systems to ensure they are developed and deployed by appropriately trained individuals and that decision-making processes are conducted by experts."

"Drawing upon dynamic capability theory as theoretical "glue," the primary objective is to investigate how specific competencies impact an organization's ability to successfully implement responsible AI principles over time, thereby maximizing the benefits derived from AI technologies and achieving enhanced performance gains."

"Through this study, I have attempted to provide organizations with a better understanding of the development of RAI capabilities in two dimensions: AI-specific and End-to-end."

Reflections on Putting AI Ethics into Practice: How Three AI Ethics Approaches Conceptualize Theory and Practice [82]

This is a machine-generated summary of:

Bleher, Hannah; Braun, Matthias Reflections on Putting AI Ethics into Practice: How Three AI Ethics Approaches Conceptualize Theory and Practice [82]

Published in: Science and Engineering Ethics (2023)

Link to original: https://doi.org/10.1007/s11948-023-00443-3

If you want to cite the papers, please refer to the original.

For technical reasons we could not place the page where the original quote is coming from.

Abstract-Summary

"Critics currently argue that applied ethics approaches to artificial intelligence (AI) are too principles-oriented and entail a theory–practice gap."

"Several applied ethical approaches try to prevent such a gap by conceptually translating ethical theory into practice."

"We explore how the currently most prominent approaches of AI ethics translate ethics into practice."

"We examine three approaches to applied AI ethics: the embedded ethics approach, the ethically aligned approach, and the Value Sensitive Design (VSD) approach."

"We outline the conceptual strengths as well as their shortcomings: an embedded ethics approach is context-oriented but risks being biased by it; ethically aligned approaches are principles-oriented but lack justification theories to deal with trade-offs between competing principles; and the interdisciplinary Value Sensitive Design approach is based on stakeholder values but needs linkage to political, legal, or social governance aspects."

"Against this background, we develop a meta-framework for applied AI ethics conceptions with three dimensions."

"This meta-framework can thus serve as a reflective tool for understanding, mapping, and assessing the theory–practice conceptualizations within AI ethics approaches to address and overcome their blind spots."

How to Bridge the Theory–Practice Gap in AI Ethics?

"Whereas in the early days of the debate, the main issue was defining which high-level principles could provide orientation for the ethics of AI, in recent times, criticism of an overly principles-based approach is increasing."

"Criticism of such principles-based approaches warns that principles alone cannot guarantee ethical AI."

"On a conceptual level, these criticisms point to a theory–practice gap in AI ethics."

"This article examines, therefore, how the theory–practice gap is addressed within current approaches to AI ethics."

"Through this exploration, this article aims to provide a meta-framework as a reflective tool for understanding, mapping, and assessing the conceptualization of theory and practice within AI ethics approaches."

"We propose three reflective dimensions to better conceptualize theory and practice in applied AI ethics approaches as well as to address and overcome their blind spots."

How Theory and Practice Are Conceptualized Within AI Ethics

"We examine in more detail how these approaches conceptualize theory and practice, as well as their interrelation."

"For our analysis, we use basic methods from coherence theory in order to understand how these three approaches conceptually link theory and practice [83]."

"For our analysis, this abductive method means that first, we hermeneutically explore the main conceptual foci by outlining the understanding of theory and practice."

"We discuss the interrelation of theory and practice within each approach to gain insights into their conceptual strengths and weaknesses."

"Along these lines, we begin the analysis with a brief overview of each approach, then we examine each approach according to three guiding questions: (1) How is practice understood? (2) How is theory understood? (3) How is the relation between theory and practice understood and conceptualized?"

Embedded Ethics

"As this overview of the embedded ethics conception by McLennan and others [84, 85] and Fiske and others [86] already indicates, the authors understand practice in relation to the technological AI development process."

"This points to a fundamental assumption of such embedded ethics approaches, namely that it is assumed that innovative and exploratory practice always raises ethical issues, and new ethical concerns arise in the specific engineering process."

"This indicates that the inclusion of ethicists in the engineering process is almost synonymous with the embedding of ethical theory in practice."

"Within this embedded ethics approach, theory and practice merge through the inclusion of ethicists given a specific ethical issue."

"This means in the case of the described concepts that the approach is driven by the engineering practice and the emerging issues identified by ethics experts and/or the stakeholders involved and guided by their ethical questions or concerns."

Ethically Aligned

"In the practice of AI engineering, this could then proceed in such a way that tools and methods are selected according to certain principles to initiate an ethically aligned process or to design ethically aligned AI artifacts."

"This concept illustrates the principles orientation of an ethically aligned approach particularly well and paradigmatically."

"Other ethically aligned approaches conceptualize their principles orientation in different ways, when they develop, for example, tools to guarantee transparency or software models that prevent discrimination."

"All, the central role of the principles regarding the understanding of theory becomes clear from the fact that the authors of this approach aim for a pro-ethical concept of ethics."

"Applying the tools is described as the conceptual point at which principled, discursive ethical theory merges with practice, namely in the design process."

"Considering this understanding of theory and practice in comparison to the embedded ethics approach, the principles orientation emerges as central in this conception."

Value Sensitive Design

"In engineering ethics, VSD is a specific approach to defining ethical values throughout the entire technological design process [87]."

"In an iterative and integrative process of ethical inquiry and interdisciplinary deliberation, this methodology is used to define values to be translated into the design by establishing standards and analyzing technical requirements that will guarantee the practical implementation of the values."

"The advocates of the VSD approach seek to incorporate value reflections into the design process in order to solve and address value problems at an early stage."

"Within this multidimensional approach, theory and practice are connected by their orientation toward the value-sensitive artifact as the objective of the design process."

"This means the practical conceptual conditions as well as ethical judgments shaped by design inherent values are formulated as contextual requirements, which are then further incorporated into the design process of a specific artifact."

A Meta-Framework for Applied AI Ethics Approaches

"However, the respective blind spots of the three approaches also reveal potentials how applied AI ethics approaches can conceptually bridge the gap between theory and practice: As we outlined in terms of the embedded ethics approach, we suggest the reflection of principles as an integral part of ethical decision-making and design to prevent subjectivity, arbitrariness, and power abuse."

"The consideration of governance aspects extends the AI ethics' understanding of practice and is crucial to keep in mind the political, legal, and social conditions, implications, and courses of action relevant to theory–practice considerations and, if necessary, to address them at a political level."

"Based on critical theory [88], we argue that the mentioned three dimensions provide important conceptual perspectives to identify blind spots and shortcomings of AI ethics approaches in terms of a theory–practice gap."

Conclusion

"This article addresses the issue of conceptualizing theory and practice in applied AI ethics approaches."

"We hermeneutically analyzed the understanding of theory and practice as well as their entanglement in each approach."

"Delineating the specific potentialities and shortcomings of the approaches rendered the conceptualization of theory and practice a multi-faceted endeavor."

"We argue in terms of critical theory that these dimensions provide a meta-framework understood as a reflective tool to understand, map, and assess current applied AI ethics conceptualizations of theory and practice."

The Ethico-Politics of Design Toolkits: Responsible AI Tools, from Big Tech Guidelines to Feminist Ideation Cards [1]

This is a machine-generated summary of:

Hollanek, Tomasz The ethico-politics of design toolkits: responsible AI tools, from big tech guidelines to feminist ideation cards [1]

Published in: AI and Ethics (2024)

Link to original: https://doi.org/10.1007/s43681-024-00545-z

If you want to cite the papers, please refer to the original.

For technical reasons we could not place the page where the original quote is coming from.

Abstract-Summary

"Drawing on a meta-review of existing 'toolkit-scoping' work, I demonstrate that most toolkits embody a reductionist conception of ethics and that, because of this, their capacity for facilitating change is limited."

"This analysis then serves to provide suggestions for future toolkit creators and users on how to meaningfully adopt the toolkit format in AI ethics work without overselling its transformative potential: how different stakeholders can draw on the myriad of tools to achieve socially desirable results but reject the oversimplification of ethical practice that many toolkits embody."

Introduction

"While the OECD repository was created to help disseminate already available toolkits for ethical AI and allow for their classification and comparative analysis, I refer to it at the outset because it points to the diversity of formats adopted by different teams in response to the challenge of translating AI ethics theory into responsible AI practice: ranging from interactive, web-based applications, to static documents featuring checklists, sets of instructions, or lists of issues to consider, aiming to intervene at different stages of the development process and targeting different stakeholder groups."

"In the concluding section, referring to broader theories and critiques of toolkitting as a method for structuring the design process, I suggest how different stakeholders can draw on the myriad of available tools, ranging from big tech companies' guidelines to feminist design ideation cards, to achieve positive, socially desirable results, while rejecting the oversimplification of ethical practice and technosolutionism that many responsible AI toolkits embody."

The Ethico-Politics of AI Ethics Toolkits

"These limitations relate to: the toolkits' foundational 'deficiencies,' reflective of the omissions in the lists of values and principles they are meant to help translate into practice; a reductionist, technosolutionist conception of ethics–seemingly dissociated from politics–that most toolkits embody; and the co-optation of concepts and methods derived from critical studies of design and technology (such as participatory or inclusive design) decontextualized in ways that foreclose their meaningful, power-sensitive implementation in the AI development process."

"Since most responsible AI toolkits embody a reductionist understanding of ethics–with the checklist as its primary 'instrument' [68]–the recommendation for future toolkits makers is to adopt different formats that reflect the complexity of ethical reasoning in design, accounting for the indirect social and environmental costs of AI development."

The Wider Landscape of AI Ethics Toolkits

"While most ethical AI toolkits embody the former approach (as the meta-critique of the toolkits landscape confirms), the alternative toolkits give an indication of what relational ethics might look like in technology design practice: how we can give this kind of critical work structure, while rejecting formulaicity and reductionism implicit in most attempts at AI ethics toolkittification."

"It is within this mirroring between the design of the toolkits themselves and the kind of design they aim to facilitate that lies a hint of what we can glean from the alternative toolkits to understand the broader process of toolkittification in AI ethics: how producing and using toolkits may help designers achieve socially desirable results without the oversimplification of ethical practice that many toolkits embody."

Towards a Conclusion: After Toolkittification

"This is because the limitations of AI ethics toolkits identified in the meta-critique might relate not to the challenges of translating the theory of ethics into AI development practice specifically, but to the pitfalls of toolkittifcation as a means of reforming design generally: a form of myopia that toolkittifcation embodies."

"While a discussion of how the approach to toolkittification as a meta-ethics of design has influenced the development of a specific toolkit (and what compromises have been made in the process) is beyond the scope of this paper–and will be addressed elsewhere–the hope is that the scaffolding proposed here, which helped our team test the limits of the toolkit format, will also help others consider what should become of AI ethics work after toolkittification."

References

1. Hollanek, T. (2024). The ethico-politics of design toolkits: Responsible AI tools, from big tech guidelines to feminist ideation cards. *AI and Ethics*. https://doi.org/10.1007/s43681-024-00545-z
2. Morley, J., Elhalal, A., Garcia, F., Kinsey, L., Mökander, J., & Floridi, L. (2021). Ethics as a service: A pragmatic operationalisation of AI ethics. *Minds and Machines*. https://doi.org/10.1007/s11023-021-09563-w
3. Taddeo, M., Blanchard, A., & Thomas, C. (2024). From AI ethics principles to practices: A teleological methodology to apply AI ethics principles in the defence domain. *Philosophy & Technology*. https://doi.org/10.1007/s13347-024-00710-6
4. Georgieva, I., Lazo, C., Timan, T., & van Veenstra, A. F. (2022). Anne Fleur from AI ethics principles to data science practice: A reflection and a gap analysis based on recent frameworks and practical experience. *AI and Ethics*. https://doi.org/10.1007/s43681-021-00127-3
5. Ibáñez, J. C., & Olmeda, M. V. (2021). Operationalising AI ethics: How are companies bridging the gap between practice and principles? An exploratory study. *AI & Society*. https://doi.org/10.1007/s00146-021-01267-0

6. Mökander, J., & Floridi, L. (2022). Operationalising AI governance through ethics-based auditing: An industry case study. *AI and Ethics*. https://doi.org/10.1007/s43681-022-00171-7
7. Amugongo, L. M., Kriebitz, A., Boch, A., & Lütge, C. (2023). Operationalising AI ethics through the agile software development lifecycle: A case study of AI-enabled mobile health applications. *AI and Ethics*. https://doi.org/10.1007/s43681-023-00331-3
8. Akbarighatar, P. (2024). Operationalizing responsible AI principles through responsible AI capabilities. *AI and Ethics*. https://doi.org/10.1007/s43681-024-00524-4
9. Lin, Z. (2024). Beyond principlism: Practical strategies for ethical AI use in research practices. *AI and Ethics*. https://doi.org/10.1007/s43681-024-00585-5
10. Morley, J., Floridi, L., Kinsey, L., & Elhalal, A. (2020). From what to how: An initial review of publicly available AI ethics tools, methods and research to translate principles into practices. *Science and Engineering Ethics, 26*(4), 2141–2168. https://doi.org/10.1007/s11948-019-00165-5
11. Floridi, L. (2016b). Tolerant paternalism: Pro-ethical design as a resolution of the dilemma of toleration. *Science and Engineering Ethics, 22*(6), 1669–1688. https://doi.org/10.1007/s11948-015-9733-2
12. Floridi, L. (2018). Soft ethics, the governance of the digital and the general data protection regulation. *Philosophical Transactions of the Royal Society A: Mathematical, Physical and Engineering Sciences, 376*(2133), 20180081. https://doi.org/10.1098/rsta.2018.0081
13. Jobin, A., Ienca, M., & Vayena, E. (2019). The global landscape of AI ethics guidelines. *Nature Machine Intelligence, 1*(9), 389–399. https://doi.org/10.1038/s42256-019-0088-2
14. Adamson, G., Havens, J. C., & Chatila, R. (2019). Designing a value-driven future for ethical autonomous and intelligent systems. *Proceedings of the IEEE, 107*(3), 518–525. https://doi.org/10.1109/JPROC.2018.2884923
15. Alshammari, M., & Simpson, A. (2017). Towards a principled approach for engineering privacy by design. In E. Schweighofer, H. Leitold, A. Mitrakas, & K. Rannenberg (Eds.), *Privacy technologies and policy* (Vol. 10518, pp. 161–177). Springer. https://doi.org/10.1007/978-3-319-67280-9_9
16. Vakkuri, V., Kemell, K.-K., Kultanen, J., Siponen, M., & Abrahamsson, P. (2019). *Ethically aligned design of autonomous systems: Industry viewpoint and an empirical study*. arXiv:1906.07946 [Cs].
17. Abdul, A., Vermeulen, J., Wang, D., Lim, B. Y., & Kankanhalli, M. (2018). Trends and trajectories for explainable, accountable and intelligible systems: An HCI research agenda. In *Proceedings of the 2018 CHI conference on human factors in computing systems—CHI'18* (pp. 1–18). https://doi.org/10.1145/3173574.3174156
18. Anabo, I. F., Elexpuru-Albizuri, I., & Villardón-Gallego, L. (2019). Revisiting the Belmont report's ethical principles in internet-mediated research: Perspectives from disciplinary associations in the social sciences. *Ethics and Information Technology, 21*(2), 137–149. https://doi.org/10.1007/s10676-018-9495-z
19. Floridi, L. (2019b). *The logic of information: A theory of philosophy as conceptual design* (1st ed.). Oxford University Press.
20. Heath, J. (2014). Rebooting discourse ethics. *Philos Soc Criticism, 40*(9), 829–866. https://doi.org/10.1177/0191453714545340
21. Yetim, F. (2019). Supporting and understanding reflection on persuasive technology through a reflection schema. In H. Oinas-Kukkonen, K. T. Win, E. Karapanos, P. Karppinen, & E. Kyza (Eds.), *Persuasive technology: Development of persuasive and behavior change support systems* (pp. 43–51). Springer.
22. PWC. (2019). *The PwC responsible AI framework*. Retrieved from https://www.pwc.co.uk/services/audit-assurance/risk-assurance/services/technology-risk/technology-risk-insights/accelerating-innovation-through-responsible-ai.html
23. Clarke, R. (2019). Principles and business processes for responsible AI. *Computer Law & Security Review*. https://doi.org/10.1016/j.clsr.2019.04.007

24. Coeckelbergh, M. (2012). Moral responsibility, technology, and experiences of the tragic: From Kierkegaard to offshore engineering. *Science and Engineering Ethics, 18*(1), 35–48. https://doi.org/10.1007/s11948-010-9233-3
25. Arvan, M. (2018). Mental time-travel, semantic flexibility, and A.I. ethics. *AI & Society*. https://doi.org/10.1007/s00146-018-0848-2
26. Cookson, C. (2018). Artificial intelligence faces public backlash, warns scientist. *Financial Times*
27. Badal, K., Lee, C. M., & Esserman, L. J. (2023). Guiding principles for the responsible development of artificial intelligence tools for healthcare. *Communication & Medicine, 3*(1), 47.
28. Correa, N. K., et al. (2023). Worldwide AI ethics: A review of 200 guidelines and recommendations for AI governance. *Patterns, 4*(10), 100857.
29. Chen, Z., Li, W., & Lin, Z. (2024). Characterizing patients who may benefit from mature medical AI models. *PsyArXiv*. https://doi.org/10.31219/osf.io/zqu43
30. Lin, Z. (2023). Why and how to embrace AI such as ChatGPT in your academic life. *Royal Society Open Science, 10*, 230658.
31. Orr, W., & Davis, J. L. (2020). Attributions of ethical responsibility by artificial intelligence practitioners. *Information Communication and Society*. https://doi.org/10.1080/1369118X.2020.1713842
32. Whittlestone, J., Nyrup, R., Alexandrova, A., & Cave, S. (2019). *The role and limits of principles in AI ethics: Towards a focus on tensions*. https://doi.org/10.17863/cam.37097
33. Mittelstadt, B. (2019). Principles alone cannot guarantee ethical AI. *Nature Machine Intelligence, 1*, 501–507.
34. Floridi, L., & Cowls, J. (2019). A unified framework of five principles for AI in society. *Harvard Data Science Review*. https://doi.org/10.1162/99608f92.8cd550d1
35. Taddeo, M., & Floridi, L. (2018). How AI can be a force for good. *Science, 361*, 751–752. https://doi.org/10.1126/science.aat5991
36. Ministry of Defence. (2022). *Ambitious, safe, responsible: Our approach to the delivery of AI-enabled capability in defence*. https://assets.publishing.service.gov.uk/government/uploads/system/uploads/attachment_data/file/1082991/20220614-Ambitious_Safe_and_Responsible.pdf
37. Stahl, B. C., Antoniou, J., Ryan, M., Macnish, K., & Jiya, T. (2021). Organisational responses to the ethical issues of artificial intelligence. *AI & Society*. https://doi.org/10.1007/s00146-021-01148-6
38. AI HLEG. (2020). *Assessment list for trustworthy Artificial Intelligence*. https://ec.europa.eu/digital-single-market/en/news/assessment-list-trustworthy-artificial-intelligence-altai-self-assessment
39. Baskerville, R. L. (1999). Investigating information systems with action research. *Communications of the Association for Information Systems, 2*, 19.
40. Daly, A., Hagendorff, T., Li, H., Mann, M., Marda, V., Wagner, B., & Wang, W. W. (2020). AI, governance and ethics: Global perspectives. *SSRN Electronic Journal*. https://doi.org/10.2139/ssrn.3684406
41. Morgan, D. L. (1997). *Focus groups as qualitative research*. SAGE.
42. Krueger, R. A., & Casey, M. A. (2000). *Focus groups—A practical guide for applied research* (3rd ed.). SAGE Publications.
43. Brown, S., Davidovic, J., & Hasan, A. (2021). The algorithm audit: Scoring the algorithms that score us. *Big Data & Society*. https://doi.org/10.1177/2053951720983865
44. Brundage, M., et al. (2020). Toward trustworthy AI development: Mechanisms for supporting verifiable claims. arXiv:2004.07213[cs.CY]
45. Koshiyama, A., et al. (2024). Towards algorithm auditing: Managing legal, ethical and technological risks of AI, ML and associated algorithms. *R Soc Open Sci, 11*(5), 230859. https://doi.org/10.1098/rsos.230859

46. LaBrie, R. C., & Steinke, G. H. Towards a framework for ethical audits of AI algorithms. In *25th Americas Conference on Information System, AMCIS 2019* (Vol. 2019, pp. 1–5).
47. Mökander, J., & Floridi, L. (2021). Ethics-based auditing to develop trustworthy AI. *Minds and Machines, 31*(2), 323–327. https://doi.org/10.1007/s11023-021-09557-8
48. Raji, I. D., & Buolamwini, J. (2019). Actionable auditing: Investigating the impact of publicly naming biased performance results of commercial AI products. In *AIES 2019 – Proceedings of the 2019 AAAI/ACM Conference on AI, Ethics, and Society* (pp. 429–435).
49. Buolamwini, J., & Gebru, T. (2018). Gender shades: Intersectional accuracy disparities in commercial gender classification. *Conference on Fairness, Accountability, and Transparency, 1*, 1–15.
50. Mahajan, V., Venugopal, V. K., Murugavel, M., & Mahajan, H. (2020). The algorithmic audit: Working with vendors to validate radiology-AI algorithms—How we do it. *Academic Radiology, 27*(1), 132–135.
51. Kazim, E., Koshiyama, A. S., Hilliard, A., & Polle, R. (2021). Systematizing audit in algorithmic recruitment. *Journal of Intelligence, 9*(3), 46.
52. Jiang, F., et al. (2017). Artificial intelligence in healthcare: Past, present and future. *Stroke and Vascular Neurology, 2*(4), 230–243.
53. Morley, J., et al. (2020). The ethics of AI in health care: A mapping review. *Social Science & Medicine, 260*, 113172.
54. Topol, E. J. (2019). High-performance medicine: The convergence of human and artificial intelligence. *Nature Medicine, 25*(1), 44–56.
55. Taeihagh, A., Ramesh, M., & Howlett, M. (2021). Assessing the regulatory challenges of emerging disruptive technologies. *Regulation & Governance, 15*(4), 1009–1019.
56. Lauer, D. (2020). You cannot have AI ethics without ethics. *AI and Ethics, 0123456789*, 1–5.
57. Schneider, J., Abraham, R., & Meske, C. (2020, November). *AI governance for businesses*.
58. Fjeld, J. (2020). Principled artificial intelligence. *IEEE Instrumentation and Measurement Magazine, 23*(3), 27–31.
59. Merton, R. K. (1987). Three fragments from a sociologist's notebooks: Establishing the phenomenon, specified ignorance, and strategic research materials. *Review: Literature and Arts of the Americas, 13*(1987), 1–28.
60. Edwards, R., & Holland, J. (2013). *What is qualitative interviewing?* Bloomsbury Academic.
61. Creswell, J., & Clark, V. (2011). *Designing and conducting mixed methods research* (3rd ed.). SAGE Publications.
62. Smith, E. (2014). Research design. In H. Reis & C. Judd (Eds.), *Handbook of research methods in social and personality psychology* (pp. 27–48).
63. Gurevitch, J., et al. (2018). Meta-analysis and the science of research synthesis. *Nature, 555*, 175–182. https://doi.org/10.1038/nature25753
64. Levendusky, M. (2013). Partisan media exposure and attitudes toward the opposition. *Political Communication, 30*(4), 565–581.
65. Thomson, R., Plumridge, L., & Holland, J. (2003). Longitudinal qualitative research: A developing methodology. *International Journal of Social Research Methodology: Theory and Practice, 6*(3), 185–187.
66. Maruyama, G., & Ryan, C. S. (2014). *Research methods in social relations*. West Sussex.
67. World Health Organization: Ethics and governance of artificial intelligence for health: WHO guidance (2021). https://www.who.int/publications/i/item/9789240029200
68. Hagendorff, T. (2020). The ethics of AI ethics: An evaluation of guidelines. *Minds and Machines, 30*(1), 99–120. https://doi.org/10.1007/s11023-020-09517-8
69. Gamble, A. (2020). Artificial intelligence and mobile apps for mental healthcare: A social informatics perspective. *Aslib Journal of Information Management, 72*, 509–523. https://doi.org/10.1108/AJIM-11-2019-0316

70. Milne-Ives, M., Selby, E., Inkster, B., Lam, C., & Meinert, E. (2022). Artificial intelligence and machine learning in mobile apps for mental health: A scoping review. *PLOS Digital Health, 1*(8), 1–13. https://doi.org/10.1371/journal.pdig.0000079
71. Damij, N., & Bhattacharya, S. (2022). The role of AI chatbots in mental health related public services in a (post)pandemic world: A review and future research agenda. In *2022 IEEE Technology and Engineering Management Conference (TEMSCON EUROPE)* (pp. 152–159). https://doi.org/10.1109/TEMSCONEUROPE54743.2022.9801962
72. The European Parliament and the Council of the European Union: General Data Protection Regulation. (2016). https://eur-lex.europa.eu/legal-content/EN/TXT/PDF/?uri=CELEX:32016R0679
73. Beck, K., Grenning, J., Martin, R. C., Beedle, M., Highsmith, J., Mellor, S., Bennekum, A., Hunt, A., Schwaber, K., Cockburn, A., et al. (2001). Principles behind the agile manifesto. *Agile Alliance*. https://web.archive.org/web/20100615234816/http://agilemanifesto.org/iso/en/
74. Nilsson, N. J. (2009). *The quest for artificial intelligence*. Cambridge University Press. https://doi.org/10.1017/CBO9780511819346
75. Meske, C., Bunde, E., Schneider, J., & Gersch, M. (2022). Explainable artificial intelligence: Objectives, stakeholders, and future research opportunities. *Information Systems Management, 39*(1), 53–63. https://doi.org/10.1080/10580530.2020.1849465
76. Vassilakopoulou, P., Parmiggiani, E., Shollo, A., & Grisot, M. (2022). Responsible A.I.: Concepts, critical perspectives and an information systems research agenda. *Scandinavian Journal of Information Systems, 34*(2) [Online]. https://aisel.aisnet.org/sjis/vol34/iss2/3
77. European Parliament, European Parliament. [Online]. https://www.europarl.europa.eu/cmsdata/196377/AI%20HLEG_Ethics%20Guidelines%20for%20Trustworthy%20AI.pdf. Accessed 2 May 2024.
78. Floridi, L., Cowls, J., Beltrametti, M., et al. (2018). AI4People—An ethical framework for a good AI society: Opportunities, risks, principles, and recommendations. *Minds and Machines, 28*, 689–707. https://doi.org/10.1007/s11023-018-9482-5
79. Arrieta, A. B., Díaz-Rodrìguez, N., Ser, J. D., Bennetot, A., Tabik, S., Barbado, A., Garcia, S., Gil-Lopez, S., Molina, D., Benjamins, R., Chatila, R., & Herrera, F. (2020). Explainable artificial intelligence (xai): Concepts, taxonomies, opportunities and challenges toward responsible AI. *Information Fusion, 58*, 82–115. https://doi.org/10.1016/j.inffus.2019.12.012
80. Microsoft: Empowering responsible AI practices|Microsoft AI. https://www.microsoft.com/en-us/ai/responsible-ai. Accessed 26 Mar 2024.
81. Someh, I., Wixom, B. H., Beath, C. M., & Zutavern, A. (2022). Building an artificial intelligence explanation capability. *MIS Quarterly Executive, 21*(2) [Online]. https://aisel.aisnet.org/misqe/vol21/iss2/5
82. Bleher, H., & Braun, M. (2023). Reflections on putting AI ethics into practice: How three AI ethics approaches conceptualize theory and practice. *Science and Engineering Ethics, 29*. https://doi.org/10.1007/s11948-023-00443-3
83. Sugarman, J., & Sulmasy, D. P. (2001). *Methods in medical ethics* (2nd ed.). Georgetown University Press.
84. McLennan, S., Fiske, A., Celi, L. A., Müller, R., Harder, J., Ritt, K., Haddadin, S., & Buyx, A. (2020). An embedded ethics approach for AI development. *Nature Machine Intelligence, 2*(9), 488–490. https://doi.org/10.1038/s42256-020-0214-1
85. McLennan, S., Fiske, A., Tigard, D., Müller, R., Haddadin, S., & Buyx, A. (2022). Embedded ethics: A proposal for integrating ethics into the development of medical AI. *BMC Medical Ethics, 23*(1), 1–10.
86. Fiske, A., Tigard, D., Müller, R., Haddadin, S., Buyx, A., & McLennan, S. (2020). Embedded ethics could help implement the pipeline model framework for machine learning healthcare applications. *The American Journal of Bioethics, 20*(11), 32–35. https://doi.org/10.1080/15265161.2020.1820101

87. Friedman, B., Kahn, P. H., Borning, A., & Huldtgren, A. (2013). Value sensitive design and information systems. In N. Doorn, D. Schuurbiers, I. van de Poel, & M. E. Gorman (Eds.), *Early engagement and new technologies: Opening up the laboratory* (pp. 55–95). Springer. https://doi.org/10.1007/978-94-007-7844-3_4
88. Waelen, R. (2022). Why AI ethics is a critical theory. *Philosophy & Technology, 35*(1), 9. https://doi.org/10.1007/s13347-022-00507-5

Chapter 5
Preparing Ethics Advisors to AI Governance: Strategies, Regulations, Global Considerations

Abstract This final chapter examines the regulatory, geopolitical, and institutional dimensions shaping AI governance and the roles of ethics advisors within these frameworks. It reviews various national and international AI governance models, evaluating their effectiveness in addressing ethical challenges and fostering global cooperation. The chapter discusses barriers such as regulatory fragmentation, cultural differences, and geopolitical tensions, proposing strategies to overcome these challenges. By providing a global perspective, it underscores the need for ethics advisors to navigate complex regulatory landscapes and contribute to the development of coherent and effective AI governance practices.

Keywords AI governance · Global regulation · Geopolitical tensions · Regulatory fragmentation · Cross-cultural cooperation

Introduction by the Editor

As artificial intelligence systems increasingly shape our societal, economic, and institutional infrastructures, the task of governing these technologies cannot be left solely to technologists or policymakers. It demands a new class of professionals—ethics advisors—equipped to navigate the dynamic intersection of normative principles, regulatory demands, and socio-technical realities. This chapter addresses the dual structure of AI governance: first, it offers a general account of governance challenges, strategies, and actors; then, it pivots to a comparative analysis of global governance models.

AI governance is more than a set of institutional rules—it is a political, cultural, and epistemic ecosystem where accountability, oversight, and trust must be continuously negotiated. At the heart of this ecosystem is the ethics advisor: no longer a marginal figure offering retrospective evaluations, but a proactive actor embedded within governance architectures. Yet, the evolving role of these professionals raises essential questions: When and how should they intervene? With whom must they collaborate? And what limits constrain their authority?

A. Carnevale, *The AI Ethics Advisor*,
https://doi.org/10.1007/978-3-032-05526-2_5

By exploring these questions through cross-cutting themes such as timing, interdisciplinarity, institutional design, and global fragmentation, this chapter argues that AI governance must be understood not only as a regulatory endeavour but as a practice of moral co-design. In doing so, it lays the groundwork for a broader reflection on how to professionalise and support the ethics advisor's role within a more democratic, decentralised, and future-proof governance landscape.

Cross-Cutting Insights

The role of ethics advisors within AI governance must be understood through a transversal lens that cuts across temporal, disciplinary, institutional, and geopolitical dimensions. Their function cannot be reduced to a single phase of AI development or confined to a specific institutional silo. Rather, ethics advisors operate within a dynamic landscape that requires anticipatory foresight, cross-sectoral collaboration, and global contextual sensitivity.

First, timing is pivotal. Ethical oversight must be conceived not as a retrospective audit but as a constitutive element of system design and deployment. When embedded early, ethical interventions contribute to value alignment and robustness, reducing the likelihood of costly corrections or societal backlash post-deployment [1, 2]. Yet, early integration is often resisted due to perceived tensions with innovation speed. Ethics advisors must therefore articulate ethics not as friction but as foresight—a form of design resilience that enhances accountability without paralysing technological development [3].

Second, interdisciplinarity is not merely a methodological preference but a structural imperative. AI governance spans legal norms, technical standards, human rights frameworks, and sociocultural values. Ethics advisors must serve as translators and negotiators across these domains, enabling co-production of norms among engineers, legal experts, policymakers, and affected communities [4, 5]. This is particularly pressing in light of the fragmented ethical landscape, where the risk of "ethics-washing" looms large without meaningful integration into institutional decision-making [6, 7].

Third, the ethics advisor's authority is often symbolic rather than operative. Lacking formal mandates or regulatory backing, many ethics officers remain marginal figures, excluded from the levers of power that shape real-world AI outcomes [8]. Strengthening their role requires embedding ethical reasoning within institutional mechanisms that can ensure not only participation but enforcement. Democratising AI governance thus entails both capacity-building and structural reform to empower the ethics advisor as a governance actor, not a mere ethical ornament [9, 10].

Finally, the international landscape of AI governance presents a pluralism of models that the ethics advisor must navigate. From state-driven systems like China's cyber-sovereignty regime [11] to multilevel, cooperative frameworks such as the Dutch public sector model [12] or South Korea's sector-specific self-regulation in healthcare [13], AI governance is characterised by regulatory divergence. Ethics advisors must be attuned to this complexity, aligning local practices with global norms while accommodating cultural and political variation [14–16]. Their ability to act as epistemic and normative intermediaries across jurisdictions is critical for fostering transnational ethical coherence amid regulatory asymmetries.

Conclusion: From Governance to Profession—Institutionalising the Ethics Advisor

As artificial intelligence governance evolves from abstract declarations to operational mechanisms, the ethics advisor is emerging as a critical—yet still under-recognised—figure in this transition. This chapter want to show that AI governance is not a monolithic domain, but a fluid and contested field where timing, collaboration, institutional architecture, and international diversity converge. Against this backdrop, the ethics advisor is uniquely positioned to mediate between normative principles and real-world constraints. Yet this potential can only be realised through a sustained effort to professionalise and institutionalise the role.

To begin with, AI governance requires that ethical oversight become a structural feature rather than an optional add-on. For this to happen, ethics advisors must be equipped with more than moral vocabulary—they need formal recognition, professional protection, and regulatory authority. Certification schemes and clearly defined competency frameworks are essential to legitimise the role and ensure it is not appropriated for reputational purposes alone. This professional infrastructure must also be complemented by standardised procedures for ethical risk assessment and auditability, adapted to the pace and scale of AI deployment across domains [7, 17].

Moreover, ethics advisors should not be left to shoulder the moral burden of AI governance in isolation. A robust ethical ecosystem requires distributed responsibility, with interdependent nodes such as algorithmic risk committees, regulatory bodies, domain experts, and civil society actors. Within this distributed network, the ethics advisor serves as a keystone—anchoring deliberation, guiding implementation, and translating abstract norms into actionable practice. This transition from isolated agent to embedded actor is key to avoiding what many scholars have warned: the professional fatigue and symbolic marginalisation of ethics within technology industries [6, 8].

Internationally, the ethics advisor must also navigate a fragmented regulatory terrain. The global comparative perspective presented in section 6.1 demonstrates that AI governance varies significantly in its institutionalisation, ranging from technocratic oversight in liberal democracies to state-led control in centralised regimes. This raises a profound challenge for professional ethics: how can a transnational role emerge when the legitimacy and scope of ethical action differ radically across jurisdictions? One response lies in the cultivation of "regulatory literacy"—the capacity of ethics advisors to map and mediate across diverse legal and cultural landscapes [15, 16, 18]. Another lies in anchoring their work within widely endorsed international frameworks, such as the UNESCO Recommendation on the Ethics of Artificial Intelligence or the forthcoming ISO standards.

In this light, AI governance becomes not only a matter of policy but a site of institutional imagination. The creation of the ethics advisor as a recognised profession is not merely a technical task; it is a political and cultural project. It requires rethinking the infrastructures of trust, authority, and participation that underpin technological development. It also requires a commitment to building institutions capable of embedding ethical deliberation into the core operations of innovation ecosystems.

Crucially, the ethics advisor cannot remain reactive. The most effective contributions to AI governance will emerge from those who are anticipatory, who engage not only with "what is" but with "what ought to be." This calls for a new generation of ethics advisors—proactive, interdisciplinary, globally aware, and institutionally grounded. Supporting them is not just a matter of professional development; it is a democratic imperative. As AI continues to reshape our societies, ensuring that ethical reflection has a seat at the table is no longer optional—it is foundational to any credible vision of responsible technological governance.

Machine Generated Summaries

AI Governance: A Systematic Literature Review [1]

This is a machine-generated summary of:

Batool, Amna; Zowghi, Didar; Bano, Muneera AI governance: a systematic literature review [1]

Published in: AI and Ethics (2025)

Link to original: https://doi.org/10.1007/s43681-024-00653-w

If you want to cite the papers, please refer to the original.

For technical reasons we could not place the page where the original quote is coming from.

Abstract-Summary

"Various AI governance frameworks have been released recently by governments, organizations, and companies to mitigate risks associated with AI."

"It can be challenging for AI stakeholders to have a clear picture of the available AI governance frameworks, tools, or models and analyze the most suitable one for their AI system."

"To fill the gap, we present the literature to answer key questions: WHO is accountable for AI systems' governance, WHAT elements are being governed, WHEN governance occurs within the AI development life cycle, and HOW it is implemented through frameworks, tools, policies, or models."

"Adopting the systematic literature review (SLR) methodology, this study meticulously searched, selected, and analyzed 28 articles, offering a foundation for understanding different facets of AI governance."

Introduction

"There are existing systematic literature reviews (SLRs) on AI governance that have provided valuable insights into national and global strategies, advanced AI governance terminologies, and ethical guidelines."

"Despite these comprehensive reviews, there is a gap in the literature concerning a detailed and layered analysis of AI governance across multiple governance levels using a systematic set of questions."

"We have employed 4 specific questions to extract relevant information from the research literature on AI governance: who is governing (i.e., stakeholders), what should be governed (e.g., data and/or system), when is it being governed (i.e., at what stage of the AI development life cycle), and how is AI being governed (i.e., frameworks, models, tools, ethics: ethics, in the context of AI governance, refers to the set of moral principles and values that aim to guide the design, deployment, and use of AI systems to ensure responsible and fair outcomes [19, 20]."

Background and Related Work

"We present a comprehensive review of existing literature on AI governance, with a focus on systematically analyzing and synthesizing the current state of knowledge in this area."

"Another study by Wang and others [21] undertook a systematic literature review on AI governance in child social care, including a total of 440 articles using the PRISMA methodology."

"The authors included a total of 35 studies on AI governance frameworks published in the last 5 years (2017–2022)."

"We have conducted a systematic literature review which differs from the existing review studies on the relevant topic in the following aspects: Focus of review: In this systematic literature review (SLR), an extensive analysis of AI governance elements has been presented using 4 specific questions (Who, What, When, How) to extract rich data about AI governance."

Systematic Review Methodology

"The same selection criteria have been applied to full papers (225), which resulted in the selection of 61 papers after mostly excluding non-empirical papers, opinion papers, and those not fitting into AI Governance."

"The selection procedure, i.e., the test-retest approach, was followed by inviting two experts of SLR to review the selected set of 61 papers in three rounds."

"The second round of the selection procedure resulted in 22 studies after reviewing the full papers."

"The final round of the selection procedure, in which two experts reviewed each set of papers, resulted in 28 papers, as again, there were a few secondary studies that were omitted."

"The selected set of 28 papers for this SLR is available in Appendix A. We have used the five-question criteria proposed by Liu and others [22] to evaluate the quality of our selected studies."

Data Synthesis and Analysis

"Study [A3] highlighted the need for governance of AI systems to mitigate various risks including ethical concerns related to military applications, ensuring safety in AI systems, addressing privacy issues, etc., associated with its rapid development."

"Five of these studies [A2], [A12], [A19], [A23], and [A25] emphasized that governance solutions should cover all stages of an AI development life cycle to ensure ethical development and deployment of AI."

"These studies emphasized the necessity of governance, particularly in addressing various ethical concerns, and indicated the importance of a comprehensive governance structure across the different stages of the AI development life cycle to ensure ethical and responsible AI deployment."

"Nine studies have proposed different solutions (frameworks, models, tools, ethical principles, policies, or guidelines) for the governance of AI."

Discussion

"As 9 studies have proposed various AI governance solutions, including frameworks, tools, and ethics principles, each study has been examined to observe which ethical AI principles as mentioned in the specific study they target to make AI ethical and responsible across different domains."

"While it is understandable that very few studies have focused on ethical principles while proposing AI governance frameworks, models, tools, etc., it is essential to introduce more structured and robust governance solutions that make AI responsible and ethical [23]."

"By highlighting these challenges, it becomes evident that AI governance solutions should be fundamentally based on ethical and responsible AI principles for fostering trust, addressing societal concerns, and ensuring the long-term success of AI technologies [24–26]."

"As AI continues to integrate into high-stakes areas like healthcare, law enforcement, and employment, governance frameworks must evolve to prioritize ethical principles such as fairness, transparency, and accountability, which are currently under-addressed."

Threats to Validity and Limitations

"Our systematic literature review (SLR) includes primary studies published over the last 10 years, up until 2023."

"By focusing exclusively on primary studies, we acknowledge that our review might exclude various AI governance frameworks or models currently in use by organizations, which are often detailed in secondary sources such as white papers, or industry reports."

"Limiting our scope to the last 10 years helps to manage the influence of rapidly evolving AI governance practices, ensuring a more consistent comparison of studies over a defined period."

"These measures ensure that our findings are robust, reliable, and attributable to the primary studies reviewed, thereby enhancing the internal validity of our SLR."

"The generalizability of these findings is limited by the scope of the selected studies, which may not capture the full spectrum of AI governance practices across diverse contexts."

Conclusion and Future Work

"This systematic literature review of 28 selected studies achieves its objectives by providing a comprehensive summary of current AI governance solutions, including frameworks, tools, models, and ethical policies."

"The challenges within existing AI governance solutions are also presented in this SLR, emphasizing the prevalent focus on ethical considerations such as fairness, transparency, privacy, etc. The analysis reveals a critical gap in addressing the who, what, and when aspects of AI governance in a holistic manner."

"This indicates the need for future AI governance solutions to closely align with ethical AI principles, fostering a holistic and principled approach to the governance of artificial intelligence."

"The primary studies included in our systematic literature review (SLR) did not adequately cover standards of AI governance, such as ISO standards, the NIST AI governance framework, etc. We have completed the collection and analysis of the grey literature on AI governance."

Defining Organizational AI Governance [2]

This is a machine-generated summary of:

Mäntymäki, Matti; Minkkinen, Matti; Birkstedt, Teemu; Viljanen, Mika Defining organizational AI governance [2]

Published in: AI and Ethics (2022)

Link to original: https://doi.org/10.1007/s43681-022-00143-x

If you want to cite the papers, please refer to the original.

For technical reasons we could not place the page where the original quote is coming from.

Abstract-Summary

"This means that ethical principles, such as fairness, need to be translated into practicable AI governance processes."

"A concise AI governance definition would allow researchers and practitioners to identify the constituent parts of the complex problem of translating AI ethics into practice."

"There have been few efforts to define AI governance thus far."

"To bridge this gap, this paper defines AI governance at the organizational level."

Introduction

"There is a lack of understanding of the position of AI governance within the organizational governance structure."

"AI governance is entering an increasingly complex organizational governance landscape, where corporate governance [27], information technology (IT) governance [28], and data governance [29] already require management attention [30]."

"The current unorganized state of AI governance literature is unfortunate because organizations deploying AI in their operations play a key role in implementing AI governance in practice [31–33]."

"We draw on previous scholarly work on AI ethics and governance [34–40] and propose a synthesizing definition of AI governance at the organizational level."

"We position AI governance as part of an organization's governance structure, together with corporate, IT, and data governance."

"Our contributions clarify the significance of AI governance as part of organizational governance that helps align the use of AI technologies with organizational strategies and legal and ethical requirements coming from the operating environment."

Defining AI Governance

"In our effort to define organizational AI governance, we also aim to include smaller organizations that use AI systems but do not exercise such leverage over global AI technology development."

"Bringing together the ethical, organizational, and technological aspects, and considering the definitions of related governance fields, we propose the following definition of AI governance at the organization level: AI governance is a system of rules, practices, processes, and technological tools that are employed to ensure an organization's use of AI technologies aligns with the organization's strategies, objectives, and values; fulfills legal requirements; and meets principles of ethical AI followed by the organization."

"The key elements of an AI governance system are rules, practices, processes, and technological tools."

"These elements are in place to govern an organization's use of AI technologies."

AI Governance as Part of an Organization's Governance Structure

"The rationale for this position is that corporate governance provides the overarching governance structure within an organization, and AI systems, as IT systems with particular capabilities [41], are governed via mechanisms that fall under IT governance."

"The models and algorithms of AI systems may not fall under data governance as it is commonly conceived."

"Because AI systems depend on data to operate and learn, certain aspects of data governance are also central to AI governance."

"The elements of data governance are relevant for AI governance, particularly regarding technical layers concerned with particular algorithmic systems."

"AI governance goes beyond governing data because data represent only one element in algorithmic systems."

"The significance of these concepts for AI governance underscores their mutual relationships: Corporate governance places AI governance in a broader frame, IT governance outlines governing mechanisms, and data governance specifies frameworks for managing the data on which AI systems depend."

Conclusion and Future Research Directions

"To contribute to tackling the unorganized state of AI governance research and practice, we presented a positioning of AI governance as part of an organization's governance structure and a definition of organizational AI governance."

"The current study indicates that AI governance literature is fragmented."

"Organizations need practical AI governance tools and frameworks, which opens avenues for design science research [42]."

"Scholars can study AI auditing literature, practices, and tools similarly to studies on AI governance and continuously build bridges to AI governance literature."

"They should not become separate silos but rather contribute to a growing general understanding of AI governance within academia and practice."

Foundations for the Future: Institution Building for the Purpose of Artificial Intelligence Governance [3]

This is a machine-generated summary of:

Stix, Charlotte Foundations for the future: institution building for the purpose of artificial intelligence governance [3]

Published in: AI and Ethics (2021)

Link to original: https://doi.org/10.1007/s43681-021-00093-w

Copyright of the summarized publication:

If you want to cite the papers, please refer to the original.

For technical reasons we could not place the page where the original quote is coming from.

Abstract-Summary

"Governance efforts for artificial intelligence (AI) are taking on increasingly more concrete forms, drawing on a variety of approaches and instruments from hard regulation to standardisation efforts, aimed at mitigating challenges from high-risk AI systems."

"This paper sketches a blueprint of such institutions, and conducts in-depth investigations of three key components of any future AI governance institutions, exploring benefits and associated drawbacks: (1) "purpose", relating to the institution's overall goals and scope of work or mandate; (2) "geography", relating to questions of participation and the reach of jurisdiction; and (3) "capacity", the infrastructural and human make-up of the institution."

"The paper highlights noteworthy aspects of various institutional roles specifically around questions of institutional purpose, and frames what these could look like in practice, by placing these debates in a European context and proposing different iterations of a European AI Agency."

Introduction

"To properly develop, support, and implement new AI governance efforts, such as legislative frameworks for AI, it is likely that a number of new institutions will need to be established over the coming years [43, 44]."

"It is, therefore, worthwhile to step back and think cautiously about the junctures we are about to lay [45] for the field of AI governance when developing these new institutions."

"Building on these calls and drawing on existing scholarship and insights, it addresses itself to those individuals who will be involved in setting up new institutions and those who are interested in conducting further research on pragmatic institution building for AI governance."

"The paper outlines the rationale for deepening the investigation of institution building for AI governance now, as well as the limitations to this paper's investigation."

Motivation, Urgency, and Limitations

"Novel AI specific governance institutions working on soft governance mechanisms, which is non-binding rules, have already come into existence."

"Given the sheer scope the new horizontal legislation for AI will introduce and the number of associated institutions, networks and processes that need to be either set up or managed, and given this political direction from the European Parliament, it is not unlikely that a European AI Agency will be on the horizon within the coming 10 years."

"The paper adopts the lens of historical institutionalism [46], suggesting that for AI governance new institutions will be built dependent on the current promise and peril of (and the associated mechanisms to enable or minimise) AI."

"The question of how to set up AI governance institutions, therefore, merits further scholarly investigation."

The Main Axes: Purpose, Geography and Capacity

"Each subsection introduces the outline of a role an institution for AI governance could take: coordinator, analyser, developer, and investigator."

"One version could be an AI observatory that is set up by EU institutions and the governments of the member states but sufficiently independent to provide meaningful insight into the actual state of AI development and deployment across the EU in addition to existing work."

"It could act as a foresight body to EU institutions, independently reviewing and analysing the landscape and, from that work, distilling noteworthy technological developments and proposing new high-risk AI systems in a timely manner."

"If several nations (in broad agreement) expect that their position towards AI governance is broadly more beneficial than that of other nations, it may be a reasonable political and future-oriented decision (from their perspective) to cooperate, coordinate and pool efforts between them through a dedicated institution."

Conclusion

"This paper highlighted the importance of thinking about institution building for AI governance in more depth and provided a conceptual framework with which one can start working on this."

"Future research directions for this topic could explore these axes for more concrete national cases or support decision making on new directions on an international level, especially as AI governance actions gain traction and clarity."

"This paper provided one proposal towards ensuring that the infrastructure we build now to action policy and other governance proposals is suitably considered and sufficiently future proof."

From the "Rush to Ethics" to the "Race for Governance" in Artificial Intelligence [4]

This is a machine-generated summary of:

Koniakou, Vasiliki From the "rush to ethics" to the "race for governance" in Artificial Intelligence [4]

Published in: Information Systems Frontiers (2022)

Link to original: https://doi.org/10.1007/s10796-022-10300-6

If you want to cite the papers, please refer to the original.

For technical reasons we could not place the page where the original quote is coming from.

Abstract-Summary

"Focusing on the role of human rights, it takes the argument that human rights offer a more robust and effective framework a step further, arguing for the necessity to extend human rights obligations to also directly apply to private actors in the context of AI governance."

"It offers insights for AI governance borrowing from the Internet Governance history and the broader technology governance field."

Introduction

"The accelerating pervasiveness and ubiquity of AI systems, combined with the growing public concern about their ethical, social, and human rights implications have brought to the forefront questions related to the steering of such technologies towards socially beneficial ends [47–50]."

"The impacts and implications of AI, algorithms and automated decision-making have emerged as important areas of human rights concern during the last decade."

"Building upon human rights and business discourse, I argue that human rights may offer more than aspirational and normative guidance in AI-DDD as well as in AI governance, if they are employed as concrete legal obligations that directly apply to both public and private actors."

"I offer a new perspective to AI governance and human rights research, providing arguments from the direct horizontality discourse and the business and human rights field."

Key Terms and Concepts

"The UN human rights system constitutes the key benchmark of international human rights protection, as most of the 193 Member-States of the UN have ratified at least one major human rights treaty, including the UNDHR."

"The states constitute the original subjects and primary actors of international law [51–53], only the states are directly bound by international human rights law and treaties."

"For now, it would suffice to note that the increasing power asymmetries between individuals and corporations, most prominently Transnational Corporations (TNCs), and the shifted balance of power to negatively affect human rights, combined with the failure of states to foster meaningful mechanisms to protect human rights at a national level, safeguarding access to meaningful remedy and redress, has intensified the discussions over a paradigm shift in international human rights law [52, 54]."

Steering AI: From Ethics to Governance

"Several non-state actors, and most prominently a handful of major technology companies, have also issued their own ethical declarations, principles, and ethical codes, expressing their commitment to the ethical and responsible development and deployment AI and algorithms, either individually (see for example [55–59]) or jointly, [60]."

"On the policy level, the wide range of ethically important and societally impactful implications of AI systems and algorithms, as well as the adverse effects of such technologies on an individual and social level, has led governments and intergovernmental organisations to progressively shift their attention from the promulgation of ethical codes and principles to specific legal instruments (see for example the

"Proposal for a Regulation laying down harmonised rules on Artificial Intelligence", by the EU Commission)."

"Although the focus on ethics has somehow overshadowed the translation of principles into concrete regulation, and the concretization of guidelines into specific binding requirements [61], the scenery is rapidly changing, as governments and intergovernmental organisations are increasingly moving towards the introduction of specific and binding rules to govern AI."

Human Rights and AI Governance

"This approach may offer "a powerful additional tool in our armour to regulate more effectively the activities of difficult regulatory targets" [62] within AI design, development, and deployment, supplementing AI governance while enhancing the level of respect and protection for human rights, independently of the states and their willingness or objective ability to hold private actors accountable for human rights violations."

"Looking beyond their function as negative rights, the direct application of human rights obligations to private actors will be valuable to ensure the ethical and socially beneficial design, development and deployment of AI systems and algorithms, not only in terms of respecting and protecting human rights in the context of AI-DDD, but also with the prospect of promoting human rights through these technologies for the flourishing of humanity."

"By introducing direct obligations, human rights will not be an afterthought anymore, but rather a guiding principle that will inform the design, development and deployment of AI systems and algorithms, not premised on the goodwill of the private actors, but on their binding duties."

AI Governance Beyond Human Rights

"As the research field that led to the emergence of AI was still developing, the Internet has been already awarded the label of "the most significant disruptive innovation" [63, 64], and the quest for developing and establishing the most appropriate governance model for the Internet started during the late 1990s."

"This movement in IG has fuelled broad discussions about human rights and human dignity in terms of technology governance, as well as concerning the necessity for adequate restriction to private power, highlighting the limitations of self-governance and market rules for governing general-purpose, disruptive and human rights-relevant technologies."

"Beyond democratic control, returning to human rights and perceiving them not merely as binding legal rights, but as a set of foundational principle that should inform and shape the design, development and deployment of new technologies, in AI governance we have the opportunity to premise AI-DDD directly on a new, more focused and actionable approach to human rights."

Concluding Thoughts

"Whereas AI Ethics have been integral in identifying several of the key risks and challenges in the field of AI systems and algorithmic decision-making, governance and hard-law instruments are necessary to ensure that AI will be designed, developed and deployed for the benefit of society [37, 65, 66]."

"Looking beyond human rights and considering the wide array of challenges in AI governance, I suggest that IG may offer several valuable insights that will allow AI governance to be a sum of informed decisions, allowing us to avoid regulatory failures and create a better governance model."

"Considering its power and effects, while learning form the IG past, it is significant to ensure that AI governance will be premised on conscious democratic decision-making, human rights-premised design, and human rights-aware designers and developers."

Policy Brief: The Creation of a G20 Coordinating Committee for the Governance of Artificial Intelligence [5]

This is a machine-generated summary of:

Jelinek, Thorsten; Wallach, Wendell; Kerimi, Danil Policy brief: the creation of a G20 coordinating committee for the governance of artificial intelligence [5]

Published in: AI and Ethics (2020)

Link to original: https://doi.org/10.1007/s43681-020-00019-y

If you want to cite the papers, please refer to the original.

For technical reasons we could not place the page where the original quote is coming from.

Abstract-Summary

"This policy brief proposes a group of twenty (G20) coordinating committee for the governance of artificial intelligence (CCGAI) to plan and coordinate on a multilateral level the mitigation of AI risks."

"Other regime complexes and international organizations, which also focus on AI governance, tend to either lack such political power or exclude major rivalry countries."

"Such inclusive centrality is necessary to counter the fragmentation of the existing cyber regime complex and effectively coordinate the mitigation of AI risks on a global level."

"The G20 CCGAI is proposed to complement and strengthen polycentric governance as well as AI governance networks."

"CCGAI's metagovernance function is presented as a task intended to institutionalize linkages between the CCGAI and relevant actors with the G20 complex and the broader AI and cyber regime complex."

"While the policy brief outlines the landscape of AI risks and proposes an agenda with AI governance challenges, the focus is on the functional and organizational features of the CCGAI and how such chartered committee can foster international collaboration."

Introduction

"There is an emerging structure based on polycentric governance as well as governance networks concerning the responsible development and use of artificial intelligence (AI)."

"Those emerging AI governance structures risk being weakened in two interdependent ways, thereby compromising on the principle of responsibly."

"The emerging AI governance structure increasingly overlaps with the existing cyber regime complex, which yet is already fragmented and thus undermines international collaboration."

"This coordinating committee is presented as a multilateral mechanism precisely to counter the structural fragmentation by actively forging collaboration concerning responsible AI governance."

"Such rather inclusive centrality is needed to counter the structural fragmentation of international relations and strengthen polycentric governance and AI governance networks."

"The challenges outlined in this first part support the conclusion that global coordination is a necessary mechanism for improving international collaboration, countering the fragmentation of the cyber regime complex, and strengthening responsible AI governance."

Challenge

"Even though the extent to which AI's benefits outweigh its harms remains unclear, the result has been a proliferation of normative and regulatory frameworks, as well as the emergence of governance networks and polycentric structures that advocate for a responsible or human-centered use of AI [67, 68]."

"Such a proliferation of normative frameworks is indicative of a global ethics and governance gap [69, 70]: a mismatch between those normative intentions (principles of responsible AI use) and existing internalized patterns of human action (actual ethics), as well as between existing and future instructions for collaborative action (governance)."

"At least three more fundamental global dynamics undermine AI governance and might turn responsible AI principles into a mere ideology of those dynamics, exacerbating rather than preventing or mitigating the cyberphysical threats and structural imbalances highlighted above: a. Economic competition: AI governance is exposed to global capitalist productivity and strategic competition over global AI leadership."

Proposal

"This policy brief proposes the implementation of a G20 coordinating committee for the governance of artificial intelligence (CCGAI) to plan and coordinate the effective prevention and mitigation of AI risks long before they become emergencies [71]."

"The advantages and limitations of polycentric governance and AI governance networks are highlighted, the functional and organizational features of the CCGAI are presented, and the main obstacles to a coordinating committee are identified."

"The CCGAI should collaborate with other international organizations, particularly those that have already established strong linkages with civil society and non-G20 nations and run programs for digital cooperation and governance."

"The G20 would need to develop its own coordination and implementation capacity to carry out the functions of a CCGAI; incorporate related work that has been done within the G20 complex; and establish linkages to existing procedures, declarations, principles, and tools."

Conclusion

"Those who advocate responsible AI governance face a lack of collaboration on national and international levels and a fragmented cyber regime complex, respectively."

"A global awareness of AI risks and the governance gap has emerged as well as the common principle of responsible AI, which makes this historical moment the right time for proposing a coordinating committee for the governance of AI (CCGAI) to the G20."

"Mandating a G20 CCGAI is a joint demand for more centrality deemed effective in forging international collaboration, reducing the fragmentation of the cyber regime complex, and strengthening polycentricity and governance networks."

"This policy brief proposes a comprehensive agenda concerning the challenges of global AI governance, but given today's lack of international collaboration, the initial focus should be on establishing the functional and operational procedures of the CCGAI and reaching a common charter."

Conceptual and Normative Approaches to AI Governance for a Global Digital Ecosystem Supportive of the UN Sustainable Development Goals (SDGs) [17]

This is a machine-generated summary of:

Gill, Amandeep S.; Germann, Stefan Conceptual and normative approaches to AI governance for a global digital ecosystem supportive of the UN Sustainable Development Goals (SDGs) [17]

Published in: AI and Ethics (2021)

Link to original: https://doi.org/10.1007/s43681-021-00058-z

If you want to cite the papers, please refer to the original.

For technical reasons we could not place the page where the original quote is coming from.

Abstract-Summary

"We suggest a conceptual and normative approach to AI governance in the context of a global digital public goods ecosystem to enable progress on the UN Sustainable Development Goals (SDGs)."

"We propose rooting this approach in the human capability concept—what people are able to do and to be, and in a layered governance framework connecting the local to the global."

"Normatively, we suggest the following six irreducibles: a. human rights first; b. multi-stakeholder smart regulation; c. privacy and protection of personal data; d. a holistic approach to data use captured by the 3Ms—misuse of data, missed use of data and missing data; e. global collaboration ('digital cooperation'); f. basing governance more in practice, in particular, thinking separately and together about data and algorithms."

"We conclude by arguing that taking a distributed but coordinated global digital commons approach to the governance of AI is the best guarantee of citizen-centered and societally beneficial use of digital technologies for the SDGs."

Conceptual Foundations

"Before we address the key issue of governance, it is important to establish a clear conceptual foundation for digital technologies in the context of sustainable development."

"Further conceptual work in promoting a shared view of Development 2.0 enabled by digital technologies would be helpful in avoiding (false) dichotomies between control and promotion of use when it comes to governing the deployment of Artificial Intelligence for the SDGsSustainable Development Goals (SDGs) or between providers of data and of AI solutions"—An example is persistent references to 'AI solutions' or 'AI for Good', presumably in opposition to 'AI for bad', begging also questions about whose good and defined by whom.

"As has been shown in the context of regulating AI use in weapons systems, a tiered and distributed approach across three levels can act like sliding doors to keep policy responses up-to-date with technology development and prevent governance gaps from emerging [72]."

"Interventions at the macro level such as minimum binding standards for the protection of personal data will be key to making the digital ecosystem safe and inclusive, for instance, for the collaborative and publicly beneficial use of health data."

Normative Approaches

"National laws and regulations must be reread in the light of advances in digital technology particularly AI replying on personal data to enhance protection; equally international organizations and forums must make a fresh interpretation of existing applicable human rights law to ensure that digital technologies are not used to erode human rights or avoid accountability."

"We need more forward-looking efforts to identify and mitigate risks in advance: companies could consult with governments, civil society and academia, for example, to assess the potential human rights impact of the digital technologies they are developing."

"As the UNSG's High-level Panel on Digital Cooperation noted companies, governments and civil society need to agree to clear and transparent standards that will enable greater interoperability of data in ways that protect privacy while enabling data to flow for commercial, research and government purposes, and supporting innovation to achieve the SDGs [73]."

A Global Digital Commons Approach to AI Governance

"There is considerable support for a toolbox approach to AI governance spanning universal principles set by international forums, national and regional regulation, non-binding industry norms, and best practices as well as individual users' settings and preferences [71]."

"A schematic for a governance mechanism for a health AI-related track inside such a digital commons architecture is described below."

"Solutions exchange architecture that: Enables exchange of governance assets in the form of best practices in co-creation, stakeholder consultations, inclusiveness, data protection principles, and regulatory mechanisms."

"Enables pooling of data power through common problem definition and research design without aggregating data; Promotes governance learning from diverse practice of AI for health, and a shared stake in global governance principles, mechanisms, and norms and best practices in stakeholder co-creation, consultation, communication."

Conclusion

"A human rights based normative framework offers not only protective, defensive rights but also entails solidarity entitlements such as participation in scientific progress and technological advancements and rights such as the right to development and the right to health."

"The human capability pillar allows us to link the human rights centered normative approaches to the practice of digital development."

"The layered governance concept links global norms to local practice."

"The global digital ecosystem is distributed across layers."

"This shift from 'command and control' to 'connect and cooperate' is at the heart of the conceptual and normative framework for a globally coordinated digital commons approach to AI governance presented in this article."

"It also shone a stark light on the fragility of living standards; many developed countries discovered their poor for the first time and hundreds of millions of informal workers in developing countries lost access to work and plunged back into poverty. [74] The planet breathed a bit better for a while only to underscore the massive effort that is needed to prevent catastrophic climate change, mass extinction of species and more pandemics via wildlife squeezed out of its living space."

"Could Artificial Intelligence (AI) fuelled by data help developing countries leapfrog to higher standards of living without straining the planet's resources further and without compromising the agency and human rights of their citizens?"

"Could they help deliver high quality and affordable health care everywhere, and prevent future pandemics from destroying lives and livelihoods at the scale we are witnessing over the past year with the novel corona virus?"

Artificial Intelligence, the Common Good, and the Democratic Deficit in AI Governance [6]

This is a machine-generated summary of:

Coeckelbergh, Mark Artificial intelligence, the common good, and the democratic deficit in AI governance [6]

Published in: AI and Ethics (2024)

Link to original: https://doi.org/10.1007/s43681-024-00492-9

If you want to cite the papers, please refer to the original.

For technical reasons we could not place the page where the original quote is coming from.

Abstract-Summary

"It indicates what we may agree on and what is and should be up to (further) deliberation when it comes to AI ethics and AI governance."

"Inspired by the republican tradition in political theory, it also argues for a more active role of citizens and (end-)users: not only as participants in deliberation but also in ensuring, creatively and communicatively, that AI contributes to the common good."

Introduction

"In discussions about AI ethics and AI policy it is often said that AI should contribute to the common good."

"The recently installed UN AI advisory body 'aims to harness AI for the common good', major AI companies such as Open AI claim that they develop AI for the common good, and already in 2018 The House of Lords Artificial Intelligence Committee's report said that AI should be developed for the common good and benefit of humanity."

"I connect political-philosophical discussions about the common good to questions concerning the governance of AI."

"After sketching a conceptual framework based on relevant political philosophy literature concerning the common good (and outlining my position in that discussion), I discuss AI and the common good to more precisely identify the democratic deficit or gap in current AI governance."

"In sympathy with the republican tradition in political philosophy (broadly construed), the paper points to the active role citizens can play in making sure that AI contributes to the common good."

The Common Good in Political Philosophy

"The common good was not only linked to the notion of the good life (flourishing) in the polis but also to democracy: power should not be arbitrary, there should be self-rule: political power is legitimized only when it is commonly accepted, when people govern themselves through a political process."

"It is fine to be governed in the name of the common good as long as citizens can participated in defining what it is and as long as there is the possibility of democratic contestation, open to anyone in society."

"This happens when technocrats or autocrats pretend that there is only one truth about the common good, that there is no pluralism or should be no pluralism, and that there is no need for consensus-making, deliberation, or political struggle."

"We need a multi-level understanding of the collective that is implied in the term common good."

AI and the Common Good

"Some of this can be seen in the current process towards the EU's AI Act, which moved from principles to concrete legal texts without a broad and transparent discussion of for instance what common goods such as security mean (and how it should be balanced with freedom and other goods) and with little or no participation of citizens."

"One would also need to discuss already at schools (and not only later in parliaments and other democratic institutions and procedures) how technologies such as AI could contribute to the common good."

"For AI governance, this means that citizens are not only heard but are also respected as potential active contributors to the common good: through their participation in democratic deliberation, but also through their development and use of AI in their everyday lives."

Conclusion: A Republican View of AI for the Common Good

"AI for democracy and AI for the common good, then, requires a recognition of the intrinsic political dimension of AI [75] and of the common good: while we may agree that AI needs to promote the common good and agree on what the common good means in general (for example we may adopt the Aristotelian, republican notion that the common good is about the flourishing and good life of the polis and its citizens and not just the pursuit of private interests), it is less clear what promoting and realizing it means in (AI governance) practice."

"If the republican approach to democracy and common good is right, then whether and how much AI contributes to the common good does not only depend on governance by "them" (nation states, international organisations, multinational corporations, unions, consumer organisations, etc) but also on (all of) us as citizens: on our creativity as tech developers and tech users and on our personal willingness and democratic commitment to publicly engage with others about how AI can contribute to more flourishing and more common good."

Against "Democratizing AI" [8]

This is a machine-generated summary of:

Himmelreich, Johannes Against "Democratizing AI" [8]

Published in: AI & SOCIETY (2022)

Link to original: https://doi.org/10.1007/s00146-021-01357-z

If you want to cite the papers, please refer to the original.

For technical reasons we could not place the page where the original quote is coming from.

Abstract-Summary

"This paper argues against the call to democratize artificial intelligence (AI)."

"The paper presents five objections against broadening and deepening public participation in the governance of AI."

"It then argues that such a democratization of AI (1) rests on weak grounds, because it does not answer to a demand of legitimization, (2) is redundant in that it overlaps with existing governance structures, (3) is resource intensive, which leads to injustices, (4) is morally myopic and thereby creates popular oversights and moral problems of its own, and finally, (5) is neither theoretically nor practically the right kind of response to the injustices that animate the call."

"The paper concludes by suggesting that AI should be democratized not by broadening and deepening participation but by increasing the democratic quality of the administrative and executive elements of collective decision making."

Introduction

"Anyone who values democracy likely welcomes the call to democratize the governance of artificial intelligence (AI)."

"Although the call to democratize AI sounds attractive, I argue that what this call demands is not persuasive upon reflection."

"I describe five objections against the demand to democratize AI."

"I take myself to be playing for the same team as those who demand to democratize AI—team democracy."

"The demand to democratize AI seems to be driven by understanding "democracy" as "rule by the people.""

"At least when it comes to the governance of AI, we might be looking to increase democracy in the wrong places (the value of participation; defending the democratic ideal) and we, thereby—perhaps—even misconstrue what democracy ought to look like."

"This paper, in its conclusion, offers an outlook to counterbalance the emphasis on participation: It is important to improve the democratic quality of the bureaucracy, that is, of the administrative and executive components of our collective decision-making."

"Democratizing AI"

"They speak of "weak AI", by which they mean what is meant with just "AI" in this paper. [T]he responsible development and deployment of weak AI will involve not just developers and designers, but the public at large. [...] [D]eveloping and deploying weak AI involves making consequential choices —choices that demand greater democratic oversight not just from AI developers and designers, but from all members of society. [...] Broaching questions of algorithmic justice via the democratic process would give members of communities most impacted by algorithmic bias more direct democratic power over crucial decisions concerning weak AI—not merely after its deployment, but also at the design stage. (Zimmermann and others [76] my emphasis) Several aspects of these claims are noteworthy."

"They contend that democratizing AI requires or consists in: (1) novel (legislative) institutions or avenues with (2) practical authority that is rooted in (3) direct individual and broad participation."

Five Reasons Against Democratizing AI

"If the call to democratize AI does not concern such systems that trigger legitimization requirements, then there are insufficient grounds to justify democracy."

"Insofar as minimalist and aggregative conceptions of democracy are only committed to formal but not to material equality, they have little, if anything, to offer in response to precisely the problems that motivate the claim to democratize AI."

"A deliberative conception of democracy may have the resources to address at least some of the problems that motivate the claim to democratize AI."

"Even on a deliberative conception of democracy, the call to democratize AI might still be incongruent to the problems that motivate it."

"Even if deliberative democracy were sufficiently normatively thick, those who call for AI to be democratized show too little concern that their emphasis on participation is in tension—theoretically and practically—with deliberation."

Conclusion

"A next question to ask is: Why should AI be democratized?"

"The call to democratize AI emphasizes participation: More people should be more involved in more decisions about the governance of AI."

"To emphasizing participation, it is also noteworthy that the proposals to democratize AI often seem to concentrate on what seems to be a legislative angle."

"How else—if participation is not the right way—can the democratic values of fairness and equality find their way into bureaucratic decision making?"

"To democratize AI, we should think about democratizing the administrative state without having to rely on broad and direct participation (e.g., Tutt [77])."

"What a democratic governance of AI would even look like—both on a theoretical level of values and on an organizational level of institutions and processes—and how the shortcomings of existing democratic institutions can be overcome are the question to ask."

International Governance of Advancing Artificial Intelligence [9]

This is a machine-generated summary of:

Emery-Xu, Nicholas; Jordan, Richard; Trager, Robert International governance of advancing artificial intelligence [9]

Published in: AI & SOCIETY (2024)

Link to original: https://doi.org/10.1007/s00146-024-02050-7

If you want to cite the papers, please refer to the original.

For technical reasons we could not place the page where the original quote is coming from.

Abstract-Summary

"We conclude that subnational governance, though prevalent and mitigating some risks, is insufficient when the individual rewards from societally harmful actions outweigh normative sanctions, as is likely to be the case with AI."

"Nationally enforced standards are promising ways to govern AI deployment, but they are less viable in the "race-to-the-bottom" environments that are becoming common."

"When it comes to powerful technologies with military implications, there is only one multilateral option with a strong historical precedent: a non-proliferation plus norms-of-use regime, which we call NPT+."

"We believe that a non-proliferation regime may, therefore, be the necessary foundation for AI governance."

"AI may exhibit characteristics that would make a non-proliferation regime less effective than it has proven for nuclear weapons."

"Verification-backed restrictions on AI development and use would address more risks, but they face challenges in the case of advanced AI, and we show how these challenges may not have technical solutions."

"It should be considered again for governing AI: a monopoly would require less-invasive monitoring, though at the possible cost of eroding national sovereignty."

"We conclude that it is too soon to tell whether a non-proliferation regime, a verification-based regime, or an International Monopoly is most feasible for governing AI."

Risks and Opportunities

"Internationally, states might attempt to prevent each other from developing technologies they consider harmful, but such regimes are likely to require intrusive monitoring of both small and great powers."

"Existing AI technologies already exhibit all three kinds of risk."

"The computing power required for many frontier applications of AI technologies is massive, currently on the order of USD 100 million."

"AI has significant economies of scale, and at least for now, its most transformative forms will likely require massive resources, resources only a large firm, and possibly only a large state, could muster."

"Because firms are vulnerable to domestic and international law in a way states are not, widespread AI cooperation may be more feasible than for seemingly similar technologies, like nuclear weapons."

"It is not yet clear how stable firms' dominance of AI will be, once the technology becomes especially powerful, and states pay more attention."

Theorizing AI Governance

"As this uncertainty decreases—for instance, as a firm becomes more confident it is likely to win an AI race—its preferred level of governance may decline, or it might prefer forms of governance that limit the actors who can join the technology club."

"In AI governance, this could mean identifying a point where actors are willing to intervene based on their subjective assessments of the risks and rewards of the technology at its different stages, from basic science to conceptualization and development through potential proliferation and deployment, with an ability to intervene based on the potential to control inputs at that stage and other factors."

"The who of AI governance depends upon the strategic environment: on the risks actors are incentivized to take, on the distribution of benefits from the technology, and on the off-the-path outcomes should governance fail."

Subnational Governance

"The celebrated Asilomar Conference on Recombinant DNA is often held up as a model for subnational AI governance."

"Asilomar-style governance requires a consensus on standards, since social sanctions will fail without broad buy-in across a given field."

"It seems reasonable to expect that social sanctions will likewise be easier to enforce around the development of AI than they were around previous technologies."

"If a technology would significantly shift the balance of power between states, or if it would fabulously enrich the firm that first invents it, then a subnational regime's enforcement mechanisms will prove too weak to govern AI."

"Subnational actors are most effective at governing technologies when (i) there is consensus around the appropriate ends of governance and (ii) the threat of social sanction is not overshadowed by other imperatives, such as actors' drive for security or profit."

National Standards

"In a transgovernmental regime, standards are enforced by national governments, but these standards are primarily articulated by mid-level officials without the direct involvement of national political figures."

"It is also an integral part of any "defense-in-depth" against a complex risk environment, especially when risks may require multiple kinds of responses; in this environment, National Standards can bridge governance efforts at the subnational, national, and supranational levels."

"The National Standards Model revolves around propagating good ideas, improving legal instruments, and harmonizing standards across like-minded states."

"Organizations like the National Institute of Standards and Technology (NIST) promote transnational standards and work with governments (including the US, via the National Artificial Intelligence Advisory Committee) to implement them."

"While it would be incorrect to attribute this gap to the European governance model, National Standards could hinder European firms' attempts to catch up."

"Like subnational governance, National Standards have an important role to play alongside other governance strategies."

The NPT+ Option

"NPT + generally has three components: a non-proliferation regime to limit development to a few actors; a set of agreements or norms to govern the technology among the few who have it; and an economic development component to compensate actors who are denied the underlying technology."

"Major powers have an incentive to provide security technologies to friendly states and to look the other way when those states violate the regime."

"The NPT regime functioned because it was a pillar of major power foreign policy—indeed, leading scholars have argued that the United States prioritized non-proliferation on the same level as European reconstruction and the Cold War balance of power."

"Non-proliferation regimes can also attract the support of powerful states more easily than other multilateral governance, because they reinforce rather than compromise these states' privileged technological positions."

Verifiable Limits

"Under the broad heading of Verifiable Limits, we consider two types of regimes: nationally enforced technology caps and International Verification."

"International Verification is bolder: it would give an international body some form of control over AI development by both firms and states, for example by making large AI training runs impossible to execute without its leave."

"There is no clear example of major powers agreeing to either governance model for restricting the development of a powerful military technology for which there is not a military substitute technology."

"Minor powers have certainly agreed to limit various technologies, for instance in the NPT."

"A full list of international arms control treaties since the mid-nineteenth century is included as Appendix A. It does not include a single precedent for a Verifiable Limits regime that would constrain the major powers."

Red-Teaming Verifiable Limits

"Any verification-based proposal must carefully analyze (i) the time to discoverability; (ii) the time to breakout; (iii) the ability of states to disrupt a program within these time frames; (iv) the position of major powers should the verification-based regime unravel, ensuring that these actors are not left worse than before; and (v) the path from the present state to the envisaged regime."

"In the case of AI, trying to parse acceptable uses of computing power will have a harder time uncovering violations than regimes that simply prohibit all uses of computing power in easily identified classes, such as those above a specified number of floating point operations per second (FLOPS)."

"If transformative AI turns out to enjoy significant economies of scale, then the market (or the balance of power) may tend to reduce the dangers of an AI race over time: as some actors draw farther ahead and consolidate their dominant positions, it would become less and less possible for other actors to close the gap."

Technical Solutions

"If certain training runs might be dangerous for one or all actors, such a technical solution could imply that training runs would only occur if an entire set of actors agreed."

"The political obstacles to Verifiable Limits are more manageable when governing AI research by firms than by states."

"If firms remain in the driver's seat, states might prefer to outsource monitoring to a third party accountable to other actors: doing so allows them to reassure other actors that their firms are obeying the rules, both because third parties can provide more credible information and because monitoring can be divorced from domestic politics."

"In such a world, the technical apparatus necessary to sustain an ambitious International Verification regime might be within reach."

"It would be dangerous, perhaps even naive, to build a regime expecting that the primary actors will not include states."

International Monopoly

"A monopoly removes this difficulty by consolidating the epistemic or physical resources necessary to develop transformative technology in a single international body."

"Even if Bohr's dream could have governed atomic mysteries, such an open world might be undesirable for other transformative technologies like advanced AI. (If AI uncovers destruction-dominant technologies, a single sociopath could wreak such damage as to make some control of the technology a matter of life-and-death.) Like the Acheson Proposal, an International Monopoly on TAI seeks to retain something of Bohr's idealism while accommodating realities of human nature and international politics."

"Both a nationally enforced technology cap and an artificially created International Monopoly might require tracking chips to ensure that no actors are developing unsanctioned capabilities."

"Unlike technology caps, an International Monopoly would not require close supervision of state training runs to determine whether the state is developing a sanctioned or unsanctioned system."

Technical Solutions

"Some forms of supranational governance would threaten state sovereignty and the balance of power much less than an International Monopoly."

"International institutions can govern civilian development and use when domestic governments support international regimes through tying market access to standards compliance."

"Without restricting access to military TAI (as in NPT + or monopoly) or monitoring its development (Verifiable Limits), international governance would not address some of the most significant risks surrounding the technology."

"International governance of civilian technologies may be a useful tool for protecting privacy, preventing human rights abuses, ensuring the safety of advanced civilian systems, and other governance objectives, but it likely cannot form the bedrock of an effective regime for governing the development and use of AI for security, any more than such a regime could hope to govern nuclear arms."

Paths Forward for Governing TAI

"There is a high likelihood that they will not suffice to govern AI on their own: the technology has too many power-political implications, and the rewards are too great, for professional and social sanctions to constrain its development."

"If substate actors will not be the primary who of AI governance when it comes to security, it would seem natural to turn to traditionally realist or liberal internationalist models instead."

"Among multilateral AI governance regimes, we see NPT + as the most feasible."

"Is to investigate how broad governance regimes might grow out of bilateral and club models."

"Whether verification can become the foundation of a governance regime rather than just its accessory will depend on verification technologies whose feasibility we do not yet know; it will also depend on how much scrutiny political leaders and great powers are willing to countenance."

Conclusions

"We analyze the broad scope of challenges and opportunities for governing transformational technologies such as advanced forms of AI."

"As we discuss in the next section, the nature of transformative AI systems (TAI) presents different incentive structures from other recent transformative technologies like recombinant DNA, and any attempt to govern TAI must account for these differences."

"AI governance has many goals, including stability, risk management, and the equitable distribution of the technology's fruits."

"Among international governance options for transformative technologies, we argue that only four are potentially viable when it comes to governing states' military sectors."

"An intrusive monitoring scheme extensively supervising AI development in all nations; this would take the form either of technology caps (if enforced by states) or International Verification (if enforced by an international body)."

Toward AI Governance: Identifying Best Practices and Potential Barriers and Outcomes [7]

This is a machine-generated summary of:

Papagiannidis, Emmanouil; Enholm, Ida Merete; Dremel, Chirstian; Mikalef, Patrick; Krogstie, John Toward AI Governance: Identifying Best Practices and Potential Barriers and Outcomes [7]

Published in: Information Systems Frontiers (2022)

Link to original: https://doi.org/10.1007/s10796-022-10251-y

If you want to cite the papers, please refer to the original.

For technical reasons we could not place the page where the original quote is coming from.

Abstract-Summary

"Firms need to introduce robust AI systems and mitigate AI risks, which emphasizes the importance of creating suitable AI governance practices."

"This study, explores how AI governance is applied to promote the development of robust AI applications that do not introduce negative effects, based on a comparative case analysis of three firms in the energy sector."

"The study contributes by exploring the main dimensions relevant to AI's governance in organizations and by uncovering the practices that underpin them."

Introduction

"This study examines how AI Governance helps top-level managers achieve their goals by introducing robust systems that automate processes and enhancing tasks that traditionally were done by intuition or simple data analysis without negatively impacting employees."

"Companies will be able to gain a better understanding of how AI technologies are used, identifying focal points and mechanisms of value generation (e.g., augmentation or automation of decision-making or processes) and what challenges AI technologies present to organizations."

"The interview questions focused on methodologies companies currently use, mechanisms and processes used in AI application development, the collection of data, and the consequences of AI application in decision making (AI risk)."

"Among the outcomes of the study, AI was found to be most helpful for (1) reducing maintenance costs, (2) increasing flexibility and robustness of the development process, (3) improving confidence in the results and final products, and (4) gaining a competitive edge over the competition."

Background

"Research studies have been conducted and supported by empirical evidence on developing AI capabilities by creating a unique set of resources that can effectively leverage investments and generate business value that leads to competitive advantage [78]."

"Researchers from Microsoft [79] approach AI governance from a technical perspective, while European Commission (EC) [80] and Singapore principles approach AI governance from a human-and ethics-centric perspective."

"According to their findings, AI governance consists of three main aspects: (1) discovering, managing, and versioning the data required for machine learning applications is more complex than a typical software application, (2) the required skills for building models and customizing them can vary based on the project, and (3) AI components might be difficult to manage if distinct modules, as well as models, exhibit non-monotonic error behavior."

"It is argued that in the existing literature researchers investigate IT governance and data governance and they suggested frameworks or procedures for improving performance or minimizing risks caused by AI."

Methodology

"Choosing these three firms from the industry allows us to compare the cases for commonalities and key differences and spot how AI Governance has been implemented."

"We described ideal candidates for interview as employees that (1) have a key position in the firm, for example, managers and leading developers, (2) have a good understanding of AI technologies and (3) have contributed to the overall development of AI either through their domain knowledge or their software development skills."

"In the course of the discussion, we identified a number of patterns that were either similar or different and explored the reasons behind them through open discussion, trying to establish consistency and cohesion, arguing which interpretation seems most reasonable to our goal and how AI Governance is created among these cases and which practices companies should adopt or introduce."

Case Analysis

"Then it depends on the type of data that you use, what data you get access to, but I would say like data scientists and developers usually we get access to basically everything because we work on everything." (Respondent 1, Company C) "The AI applications focus on specific needs, which usually involve forecasting ancillary services, customer needs (AI assistants) and reducing maintenance costs by minimizing business risks at the same time."

"Taking away this fear that we were coming from the outside as aliens and our work is to identify patterns (basically) it helped a lot". (Respondent 1, Company A) What is more, AI teams explained what AI is all about and how it works because most employees who started using AI as assistant in their decision-making processes misunderstood very often AI's ability to predict certain patterns (especially true when AI models were updated): "You need to ensure that model operates in a way that the operators understand and they agree with how it was developed … allow an operator to make changes to the decision, what you often see is that the performance gets much worse." (Respondent 6, Company A) "Firms encounter various enablers and inhibitors when they innovate their business model."

Discussion

"The study reveals not only that AI governance is a multi-faceted issue for organizations but that it spans multiple levels, therefore requiring a structured approach when it is deployed."

"Information analysis refers to the opportunity of developing unbiased approaches for evidence-based data analysis [81], where AI can foster digital process and service innovation as companies did in this study."

"AI governance in this article is not seen as a process but as a set of important aspects that need to be considered when designing and deploying practices and mechanisms, in order to ensure that the main challenges are overcome successfully and that AI applications are operating as planned."

"Our proposed model suggests that although there are inhibitors and barriers and despite the different ways of approaching AI governance, it offers positive outcomes, if best practices are followed, and this study identified specific procedural, structural and relational components that are necessary for achieving this."

Mapping Global AI Governance: A Nascent Regime in a Fragmented Landscape [10]

This is a machine-generated summary of:

Schmitt, Lewin Mapping global AI governance: a nascent regime in a fragmented landscape [10]

Published in: AI and Ethics (2021)

Link to original: https://doi.org/10.1007/s43681-021-00083-y

If you want to cite the papers, please refer to the original.

For technical reasons we could not place the page where the original quote is coming from.

Abstract-Summary

"The rapid advances in the development and rollout of artificial intelligence (AI) technologies over the past years have triggered a frenzy of regulatory initiatives at various levels of government and the private sector."

"This article describes and evaluates the emerging global AI governance architecture and traces the contours of a nascent regime in a fragmented landscape."

"To do so, it organizes actors and initiatives in a two-by-two matrix, distinguishing between the nature of the driving actor(s) and whether or not their actions take place within the existing governance architecture."

"The nascent AI regime that emerges is polycentric and fragmented but gravitates around the Organisation for Economic Co-Operation and Development (OECD), which holds considerable epistemic authority and norm-setting power."

Introduction

"Researchers look at questions pertaining to ethics, regulation, and governance, with a strong normative push to ensure that the potential malign consequences of AI are controlled and the benefits fairly distributed [82–86]."

"As the AI ethics research community develops frameworks and technical governance models to ensure that AI is designed and employed ethically, it must not forget about the global dimension of AI policy [87, 88]."

"Big parts of the discussion around ethical AI and AI governance, just as this article, focus on the international level."

"This article sets out to describe and evaluate the rapidly evolving emergent global AI governance landscape."

"Even though AI is a novel technology going beyond the scope of established regulatory or legal governance mechanisms, there is a tendency to address these new challenges within existing frameworks."

Literature Review

"Literature specifically addressing global AI governance or international AI policy is rare to find."

"This article aims to contribute to recent work on the important intersection of AI ethics and governance [87, 89, 90]."

"In outlining a research agenda for AI governance, Dafoe (2018) laments the neglect of political science in understanding problems of AI governance."

"He emphasizes the role of the discipline in shaping AI politics and devising visions for ideal governance [91]."

"In light of this, the contribution of this article is three-fold: (1) the two-by-two matrix provides a useful analytical tool for organizing and evaluating the current governance landscape, serving as a reference point. (2) The empirical work on important governance actors and initiatives, together with the analysis of their trajectories and connections, helps answer important questions about the dynamic evolution of AI governance. (3) The discussion of these findings brings to light important features and patterns of the nascent AI regime."

Mapping the Current Global AI Governance Landscape

"The current global AI governance landscape displays a multitude of governance initiatives by various actors, some dealing with the regulation of very specific AI applications and others with more general, abstract principles of AI ethics and policy."

"Since the membership includes a diverse set of actors with at times opposing interests regarding AI development (e.g., Russia is a member of the CoE as well), agreement on actual binding outcomes seems unlikely—though this would no doubt be a substantial step towards global AI governance."

"With the release of its AI strategy in April 2018, it established the High-Level Expert Group on Artificial Intelligence, whose 52 members have been at the fore of global debate around AI regulation and governance questions."

"Another well-known international organization that has sought ownership of AI-related governance issues is the Organisation for Economic Co-operation and Development (OECD)."

Discussion

"International standards organizations play a role in the development of AI governance, as is the case for most emerging technologies."

"As standards cannot be completely detached from the policy world, scholars of global AI governance need to have a sound understanding of the proceedings in the international standard-setting arena."

"Sub-state actors from the public sector are practically not present in the discussions around global AI governance."

"Through its close collaboration with other multilateral actors such as the European Commission, the UN, and the CoE, and by using the GPAI as a dedicated tool for advancing global AI governance, it may continue to play a leading role."

"As with other polycentric governance architectures, global AI governance will likely continue to struggle with the challenge of coordination [92]."

"The government has signaled willingness to engage in global governance as a responsible actor, and specifically on AI ethics has made some steps towards conciliation."

Conclusion

"This article outlined the current state of play in global AI governance by describing the most important multilateral initiatives."

"It thus contributes to the growing body of literature aimed at understanding and engaging with the rapidly evolving global AI governance architecture."

"Supranational organizations such as the EU and the OECD have demonstrated remarkable agency in shaping global AI governance."

"The complementary future analysis could look in more detail at the strategies and actions of nation-states and how these engage on the global level in shaping AI governance."

"We might ask, for instance, how this nascent global AI governance system fits into the wider global governance architecture (see [93])."

Overcoming Barriers to Cross-Cultural Cooperation in AI Ethics and Governance [14]

This is a machine-generated summary of:
ÓhÉigeartaigh, Seán S.; Whittlestone, Jess; Liu, Yang; Zeng, Yi; Liu, Zhe Overcoming Barriers to Cross-cultural Cooperation in AI Ethics and Governance [14]
Published in: Philosophy & Technology (2020)
Link to original: https://doi.org/10.1007/s13347-020-00402-x

If you want to cite the papers, please refer to the original.
For technical reasons we could not place the page where the original quote is coming from.

Abstract-Summary

"Achieving the global benefits of artificial intelligence (AI) will require international cooperation on many areas of governance and ethical standards, while allowing for diverse cultural perspectives and priorities."

"We suggest that there is reason to be optimistic about achieving greater cross-cultural cooperation on AI ethics and governance."

"Even where fundamental differences exist, these may not necessarily prevent productive cross-cultural cooperation, for two reasons: (1) cooperation does not require achieving agreement on principles and standards for all areas of AI; and (2) it is sometimes possible to reach agreement on practical issues despite disagreement on more abstract values or principles."

"We believe that academia has a key role to play in promoting cross-cultural cooperation on AI ethics and governance, by building greater mutual understanding, and clarifying where different forms of agreement will be both necessary and possible."

Introduction

"By 'cross-cultural cooperation', we mean groups from different cultures and nations working together on ensuring that AI is developed, deployed, and governed in societally beneficial ways."

"Examples include (but are not limited to) the following: AI researchers from different countries collaborating on projects to develop systems in safe and responsible ways; establishing networks to ensure that diverse global perspectives can feed equally into international discussions about the ethical issues raised by AI; and involving a range of global stakeholders in the development of practical principles, standards, and regulation."

"International cooperation is also important for more practical reasons, to ensure that applications of AI that are set to cross-national and regional boundaries (such as those used in major search engines or autonomous vehicles) can interact successfully with a sufficient range of different regulatory environments and other technologies in different regions [94]."

"Drawing on the insights of a group of leading scholars from East Asia and Europe, we analyse current barriers to cross-cultural cooperation on AI ethics and governance, and how they might be overcome."

The Role of North America, Europe, and East Asia in Shaping the Global AI Conversation

"The prominence of North America, Europe, and East Asia is further seen in the leadership and composition of multi-stakeholder and nongovernmental initiatives such as the Partnership on AI, the Future Society, the International Congress for the Governance of AI, and the Global Partnership on AI [95].A large majority of the most prominent conferences on AI ethics and governance have taken place in these regions, including the US-based Beneficial AI conference series, the Beijing Academy of AI Conference series, the Beijing Forum, the US-based Artificial Intelligence, Ethics, and Society conferences, governance and ethics workshops attached to the leading machine learning conferences, and many more."

"This combination of: a. technological leadership in North America, Europe, and East Asia; b. the outsized role of these regions in shaping the global ethics and governance conversation; and c. the underlying tension introduced by progress being framed through a competitive lens, and a perception of disagreements on fundamental ethical and governance issues leads us to focus on the barriers that exist to productive intellectual exchange and cooperation between these regions and cultures in particular."

Barriers to Cross-Cultural Cooperation on AI

"Despite the emergence of several international alliances in AI ethics and governance, many barriers remain to achieving real cross-cultural cooperation on the norms, principles, and governance frameworks that should guide how AI is developed and used."

"Mistrust between different regions and cultures is one of the biggest barriers to international cooperation in AI ethics and governance."

"This culture of mistrust is underpinned by both: a. a history of political tensions between these two powerful regions that has increased significantly in recent years, and is currently contributing to the competitive framing of AI development as a 'race' between 'Eastern' and 'Western' nations."

"A continued exacerbation of this culture of mistrust could severely undermine possibilities for global cooperation on AI development and governance."

"International agreement will also be of particular importance for all cases in which AI technologies are developed in one region, but used or deployed in a different region."

Overcoming These Barriers to Cooperation

"While cross-cultural cooperation in AI ethics and governance will be genuinely challenging, we suggest that there are steps that can be taken today to make progress, without first needing to tackle the greater problems of finding consensus between cultures on all fundamental ethical and philosophical issues, or resolving decades of political tension between nations."

"Given the rich history of misunderstanding between nations, to build greater cross-cultural cooperation, we should start by focusing on identifying those misperceptions most relevant to AI ethics and building greater mutual understanding of where more substantive disagreements exist and are likely to impact governance approaches."

"A key outstanding challenge for AI ethics and governance is identifying those areas where cross-cultural agreement on norms, standards, or regulation is crucial, and where different interpretations and approaches are acceptable or even desirable."

Recommendations

"Academia has an important role to play in supporting cross-cultural cooperation on AI ethics and governance: both through research into where and what kinds of cooperation are most needed, and by establishing initiatives to overcome more practical barriers to cooperation."

"Our discussion in this paper, especially in section 4, has pointed to many research areas in need of further exploration, including the following: Exploring, identifying, and challenging perceived cross-cultural differences in values, assumptions, and priorities relevant to AI ethics and governance, on multiple different levels, including the following: Analysing similarities and differences in technology ethics across different philosophical traditions, and exploring how these may affect AI development, deployment, impacts, and governance in practice; Exploring the empirical evidence behind claims of key value differences between cultures."

Limitations and Future Directions

"We believe that academia has an important role to play in supporting cross-cultural cooperation in AI ethics and governance: that it is possible to establish effective communities of mutual understanding and cooperation without needing to resolve all fundamental value differences, and that reducing misunderstandings and misperceptions between cultures may be of particular importance."

"We recognize that the suggestions in this paper cannot go all the way to overcoming the many barriers to cross-cultural cooperation, and that much more work needs to be done to ensure AI will be globally beneficial."

"More research on how these issues present barriers to cross-cultural cooperation in AI ethics and governance would therefore be particularly valuable, helping us to understand the limits of academic initiatives in promoting cooperation, and in what ways these approaches need to be embedded within a broader analysis of power and political dynamics."

Conclusion

"Even if this were the case, it would not be desirable for these regions to be overly dominant in shaping the ethics and governance of AI globally; all global communities to be affected by AI must be included and empowered."

"For a well-functioning system of global cooperation in AI, the challenge will be to develop models that combine both principles and standards shaped and supported by global consensus, and the variation that allows research and policy communities to best serve the needs of their societies."

"On a more practical level, the international AI research community, and AI ethics and governance communities, must think carefully about how their own activities can support global cooperation, and a better understanding of different societal perspectives and needs across regions."

"With political winds increasingly favouring isolationism, it has never been more important for the research community to work across national and cultural divides towards globally beneficial AI."

Cultural Differences as Excuses? Human Rights and Cultural Values in Global Ethics and Governance of AI [15]

This is a machine-generated summary of:

Wong, Pak-Hang Cultural Differences as Excuses? Human Rights and Cultural Values in Global Ethics and Governance of AI [15]

Published in: Philosophy & Technology (2020)

Link to original: https://doi.org/10.1007/s13347-020-00413-8

If you want to cite the papers, please refer to the original.

For technical reasons we could not place the page where the original quote is coming from.

Abstract-Summary

"Cultural differences pose a serious challenge to the ethics and governance of artificial intelligence (AI) from a global perspective."

"One response to this challenge is the human rights approach to AI governance, which is intended to be a universal and globally enforceable framework."

"This commentary examines the human rights approach to AI governance with an emphasis on cultural values and the role of culture."

"I show that the consideration of cultural values is essential to the human rights approach for both philosophical and instrumental reasons."

Introduction

"Deference to cultural differences, therefore, can pose a serious challenge to the ethics and governance of AI from a global perspective, and it calls for an approach to AI ethics and governance that respects basic human values while also providing legal and ethical frameworks that are applicable and enforceable across different cultures."

"The human rights approach to AI governance (see, e.g., [37, 96–101]) intends to be a universal and globally enforceable framework."

"The aim of this commentary, therefore, is to foreground the importance of cultural values and the role of culture in the human rights approach to AI governance."

"In the concluding remarks, I draw some lessons from my discussion for engaging with cultural values for the human rights approach and for global ethics and governance of AI technologies more generally."

A Sketch of the Human Rights Approach to AI Ethics and Governance

"Scholars and practitioners have made explicit reference to the major European and international human rights documents in their works on AI governance, including, for example, the Universal Declaration of Human Rights (UDHR), the International Covenant on Civil and Political Rights (ICCPR), the International Covenant on Economic, Social and Cultural Rights (ICESCR) (e.g., [96, 98, 99]), the UN Guiding Principles on Business and Human Rights (GPs) (e.g., [98, 101]), and the European Convention on Human Rights (ECHR) (e.g., [37])."

"Central to HRA is the explicit reference to major European and international human rights instruments as the normative standard for the development and implementation of AI technologies."

"Proponents of HRA draw attention to the wide acceptance of the UDHR and related documents and argue that human rights provide a global normative standard, as well as a shared normative language, to assess and deliberate on the potential social, ethical, and political implications of AI technologies."

Questioning the Human Rights Approach

"In the current conversation about human rights and AI technologies, however, the proponents of HRA have not sufficiently acknowledged the contested nature of human rights and the extent of disagreement over their interpretation."

"There are also issues with conflicting interpretations of specific human rights and their implementation and the criteria to evaluate and settle conflicts between the different interpretations (see, e.g., [102, 103])."

"Proponents of HRA should be wary of the missing discussion on the contested nature of human rights and the possible disagreement over their interpretation and, relatedly, the implications of a plurality of reasonable moralities."

"While some accounts of HRA have made explicit their normative ground or their understanding of human rights, e.g., Latonero [99] mentioned human dignity,

Yeung and others [37] referred to the value of democracy, and Raso and colleagues adopted a "legal conception of human rights" [98], they have not further explored the normative and pragmatic implications of using these normative grounds and understandings of human rights."

Cultural Values and the Two Conceptions of Human Rights in the Human Rights Approach

"Pace Ni, proponents of HRA can draw from Irene Bloom's [104] Confucian account of human dignity, which stresses instead the potentiality to become morally excellent as shared by all individuals, to defend the normative significance of human dignity for human rights and for HRA."

"The political conceptions overcome the justified concerns about the plurality and incommensurability of reasonable moralities by grounding human rights in their functions that are independent of specific cultures and would be acceptable to those who share the need for a well-functioning international order."

"Cohen's justificatory minimalism entails that the proponents of HRA need to look into the values in other reasonable moralities if they are to justify a broad(er) range of human rights for normative evaluation of AI technologies in a cross-cultural context."

"The accounts of HRA based on a political conception also need to be open and responsive to justifications for divergence from the existing set of human rights in other cultures."

Concluding Remarks: Cultural Values and Global Ethics and Governance of AI

"I draw some lessons from the prior discussion for engaging with cultural values for HRA and for global ethics and governance of AI technologies more generally."

"The discussion demonstrates that normative standards for the global ethics and governance of AI technologies should be viewed not as a pre-determined endpoint but as an on-going process of negotiation and construction, and thus ought to be open and responsive to cultural values."

"Doing so can mitigate the misuse of cultural differences, and it can also enrich the normative foundation of HRA and other approaches for the global ethics and governance of AI."

"This can only be done if the proponents of HRA and other approaches to global ethics and governance of AI technologies are willing to work with and in other cultures."

A Roadmap for Governing AI: Technology Governance and Power-Sharing Liberalism [105]

This is a machine-generated summary of:

Allen, Danielle; Hubbard, Sarah; Lim, Woojin; Stanger, Allison; Wagman, Shlomit; Zalesne, Kinney; Omoakhalen, Omoaholo A roadmap for governing AI: technology governance and power-sharing liberalism [105]

Published in: AI and Ethics (2025)

Link to original: https://doi.org/10.1007/s43681-024-00635-y

If you want to cite the papers, please refer to the original.

For technical reasons we could not place the page where the original quote is coming from.

Abstract-Summary

"This paper aims to provide a roadmap for governing AI."

"To the reigning paradigms, we argue that AI governance should be not merely a reactive, punitive, status-quo-defending enterprise, but rather the expression of an expansive, proactive vision for technology—to advance human flourishing."

"We build on a new normative framework that will give humanity its best chance to reap the full benefits, while avoiding the dangers, of AI."

"To lay out how Power-Sharing Liberalism can be applied to AI governance, we take four steps."

"We define central concepts in the field of AI governance, disambiguating between forms of technological harms and risks."

"We review current normative frameworks around the globe and argue that Power-Sharing Liberalism is a better fit for governing AI."

"We walk through the six governance tasks that should be accomplished by any governance framework and analyze them through the Power-Sharing Liberalism framework."

Introduction

"Whereas those approaches aim merely (if still ambitiously) to reduce harms, we argue that AI governance also requires an expansive, proactive vision for the way this breakthrough technology can advance human flourishing, safety, happiness, and well-being."

"To lay out this expansive vision, we take four steps. (1) We define central concepts in the field, disambiguating between various forms of technological harms and risks. (2) We review normative frameworks governing emerging technology that are currently in use around the globe, and then outline key elements of the normative framework, Power-Sharing Liberalism, which we propose to use; (3) Applying that normative framework, we make recommendations that would delegate responsibility for different modalities of harm and opportunity to various public institutions and democratic mechanisms."

Key Concepts

"Interaction effects: Because AI systems are deployed in use cases that are themselves connected to other social and biological systems and phenomena (for instance, legal structures, economic structures, labor arrangements, family structures), effects of AI systems may emerge that flow not from the specific technical capabilities of the system but rather from how that capability interacts with other systems and phenomena."

"In today's context of AI development, harms and benefits are present at each level of social experience, from the individual to collectivities at different scales At an individual level, people have experienced harms of bias and discrimination [106] due to the use of AI in consequential systems."

"Capabilities Risk and interaction risk: As we seek to govern AI, we must not only distinguish between harms and benefits at the level of the individual vs. the group (up to the scale of all of humanity), but also between the risks that flow from the capabilities themselves and those that flow from how those capabilities interact with other biological and social systems."

Normative Frameworks: The Current Ones and Our Proposal

"The AU strategy has five focal areas aimed at maximizing benefits through development-oriented use cases of AI: building core AI capabilities; minimizing risks with an intent to ensure ethical, safe and secure development and deployment of AI; promoting public and private sector investments; and fostering regional and international cooperation and partnerships in the governance of AI."

"As public sector leaders try to govern new AI technologies, they should ask themselves and require technology companies to answer—whether and how the product in question erodes or advances human flourishing."

"The existing paradigms for protecting consumers and human subjects in research and, by extension, for protecting people from harms from AI technologies, tend to be organized around protection of the negative liberties: rights to bodily autonomy, privacy, and non-discrimination with regard to civil, political, and social rights."

Governance Tasks

"The tasks involved in governing AI technologies are: (1) blocking and mitigating harm from both the production and use of AI tools, (2) equipping ourselves to see and maintain human mastery over possibly emergent capabilities, (3) blocking malicious actors, (4) steering toward public goods, including through investment in R&D, (5) building human capital, and (6) investing in the sustainability of democratic steering capacity."

"While some existing frameworks are moving in these directions, all could use further broadening. (2) Existing legal frameworks to protect individual rights and to achieve non-discrimination can function to address many near-term potential harms from AI, but the relevant agencies will require new capacities within their staffs to do this work. (3) A need for cross-domain learning about how best to integrate review and evaluation of AI-based tools and use cases makes it imperative to coordinate across agencies, as the recent U.S. Executive Order and European legislation recognize; a strengthened AI Safety Institute could advance this work."

Implementation Vehicles

"The harder challenges will be to secure global governance frameworks necessary to provide stability for governance in any given domestic context and to secure governance frameworks for AI companies themselves that tether them to public goods and social accountability."

"Policymakers should develop international agencies or organizations for global standards-setting on weaponized AI."

"The UN report, although stating the limits of the nuclear energy analogy for AI global governance, and although identifying the Geneva Convention as an extant governing framework for protection of persons against weaponized AI, acknowledges the likely need for global mechanisms for formalizing red lines and sharing benefits, drawing on the experience of bodies like the IAEA. [107], pp."

"Ensuring that this generates a stable regime of incentives will also require a global governance framework that reinforces treatment of AI research in this way."

Conclusion

"Decisions we make in the next few years about how to govern AI will be critical."

"Applying that framework to the tasks of technology governance, we propose pathbreaking ways to allocate responsibility and authority, to ensure that incentive structures reinforce the pursuit of public goods, and to harmonize efforts across jurisdictions in order to erect a stable global framework for governing AI."

"The consideration of how to govern AI is a chance not merely to categorize and manage narrowly construed risk, but to construe both risk and opportunity more broadly and accurately, and therefore to recommend correspondingly large investments in public goods, personnel, and democracy itself."

"Humanity is involved in an era-defining phase of collective learning."

AI Governance Models: A Comparative Perspective

AI Governance in a Complex and Rapidly Changing Regulatory Landscape: A Global Perspective [16]

This is a machine-generated summary of:

Zaidan, Esmat; Ibrahim, Imad Antoine AI Governance in a Complex and Rapidly Changing Regulatory Landscape: A Global Perspective [16]

Published in: Humanities and Social Sciences Communications (2024)

Link to original: https://doi.org/10.1057/s41599-024-03560-x

If you want to cite the papers, please refer to the original.

For technical reasons we could not place the page where the original quote is coming from.

Abstract-Summary

"The rapid advancement and deployment of Artificial Intelligence (AI) poses significant regulatory challenges for societies."

"The lack of technical capabilities to regulate this sector despite the urgency to do so resulted in regulatory inertia."

"This article focuses on the theoretical framework being established in relation to the development of international law applicable to AI and the regulatory authority to create and monitor enforcement of said law The authors argue that the road ahead remains full of obstacles that must be tackled before the above-mentioned elements see the light despite the attempts being made currently to that end."

Introduction

"The problems identified require coordination via a new global AI regulatory authority to tackle current and future issues emerging in this field."

"The objective is to anticipate and respond to rapidly changing technological developments, balance the interests of different stakeholders, and provide the necessary technical expertise and resources to effectively regulate this sector."

"This article discusses the framework to be created globally based on which a regulatory authority is established with the mission of enacting and monitoring enforcement of international law considering the relevant stakeholders."

"They will also highlight current attempts towards that direction showing that further efforts are needed to that end and that many factors and circumstances must be considered including the current state of international law and organizations, their effectiveness, and states participation."

"The role of the AI regulatory authority with establishing and monitoring international law is later discussed."

AI Risks for the International Community

"The use of AI presents various risks that directly or indirectly impact the international community."

"These risks depend on the level of AI development and human agency [86]."

"Other risks involve dependence on technology, loss of human connection, fairness, interpretability, safety, robustness and security, lawfulness, misinformation and manipulation, lack of compliance, and economic inequality and taxation [108–111]."

"Regarding human society, risks include AI's impact on the market economy, potential human replacement by robots, brain modification technologies, a transnational totalitarian computer system, dangerous scientific progress, global health issues, and the potential for AI to control the planet."

"These risks can emerge at various stages of AI development [86, 112]."

AI Benefits for the International Community

"The use of AI brings a wide range of benefits, including economic growth, improved performance, increased comfort and efficiency, enhanced safety through crime detection, and sustainability improvements."

"There are calls for frameworks to guide AI development to benefit all humanity equally [113], with global governance playing a crucial role in ensuring this [114] by prioritizing ethics, the rule of law, and addressing challenges [115, 116]."

"International groups, such as the AI Alliance, have been established to ensure the responsible use of technology for everyone's benefit [117, 118]."

"The AI advisory body of the UN, in its report "Governing AI for Humanity," established the first guiding principle that AI should be governed inclusively, by and for the benefit of all."

Why AI Needs to Be Regulated Internationally?

"This is where international laws play a crucial role, setting goals and standards to reduce the likelihood of risks (Cha [119], depending on their level and potential damage [120], which can occur in any territory [121])."

"Key issues requiring regulation include human rights protection, questions of sovereignty, state responsibility, dispute settlement, and the North-South divide [122]."

"Since the AI industry is global, with networks and computing resources spread across many countries, international cooperation is essential [121]."

"Domestic regulations face criticism for failing to provide a unified definition of AI, adequately address key issues, and ensure compliance [123]."

"International organizations have begun recognizing the need for transnational AI regulations [124], including private ones [125], where limitations have been noticed [126]."

"Relying solely on national approaches could lead to fragmented global regulations, as nations compete for AI development and potentially implement inadequate rules [94]."

"The extensive experience of international law can provide crucial support to a new field where these questions will arise [127]."

Theoretical Framework

"This is a complicated task that requires great efforts to adopt laws that consider the interests and needs of all of them mainly states whose consent is crucial to establish and enforce AI rules domestically [128]."

"It also includes the representation of the different actors involved in the regulatory process mainly states, other organizations, private companies, and civil society."

"This is happening in a context where the development of international law is a very complicated process that spans upon years and decades depending on the field and the sensitivity of the issue."

"This is because the international community and global governance mechanisms do not have the necessary legitimacy to force a shift in a state's behavior [129]."

"Scholars will disagree among each other over the shape, functions, and even whether an international structure should be created to address the global AI governance regime."

Literature Review

"The interplay between the law and AI as a subject is not novel if one considers the literature related to regulations and technology over the decades [130], particularly this topic [131–133] where governance represents one fundamental aspect tackled [134]."

"AI rules are conceived as means for the protection of public interests and ethics as well as avoiding and tackling existing inequalities resulting from such technologies [135]."

"All these norms and rules represent international law's initial response to AI [136], as the rules often follow technological developments [137], considering the multilateral context and the different institutions [138]."

"This is in contrast to others who claim that AI may result in the displacement even destruction of international law [139] or the revaluation of the existing rules [136], as the law reaches its limits in its regulatory attempts [140]."

"Some claim that reliance on public international law would not yield the expected results in terms of controlling and tackling AI developments [141], as structural changes to this framework are being noticed [142]."

"It is worth mentioning that for the time being, international law lags behind when it comes to the adoption of appropriate rules for governing AI [143], given the complexity surrounding the adoption of a suitable regulatory design especially concerning the question of the exact time to make a regulatory intervention [144]."

Overview of Most Pertinent Legal Initiatives and Regulations

"It outlines responsibilities for providers, users, and other stakeholders involved with high-risk AI systems."

"Governance structures are put in place, including the European AI Board, national competent authorities, and an EU database for standalone high-risk AI systems."

"This document includes became a binding treaty covering general provisions and obligations; principles related to activities within the lifecycle of artificial intelligence systems; remedies; assessment and mitigation of risks and adverse impacts;

convention implementation; follow-up mechanism and cooperation and final clauses [145]."

"The UN Educational, Scientific and Cultural Organization (UNESCO) adopted recommendations on the ethics of AI, covering various systems primarily related to education, science, culture, communication, and information."

"China adopted the Interim Measures for Generative Artificial Intelligence Service Management, through which legislators seek to balance innovation with legal governance based on specific principles [146]."

Artificial Intelligence, International Law, and Global Actors

"Companies play a vital role in the development of AI nationally and internationally as their products cross national borders where rules vary [99]."

"These include conditional support from international organizations such as the World Bank; the adoption of a global corporation treaty stipulating the responsibilities of AI use creating obligations for companies having a state's nationality and having periodic monitoring [147]."

"The goal is to create consensus among nations parties to these organizations on regulatory AI elements without for the time having binding obligations upon states or being able to intervene in domestic decisions in relation to this topic [148]."

"International organizations create a space for states and other stakeholders to adopt AI norms and attempt to facilitate the reaching of an agreement among the parties [134]."

"The work of the various entities is not connected, suggestions are made for the creation of instruments for the coordination of activities of international organizations for regulating AI [149]."

AI Regulatory Authority

"This section will examine the two main functions of a global AI organization: adopting international law and monitoring its enforcement domestically."

"Some call for considering the EU AI Act as global AI law [150], while similar proposals are expected to occur with regards to the Council of Europe Framework Convention on Artificial Intelligence [145]."

"A global AI authority should start by using nonbinding instruments such as recommendations, guidelines, and standards [151], while considering the provisions established within AI treaties."

"The global entities establish mechanisms to monitor whether a government is indeed implementing its commitments [128, 152–155]."

"These same authorities would have the task of implementing global agreements [156]."

"Monitoring is needed due to the high degree of complexity and uncertainty surrounding AI activities affecting the implementation of sound domestic rules due to the nature of this technology [157]."

"Some even expect the monitoring to occur by a separate structure within the global regulatory authority [71], on a continuous basis in the various fields [158]."

AI and International Law: The Road Ahead

"Despite the importance of international law in the regulation of AI [159], the field is nascent resulting in numerous legal questions among others."

"Concerned stakeholders did not reach an understanding of how international law would regulate AI developments [160] and the aspects as well as matters to be regulated [161]."

"International lawyers are extremely relevant in guiding the technological developments by creating a new regulatory framework via binding and nonbinding instruments, addressing transnational disputes and strengthening international law overall [162]."

"The universal and general scope of AI in addition to its technical and practical nature makes international law the main framework to regulate it given the inability to address such elements on a territorial basis."

"Such laws require international harmonization as technological differences concerning AI among the different nations persist [163], and as the number of nations adopting national AI laws increases [164]."

"One may also argue that international AI law as a field is starting to emerge resulting in nations having to clarify their positions concerning this matter globally."

Conclusion

"One must also stress upon the efforts made by various scholars and experts in their attempts to propose ways and means to regulate this sector as eventually the accumulated efforts over the years would likely lead to a global regulatory framework tackling AI."

"Leaders from UN, academia and industry are setting the stage globally for what is coming: an extremely difficult conversation on the governance of AI leading to the establishment of binding law and a regulatory authority."

"The study is limited by its focus on global developments related to AI law It did not consider the interplay between international and national laws, although some domestic rules are mentioned."

"The emphasis is more on the law, while other fields such as politics, economics, and so on, also play a role in the creation of global AI frameworks."

Exploring China's Cyber Sovereignty Concept and Artificial Intelligence Governance Model: A Machine Learning Approach [11]

This is a machine-generated summary of:

Hung, Ho Ting Exploring China's cyber sovereignty concept and artificial intelligence governance model: a machine learning approach [11]

Published in: Journal of Computational Social Science (2025)

Link to original: https://doi.org/10.1007/s42001-024-00346-8

If you want to cite the papers, please refer to the original.

For technical reasons we could not place the page where the original quote is coming from.

Abstract-Summary

"Dissatisfied with the status quo, some developing countries like China embrace another governance concept called cyber sovereignty, which advocates more state control."

"This gives rise to the question: what explains China's approach to cyber and AI governance?"

"Current studies on cyber sovereignty and China's AI governance model are mostly qualitative and/or have a small sampling frame, while the meaning of cyber sovereignty is debatable."

"This article applies topic modelling to official/semi-official texts about cyber and AI governance to understand the cyber sovereignty concept and how it shapes China's approach to AI governance."

"Since the global community has not reached a consensus over global AI governance, China is exploiting this gap to promote its own set of cyber visions."

Introduction

"To examine what norms govern the emergence of AI, one place to seek the answer would be China's existing approach to cyber governance."

"This article will show how China's cyber norms are structuring China's approach to a new technological area: the AI realm, with the scope lying in the political and international governance aspects."

"I address the following questions by applying topic modelling to official/semi-official textual materials: What norms underpin China's approach to cyber and AI governance?"

"It fills the literature gap about the relationship between China's development of cyber sovereignty and AI governance, thus facilitating the study of the evolvement of China's role in emerging realms."

"It introduces the first quantitative machine learning study on China's cyber sovereignty and AI governance, covering both official and state-affiliated textual materials."

"I review existing literature on China's cyber sovereignty and AI governance approach."

Literature Review

"This implies that cyber sovereignty can be an underpinning value of AI governance and examining China's developing country status is crucial to understanding its norm promotion."

"This article provides an empirical test about how China's subsidiary status explains its desire to rewrite norms about cyber and AI governance, while adjudicating the academic debate about how state-centric China's approach is."

"As the literature review suggests the need to consider China's developing country status, this article applies the norm subsidiarity theory to explain what drives China's approach to cyber and AI governance."

"This leads to a hypothesis testing whether China is a norm follower or a reviser, thus assessing whether China's cyber vision is liberal: Due to its state-centric approach to sovereignty, China has also applied a state-centric official discourse on global cyber governance."

Methodology

"To test the hypotheses, I apply topic modelling to study texts discussing cyber sovereignty and AI governance."

"Topic model's extractions of themes from discussions about cyber and AI governance allow us to infer what is valued and actively promoted by China effectively."

"Topic modelling is not a panacea for addressing text analysis problems."

"It is expected that the number and the category of topics generated by models analysing Chinese and English texts respectively are vastly different."

"I will perform additional analysis on a subset of documents by removing texts discussing cyber governance only but not cyber sovereignty."

"Topic modelling is ultimately an automated method for identifying the statistical correlation between words, so not all topics are interpretable or useful for answering a particular research question [165, 166], especially when government texts are long and cover many matters."

Results

"For China (English) texts, Topic 4 discusses China's worldview that all countries share common interests in cyberspace and should promote openness in cyber governance."

"For China (Chinese) documents, they cover five main themes: First, China encourages AI development, while stressing the need to ensure safety to maximize AI benefits (Topics 26, 29); Second, all human has a shared destiny and China has a responsibility to help mankind grasp the opportunity provided by AI (Topic 21); Third, China encourages cooperation in building AI governance and addressing AI risks (Topic 10); Fourth, regarding the risks, the documents have a specific emphasis on ethics (Topics 6, 16), the black-box nature of generative AI regulations (Topics 7, 19), and data security issues (Topic 15); Fifth, regarding participation in risk management, the relevant texts request equal and fairer participation in AI governance (Topics 2, 12, 23)."

Discussion

"This seems to imply that China hopes to promote international efforts in addressing cyber and AI development which are issues of all countries' common interests to promote common prosperity."

"Although sovereignty does not form a topic in China's discussions of AI governance, China has expressed a need for national security and state control in both discussions."

"The findings support H2 (Due to its residual identity as a developing country and non-Western power, China stresses developing countries' participation in cyber governance)."

"China has indicated its firm support for promoting fair participation in both cyber and AI governance."

"The findings thus reiterate the need to consider China's subsidiary status as a developing country in understanding its cyber and AI governance approaches."

"Although sovereignty is not explicitly listed as a theme in discussions of AI governance, China has been continually stressing the need to protect national security, promote sovereign equality, and ensure non-interference."

Conclusion

"This article seeks to understand China's cyber and AI governance approaches by performing a topic model analysis and comparing relevant Chinese discussions with their US counterparts."

"This article confirms that sovereignty protection and state control characterize China's approach to governing cyberspace and AI development, which reflects an extrapolation of Chinese cyber norms to an emerging field."

"As this article identifies the Chinese government's emphasis on its inferior status in its textual discussion of cyber sovereignty and AI governance, it reflects the norm subsidiarity theory's applicability to explaining China's position in emerging technology governance and its promotion of alternative norms."

"Scholars may analyse China's diplomatic discourse and interactions in international organizations or negotiations, developing countries' perception of China's alternative cyber and AI governance model, or the US reaction to China's vision."

"This article explores how China communicates its cyber and AI governance vision in its official texts broadly, thus examining their conceptual meanings."

AI Governance Systems: A Multi-scale Analysis Framework, Empirical Findings, and Future Directions [167]

This is a machine-generated summary of:

Attard-Frost, Blair; Lyons, Kelly AI governance systems: a multi-scale analysis framework, empirical findings, and future directions [167]

Published in: AI and Ethics (2024)

Link to original: https://doi.org/10.1007/s43681-024-00569-5

If you want to cite the papers, please refer to the original.

For technical reasons we could not place the page where the original quote is coming from.

Abstract-Summary

"We apply our analysis framework to an empirical study of Canada's national AIG system."

"Drawing upon qualitative data collected from 20 leaders of Canadian AIG initiatives and subject matter experts, we identify and discuss the actors, impacts, resources, networks, activities, logics, norms, and rules involved in structuring and operating a national AIG system, using Canada as a case study."

"Based on our findings, we propose three directions for future research: (1) conduct additional analysis of the 610 topics in our dataset, (2) further investigate institutional and ecosystem-level structures and dynamics in Canada's national AIG system, (3) apply our framework, data, and findings to study AIG systems in other contexts."

Introduction

"As a system, AI governance (AIG) is an interdependent set of components that are (1) situated in a context, (2) structured by the perceptions of "AI" that exist within that context, and (3) intended to maximize benefits and minimize harms that actors within that context perceive as being caused by "AI.""

"Although AIG is a fast-growing field of research and practice, AIG is not well understood or studied as a systemic phenomenon composed of several interdependent structural and functional components."

"These gaps indicate a need for more integrative theories, analysis methods, and empirical studies of the components of AIG systems across multiple contexts and scales of activity."

"RQ3—ecological question: How can those components be empirically studied in a macro-scale AIG system that contains a population of AIG systems within it, such as a national AIGS?"

Theoretical Background

"To the scale of individual organizations, AIG components (e.g., resources, networks, and ecosystems) have been empirically studied within larger scale systems, such as the AIG systems of economic sectors, geographic regions, nations, and international groups [125, 168–170]."

"Of interactions between national and subnational AIG initiatives in Germany, Liebig and others [168] demonstrate that a multi-level perspective is needed to analyze macro-scale systems that contain multiple levels of smaller scale systems within them, such as Germany's national AIG system that contains within it the AIG systems of the nation's subnational regions, economic sectors, and individual organizations."

"The service systems analysis framework was originally developed for context-independent analysis of micro-scale organizational contexts (e.g., activity within companies, government departments, research institutes) rather than macro-scale organizational contexts that contain a population of organizations within them (e.g., governments, sectors, nations)."

Research Context: AI Governance in Canada

"This dual mandate has resulted in ISED occupying a highly central role in Canada's national AIGS, with ISED leading many AIG initiatives that are intended to both promote the growth of the Canadian AI industry and to create a regulated marketplace for the Canadian AI industry."

"ISED has undertaken many AIG initiatives in support of this dual mandate, but the two most notable are the Pan-Canadian AI Strategy (PCAIS) launched in 2017, and the Artificial Intelligence and Data Act (AIDA) tabled in Parliament in 2022 as one of three parts of a larger bill entitled the Digital Charter Implementation Act)."

"In 2023, ISED created another new policy instrument: a Voluntary Code of Conduct intended to support organizations across Canada in responsibly developing and managing generative AI systems [171]."

"ISED is also responsible for the Global Innovation Clusters, an initiative launched in 2018 to support innovation in five regional economic clusters across Canada, including innovations in AI technologies [172]."

Research Design and Methodology

"We selected participants for inclusion in this subset based on two criteria: (1) their leadership roles or subject matter expertise required them to have knowledge of the topics, categories, trends, and gaps that most frequently emerged during the primary data analysis phase, and (2) their leadership roles or subject matter expertise required them to have knowledge of many public sector, private sector, and civil society perspectives on AI governance."

"Prior to each follow-up interview, we distributed to the participant a short preliminary report on findings that emerged from primary data analysis."

"During interviews, we posed three questions to participants that were intended to elicit their perceptions on subjects of interest to them in the report, as well as their assessment of the report's accuracy and completeness (see "Appendix 4″)."

"This secondary data analysis was conducted on the initial topics, categories, and quantitative data recorded in our codebook in addition to the new interview data that was collected during the quality assurance phase."

Findings

"Participants perceived many potential benefits, risks, and harms of AI systems and/or AI governance activities within Canada's AIGS."

"Awareness of and literacy with a variety of AI-related topics is also an important cognitive resource, and here too, participants frequently perceived gaps in the awareness and literacies of many different actors as constraining the development and quality of Canada's AIGS."

"The capacity gaps perceived by participants include incapacities of organizational actors, government institutions, civil society, and the broader ecosystem to effectively develop, use, manage, make sense of, and share knowledge about AI systems, impacts, policy instruments, and other governance mechanisms."

Limitations

"Our data and findings represent the most significant components of Canada's national AIGS as perceived by our participants during the data collection phase of our study (February 2023–July 2023)."

"Our study is not intended to provide an exhaustive or immutable account of Canada's AIGS–our data and findings provide a time-sensitive, accurate, and reasonably complete representation of Canada's AIGS, as confirmed by participants during the quality assurance phase of our study (October 2023–December 2023)."

"Our data and findings may contain minor gaps in timeliness and completeness due to the complexity and fluidity of the field, and new minor gaps will likely continue to emerge as Canada's AIGS continues to evolve."

"Our data and our discussion of findings are therefore also subject to the perceptual limitations of our participants and ourselves."

"Additional lower-frequency topics perceived by one or few participants could emerge through further interviews, these additional topics would not have a significant impact on the overall quality or accuracy of our findings."

Implications for Future Research, Practice, and Policy

"We divide this agenda into three future research directions: (1) conduct additional analysis of topics in our dataset, (2) further investigate institutional and ecosystem phenomena, (3) apply our framework, data, and findings to other AIG research contexts."

"These studies shed greater light on many of our own findings regarding the political and economic logics, resource constraints, power structures, and international relations that influence Canada's national AIGS, many of our other findings regarding institutional and ecosystem phenomena have not been well-studied in the research literature."

"Comparative analysis of Canada's national AIGS and other contexts could then also be conducted to further enrich the data and findings generated from across the studies."

Conclusion

"RQ3—ecological question: How can those components be empirically studied in a macro-scale AIG system that contains a population of AIG systems within it, such as a national AIGS?"

"These systems are structured by the perceptions, values, and activities of many actors within and outside of Canada, and can be empirically studied by applying service system analysis methods to analyze AIG activities within and across scales (RQ2 and RQ3)."

"Our study contributes new empirical data and findings to researchers, practitioners, and policymakers who wish to better understand or intervene in the systems through which a nation's governance of AI is structured and operated."

"Our study also contributes novel theoretical and methodological frameworks to researchers, practitioners, and policymakers who wish to transfer our theories and methods to their own studies of national AIG systems or AIG systems at other scales of activity."

Artificial Intelligence Politics and Sanctions: Comparing the Cases of Russia and Iran [173]

This is a machine-generated summary of:

Bolgov, Radomir Artificial Intelligence Politics and Sanctions: Comparing the Cases of Russia and Iran [173]

Published in: (2023)

Link to original: https://doi.org/10.1007/978-981-99-3467-6_4

If you want to cite the papers, please refer to the original.

For technical reasons we could not place the page where the original quote is coming from.

Abstract-Summary

"The purpose of this study is to identify similarities and differences in the Artificial Intelligence (hereinafter AI) policies of the states claiming global (Russia) and regional (Iran) influence."

"We analyze legislation and strategic documents, as well as institutions and practices in the field of artificial intelligence development in these states."

"In order to conduct a comparative analysis of legislation, we developed a set of parameters for comparison: (1) AI development goals, (2) authorities responsible for the implementation of AI projects, (3) AI development priorities, and (4) positions of countries in the global AI development rankings."

"The basis of the study is the analysis of AI development indices (Government AI Readiness 2021 by Oxford Insights, Nature Index 2020 Artificial Intelligence, and Global AI Index 2021 by Tortoise Media), official statistics, national legislation, and media publications."

Introduction

"The cooperation of countries on AI is strategically necessary."

"The UN Security Council has sanctions mechanisms, the implementation of which is mandatory for all member states of the Organization."

"The purpose of this study is to identify similarities and differences in the AI policies of the States claiming global (Russia) and) influence."

"The context of this study is the sanctions of Western countries, which significantly influenced the AI policies of these States."

"In order to conduct a comparative analysis of legislation, we developed a set of parameters for comparison: (1) AI development goals, (2) authorities responsible for the implementation of AI projects, (3) AI development priorities, (4) positions of countries in the global AI development rankings."

"The study is based on the analysis of AI development indices (Government AI Readiness [174] by Oxford Insights, Nature Index [175], and Global AI Index [176] by Tortoise Media), official statistics, national legislation, and media publications."

Methodology of Case Selection

"Direct parallels should not be drawn."

"Unlike Russia, Iran is a theocratic state headed by a religious were introduced gradually over decades, while in Russia it was a one-time shock imposition of sanctions."

"There are many similar things, especially when it comes to sanctions."

"Almost all the Western brands left these countries (as declared)."

Theoretical Framework

"The growing confrontation between the political regimes and military machines of Western countries and Russia shifts to the technological sphere [177]."

"Several experts consider the conflict of the modern superpowers for the leading position in the field of new technologies as a manifestation [178], a new type of mercantilism that plays a key role in industrial policy and world trade of the world's leading economies [179]."

"Valdai Club experts note that there are only two technological platforms in the world (American and Chinese) and consider it a priority for to decide whether to join one of these platforms or build their own, competing with the two already established ones [180]."

"The problem of sanctions effectiveness in technology was discussed by Tkachenko and colleagues [178]."

"As a retaliatory measure, Russia may limit the export to Western countries of chemical elements on which the production of semiconductors depends."

AI Development Experience in Russia and Iran

"This is an experiment that aims to create a favorable legal environment for the development of AI-related technologies and the testing of AI-based applications."

"As part of the Digital Economy of Russia program, a multilateral body has been created that is responsible for coordinating the development of AI in Russia and the implementation of the National Strategy for the Development of AI."

"The Technical Committee for (TK 164) was established in 2019 on the basis of the Russian Venture Company in accordance with the order of Rosstandart to improve the efficiency of the development of the regulatory and technical base in the field of AI."

"purchases almost 85% of IT products in Asia, but often its quality leaves much to be desired (for example, among Chinese chips purchased by Russia, also buys, 40% turn out to be defective) and they are based on technologies from foreign companies that can limit exports and impose anti-Russian "secondary sanctions.""

AI Development in Russia and Iran from a Comparative Perspective

"A number of projects are tested first at the regional level (in particular, an experiment on the trial operation of highly automated vehicles on public roads in Moscow and the Republic of Tatarstan) [181], and only then a decision is made to replicate the experiment to other regions [182]."

"In Iran, in the system of bodies responsible for the development of AI, powers are divided between line ministries and departments (Ministry of Trade, Ministry of Defense, Ministry of Health, etc)."

"A number of departments (in particular, the Ministry of Defense) have their own AI development strategies."

"Both countries have adopted a number of special documents regulating the development of AI."

"A number of broader initiatives and programs are already addressing aspects of AI development (in particular, the Russian National Program "Digital Economy")."

Conclusion

"Since Russia is larger and stronger economically and technologically, technology sanctions will not have the same devastating impact on as on the Iranian one."

"If Russian IT professionals decide to cut ties with Russia, could face consequences and the educational system should be ready for it, by intensive teaching in the IT field."

"The Iranian theme can hardly be considered a stumbling block in the ranks of the EU."

"As an attempt to get out of this situation, one can consider Russia's cooperation in this area, in purchase of Iranian UAVs or other common technological projects."

"Sanctions intensify Russian technological cooperation with China, which is another country facing Western sanctions."

Developing a Framework for Self-Regulatory Governance in Healthcare AI Research: Insights from South Korea [13]

This is a machine-generated summary of:

Kim, Junhewk; Kim, So Yoon; Kim, Eun-Ae; Sim, Jin-Ah; Lee, Yuri; Kim, Hannah Developing a Framework for Self-regulatory Governance in Healthcare AI Research: Insights from South Korea [13]

Published in: Asian Bioethics Review (2024)

Link to original: https://doi.org/10.1007/s41649-024-00281-w

If you want to cite the papers, please refer to the original.

For technical reasons we could not place the page where the original quote is coming from.

Abstract-Summary

"In developing the guidelines, a four-phase clinical trial process was expanded to six stages for healthcare AI research: preliminary ethics review (stage 1); creating datasets (stage 2); model development (stage 3); training, validation, and evaluation (stage 4); application (stage 5); and post-deployment monitoring (stage 6)."

"Researchers identified similarities between clinical trials and healthcare AI research, particularly in research subjects, management and regulations, and application of research results."

"To clinical trials, this procedural approach to healthcare AI research governance effectively highlights the distinct characteristics of healthcare AI research in research and development process, evaluation of results, and modifiability of findings."

"To overcome the limitations, the researchers' ongoing efforts for educating AI researchers and public and the revision of the guidelines are expected to contribute to establish an ethical research governance framework for healthcare AI research in the South Korean context in the future."

Introduction

"Corresponding with this trend, the Korean National Institutes of Health (KNIH) published the 'Research Ethics Guidelines for AI Researchers in Healthcare' in August 2023, marking an initial effort to offer an actionable guidance to healthcare AI researchers in the country [183]."

"The guidelines aim to establish ethical standards for all stages of healthcare AI development by presenting ethical principles and detailed values."

"These guidelines are designed to assist support healthcare AI researchers in conducting ethical research by presenting providing part I principles to consider in relation to research, part II corresponding relevant research codes, regulations and related ethical cases, and part III an expanded framework, aligning with that applies for the existing governance framework for phase I–IV clinical research, tailored for to the context of healthcare AI research."

"This paper presents a healthcare AI research governance system, expanding upon the existing human subjects research."

Procedural Considerations for Conducting Healthcare AI Research

"Based on the legal background, part III introduces a six principle-based framework and explanations with specific ethical cases, aligning with the procedural considerations when researchers conduct healthcare AI research."

"Healthcare AI research and development begins with the establishment of a robust ethical framework, grounded in the aforementioned six ethical principles."

"Each steps follows a structured ethical framework, integrating the principles, thereby ensuring the ethical integrity of healthcare AI research and development."

"For research institutions, the guidelines play a pivotal role in ensuring ethical standards of healthcare AI research and development."

"The research institutions can utilize the guidelines to evaluate the design procedure, algorithm development, and application of AI technologies in their own research endeavours."

"Through such feedback and societal discussion, the developers of this guidelines strive for continuous refinement, aiming to foster a research environment that esteems ethical principles and values."

Stage 1. Preliminary Ethics Review

"Prior to the commencement of healthcare AI research and development, it is imperative to establish a clear ethical framework guided by specific guidelines."

"It is essential to establish and consider ethical guidelines that are particularly relevant to the research and development process, setting a strong foundation for responsible and ethical AI innovation in healthcare."

"Is the objective to develop a medical device or other health and public health objectives? (Specify clinical diagnosis-treatment decision, patient decision support, prevention, behavioural intervention, public health, and if others, additional descriptions should be included in the protocol.) (b) Is it human subject research or research utilizing datasets? (check bioethics exemptions and compliance requirements.) If human subjects research, does the plan include interventions or interactions? (c) Does the plan address potential or manifest harms? (Provide a risk-benefit analysis.) (d) Is there evidence or potential for sample bias in the plan?"

Stage 2. Creating Datasets

"Conducting ongoing quality control is imperative to minimize data bias and ensure the diversity and representativeness of the datasets, which are fundamental for the development of fair and effective healthcare AI systems."

"Related questions: (a) Is the data collection plan comprehensive? (identification and consultation with data subjects or maintaining organizations, data types and details, collection techniques, frequency selection, inclusion and appropriateness of purposes of use) (b) Are anonymization measures considered? (detailed technical and administrative/physical measures; if not anonymized, justification and additional measures required) (c) Is the dataset size aligned with the learning task and model complexity? (d) Is the data quality recognized as high? (e) Are the data appropriately visualized and exploratory analyses conducted? (f) Is the raw data collected according to approved clinical standards and protocols, utilizing valid and reliable techniques? (g) Are regular and continuous data quality control measures implemented?"

Stage 3. Model Development

"To ensure transparency, a concise description of the development plan should be publicized, detailing the steps and intentions behind the model's construction."

"Standardizing the data before training the model is essential to ensure consistency and accuracy."

"Related question (considerations in Stage 1 should be considered in conjunction with those below) (a) Does the plan provide an adequate accounting of human subjects and data subjects? (b) Are the methods of split cross-validation of datasets and datasets utilized in the plan appropriate? (correcting erroneous data, resolving inconsistencies in data, deleting unnecessary data, ensuring quality assurance and accuracy of data) (c) Are potential issues with privacy addressed? (review for possible data breach) (d) Does the plan assess the sources or likelihood of sampling/evaluation/algorithmic bias? (considering resampling, algorithmic fairness, etc)"

Stage 4. Training, Validation, and Evaluation

"The phase of training and validating algorithms using the collected data, followed by an evaluation of their applicability for research purposes, is crucial for crafting robust AI systems."

"Training AI models meticulously is fundamental to boost their reliability and accuracy."

"This includes evaluating the AI's accuracy, its relevance to clinical applications, the fairness of its decision-making processes, and the level of trust or acceptance these systems receive from both patients and healthcare professionals."

Stage 5. Application

"Ensuring compliance with ethical frameworks and legal regulations is paramount when governing AI models in the real-world application."

"Supervising and maintaining the models involve assessing their ethical integrity and making continuous improvements as necessary."

"Designate a specific individual or entity responsible for the ethical management of the model."

"Related questions: (a) Is there a match between the dataset and the population setting for model application? (b) Are the results interpretable? (c) Have they been assessed for major biases? (e.g., gender, race) (d) Has the model been externally validated using datasets from other settings? (e) Has the model been empirically evaluated for validity, clinical utility, and cost-effectiveness?"

Stage 6. Post-deployment Monitoring

"It involves regularly reviewing the model's performance in real-world applications, aligning with the self-constructed ethical framework previously established."

"Maintaining open communication and collaboration with all stakeholders, including AI providers, users, patients, the public, and government agencies, is crucial for ongoing development and alignment with user needs and ethical standards."

"Related questions: (a) Do you regularly monitor the product whether the entire data process is correctly aligned or when the entire process is performed automatically without the need for human intervention? (b) Does the user (healthcare provider), user organization (healthcare organization) regularly disclose usage results, both positive and negative? (c) Are there communication and recovery protocols established for model application errors? (d) Are there improvements needed in the relevant ethical framework and guidelines?"

A Step-by-Step Explanation of Healthcare AI Research Governance Framework

"Human subjects, biospecimens, or populations in clinical trials share qualitative similarity with health data, their constructs, or databases utilized in healthcare AI research."

"Just as clinical research with human subjects has established protocols to ensure respect and protection of individuals involved and affected by research process and its outcome [184], healthcare AI research also confronts to address ethical considerations arising from both the research process and the utilization of its outcomes."

"As human clinical trials aim to apply developed treatments and new drugs to humans by assessing efficacy and safety, healthcare AI research endeavours to apply developed algorithms and applications to humans to demonstrate effectiveness."

"It is practical for governing healthcare AI research governance to consider adopting elements maintainable from the human subjects clinical research governance system while modifying them to suit the development and application dynamics of healthcare AI."

Six-Stage Process for Healthcare AI Research

"The introduction of <Stage 1: preliminary ethics review > and < Stage 2: creating datasets > reflects the unique nature of healthcare AI research and emphasizes the necessity for comprehensive and sustainable research guidelines from data collection stage onwards."

"< Stage 3: model development >, < Stage 4: training, validation, and evaluation >, < Stage 5: application >, and < Stage 6: post-deployment monitoring > align with the concepts of phases I–IV of clinical research but are specifically tailored to address the characterized process of developing and applying healthcare AI algorithms."

"This entity would review the data collection and management system before commencing healthcare AI research."

"Compared to the UK guidelines, the six stages presented in this paper add a preliminary ethical framework design and committee verification of data collection and management, distinguishing stages between algorithm determination and subsequent training, validation, and evaluation."

Limitations and Future Research

"In the case of healthcare AI research and application involving multiple parties, it is necessary to examine whether the harm caused can be assumed the same as the existing medical liability process."

"While the governance of healthcare AI research needs to address the issue of liability, it is limited by the fact that the guidelines in the study focus on proposing an ethical model grounded in self-regulation, addressing the intricacies of liability remains a significant challenge."

"This is an area that requires empirical verification by applying the guidelines to actual healthcare AI research governance."

"This paper calls for further research on the healthcare AI governance guidelines presented here to address the issues identified above, especially linking it the legal standard to regulation."

Conclusion

"The aims of this study are to present a healthcare AI research governance system founded on the South Korean 'Research Ethics Guidelines for AI Researchers in Healthcare' and to elucidate each procedural step."

"The six-stage healthcare AI research governance framework mirrors the healthcare AI research and development process, and is designed in harmony with the existing clinical research management systems."

"This parallel structure facilitates the utilization of established research management resources and foster mutual understanding among researchers and institutions for conducting ethical research procedures."

"The guidelines are likely to reflect the specificities of the Korean healthcare environment, emphasizing the need for further international dialogue and refinement."

Frontrunner Model for Responsible AI Governance in the Public Sector: The Dutch Perspective [12]

This is a machine-generated summary of:

Popa, Diana Mariana Frontrunner model for responsible AI governance in the public sector: the Dutch perspective [12]

Published in: AI and Ethics (2024)

Link to original: https://doi.org/10.1007/s43681-024-00596-2

If you want to cite the papers, please refer to the original.

For technical reasons we could not place the page where the original quote is coming from.

Abstract-Summary

"Across the European Union, considerable discrepancies can be observed regarding the current state of AI adoption in the public sector and the complexity of functioning AI governance structures."

"In the field of AI implementation and AI governance models in the public sector the frontrunner is the Netherlands, scoring first in the Global Index on Responsible AI."

"The article looks into the structure of the public Dutch Algorithm Register which currently contains over 400 entries, the AI framework for the public sector, supervisory structures in place and risks management approaches, addressing the importance of values in the development and deployment of AI systems and algorithms."

Introduction

"With the coming into force of the Artificial Intelligence Act [185, 186] in the EU, public entities have been simultaneously working on shaping internal structures for regulating and governing national AI landscapes and developed different open instruments for giving citizens insight into what and how algorithms are being used in the public administration act, in line with principles of political legitimacy and responsible AI governance."

"Different public entities within the national AI oversight system such as the Dutch Data Protection Authority, the Netherlands Court of Audit, Ministry of Interior are conducting investigations on the best way to involve citizens in the decision making process of AI development and deployment [187]."

"Numerous instruments for transparency and responsible deployment of AI system have been developed by the government and put at the disposal of both public authorities and public in general."

Theoretical Frames

"The user centric approach could also be considered as having an indirect spillover effect in cases where the citizen, as end user of an AI application in a commercial or private setting, has had either a positive or negative experience with the technology and that result influences their perception of the usage of AI by public authorities, either with an impact on the self or in relation with the impact the technology has when deployed at societal level."

"Of relevance is not only trust in AI, but also in the deployer of the technology, namely the public authorities and government, that use the AI in the interest of the citizen (end-user of the result)."

The Digital Landscape

"The Global Index on Responsible AI looks into three thematic dimensions Responsible AI capacities, Human Rights and AI and Responsible AI Governance across three pillars: government frameworks, government actions and non-state actors [188] and of the three, the Netherlands scores highest for the pillar "government actions"."

"The Responsible AI index lists 19 public initiatives in the Netherlands for Responsible IA governance, Responsible AI capacities and Human Rights and AI, with the Algorithm Register being a dimension of Responsible AI governance and a binding framework [188]."

"This ambition has been concretized by the lead position the Netherlands has in the Responsible AI global index, through (among the elements named above) the application of transparency principles into low threshold instruments and reports available to the general public and to different public and civic actors that might have an interest into to the way AI applications and algorithms are used in actions impacting individuals."

The Algorithm Register and Algorithm Framework

"Based on an envisioned uptake of the use of both the algorithm register (not only in the case of compulsory high risk systems) and the framework as daily work instrument, what now is being a bottom up daily practice of policy making and execution at local level will move towards a (more) uniform practice when it comes to the governance and use of AI systems with consistent sector or regional patterns starting to form."

"In line with the digitalisation strategy of the Netherlands and because it is a subject pertaining to many aspects of social life across different public bodies, both the algorithm register and the algorithm framework require considerable resources, both financial and human resources, with a so called digital triangle for digitalisation (Ministry for the Interior as the coordinating entity, ministry of Justice and Security and the Ministry for Economic affairs and Climate) and specialists from different ministries, other public organisations using AI applications, and also researchers come together in a co-creation exercise to work on the public interface of the algoritmekader, to find and test solutions, present progress, relevant case studies and good practices to other target groups."

Values Centred Responsible AI Governance

"The use of AI in the public sector has as benefits a faster decision on a certain request from the individual and a facilitation of repetitive processes for the public institutions."

"In a bilateral influencing relationship, values also shape technological use through the ways in which both authorities and the public use technology, what norms are enforced in a given ecosystem and how, in what measure individuals can exercise their rights in relation to the decisions taken and how often they do so etc. Even if in the case of AI actual alignment with public values is not required by the legislation, it is a practice in line with democratic values that increases transparency of the act of governing and public decision making and it is a reflection of the governing style of a certain nation state, such as is the case of the Netherlands."

Risk Management Approaches

"In the case of AI, a unique combination regarding risk management is observed: seen that AI is deployed as a product to be deployed on the unique market, it reflects the product risk management approach, and if it uses personal data for training purposes, or when deployed it uses personal data in a manner which could result in a decision with possible high impact on the individuals, the human rights framework also applies."

"For the purpose of an in depth analysis at national level of the risks and mitigation measures in place when using AI and algorithms in public decision making, the singular use of the algorithm register seems restrictive, requiring additional requests for information, for example based on the Open Government law (Wet Openbaare Overheid) named above."

Conclusion

"Transparency instruments facilitate the build-up of trust in the way AI systems were developed and in the way they are deployed by public authorities."

"With the role of early adopter and frontrunner in the development and implementation of AI transparency instruments comes the responsibility of influencing current behaviour and shaping future behaviour, since the frontrunner will become an example to be analysed currently and retrospectively, writing lessons of success or of failure."

"As the Dutch AI governance and transparency instruments preceded in development and implementation their EU equivalents and also other national initiatives, proactively sharing good practices and lessons learned from technology deployment gone wrong can benefit the European market as a pull factor, since mature and tested initiatives can be easier taken up and implemented as standard product by others, saving time and resources."

Governing Silicon Valley and Shenzhen: Assessing a New Era of Artificial Intelligence Governance in the United States and China [18]

This is a machine-generated summary of:

Hine, Emmie Governing Silicon Valley and Shenzhen: Assessing a New Era of Artificial Intelligence Governance in the United States and China [18]

Published in: Digital Society (2024)

Link to original: https://doi.org/10.1007/s44206-024-00138-7

If you want to cite the papers, please refer to the original.

For technical reasons we could not place the page where the original quote is coming from.

Abstract-Summary

"This article examines recent developments in artificial intelligence (AI) governance in the United States (US) and China, exploring their implications for each country's development trajectory."

"Despite China's expressed desire for values-pluralistic international governance, existing tensions between the two, coupled with the US's burgeoning coalition centered around AI with "democratic values," might pose challenges to collaboration and international governance."

"The article contends that both systems can be accommodated within a values-pluralistic human rights framework, potentially paving the way for meaningful international governance efforts."

Introduction

"While domestic AI regulation is necessary to ensure that the risks and benefits of AI do not disproportionately fall on specific groups, global AI governance—in the form of an international governing body, treaty, or other mechanism—may be necessary to ensure a broad, equitable distribution benefits and harms."

"Previous work has examined AI governance efforts in the US and China [189] compared AI governance in the US and EU, while [190] did the same for China and the EU."

"Considering these three factors, this paper will examine recent governmental AI governance efforts in the US and China, analyzing official governance documents from each, plus international documents that show how each Good AI Society is evolving in the global context."

"For China, this is primarily new AI-related legislation, plus updated funding and local documents revealing shifts in where AI governance is concentrated."

"While these competitive dynamics may make cooperation on AI governance less likely, I reject the claim that the two countries' values are fundamentally misaligned."

United States

"Innovation and the promotion of American values have been consistent themes, but now regulatory efforts are increasing and attempting to support the Biden administration's community-centered and fundamental rights-based vision of AI, centering trustworthy AI in a way more in line with international definitions."

"The US's Good AI Society involves the executive branch and national agencies promoting domestic values and government innovation, as well as private-sector innovation through light-touch regulations."

"In a US House of Representatives hearing called "Artificial Intelligence: Advancing Innovation Towards the National Interest," Republican Representative Frank Lucas said, "embedding our values in AI technology development is central to our economic competitiveness and national security," and later that "We cannot and should not try to copy China's playbook, but we can maintain our leadership role in AI and we can ensure its development with our values of trustworthiness, fairness, and transparency" ("Artificial Intelligence: Advancing Innovation in the National Interest" [191])."

China

"After the release of high-level guiding documents and ethics principles, the past several years of AI governance in China have seen a proliferation of hard laws and ethics principle-sets that show that the Chinese Good AI Society is a stable yet innovative one intending to lead globally."

"China began its AI regulation with an attitude of cautious innovation and used "fragmented authoritarianism" to delegate AI development to local governments and see what approaches bubbled to the top while explicitly aiming for global leadership, including in development, standards, and ethics [192]."

"Guiding documents from 2019 were the Beijing AI Principles [人工智能北京共识, rengong zhineng Beijing gongzhi], created by the coalition Beijing Academy of Artificial Intelligence (BAAI) and the New Generation Artificial Intelligence Governance Principles: Developing Responsible Artificial Intelligence [新一代人工智能治理原则——发展负责任的人工智能, xin yidai rengong zhineng zhili yuanze—fazhan fuze de rengong zhineng] (Governance Principles), created by a Ministry of Science and Technology expert group."

Discussion

"The US's Good AI Society is generally outward-facing, reflecting the Protestant Ethic's drive for "world mastery" [192] that encouraged expansionist and imperialist foreign policy ([193], 237)."

"China's Good AI Society is influenced by Confucianism, but it—and the country as a whole—is not a monolithic embodiment of Confucian thinking."

"In the Confucian Good AI Society, innovation is harnessed by the government, which issues centralized guidance and funding, while in the Protestant Ethic Good AI Society, it is unleashed with minimal (though increasing) interference."

"The co-existence of two Good AI Societies under different value-sets is permissible from the Confucian perspective and reflects in the calls for ethical pluralism emanating from China."

"A global evolution of the Confucian Good AI Society, justified by China's stated desire to be a world leader and work with other countries, could discourage these human rights-violating actions."

Conclusion

"It also anticipates working with values-aligned countries to strengthen global AI governance [189, 192]."

"Anti-China sentiment is a unifying force for Democrats and Republicans, but while it might facilitate domestic AI governance, it is a major block for global governance efforts."

"Although China's rhetoric is less explicitly competitive, its intention to become a global leader in AI ethics and governance will be perceived as threatening by the US."

"China does profess a desire for collaborative international governance, but whether this extends to accepting a multipolar AI governance situation remains to be seen, and foreign policy precedent suggests that it may be disingenuous."

"In light of both the US and China's Good AI Societies emphasizing international governance, reflecting on underlying philosophies of technology may help establish a base for cooperation on global governance."

"China, rhetorically and philosophically, seems willing to entertain global, value-pluralistic AI governance."

References

1. Batool, A., Zowghi, D., & Bano, M. (2025). AI governance: A systematic literature review. *AI and Ethics*. https://doi.org/10.1007/s43681-024-00653-w
2. Mäntymäki, M., Minkkinen, M., Birkstedt, T., & Viljanen, M. (2022). Defining organizational AI governance. *AI and Ethics*. https://doi.org/10.1007/s43681-022-00143-x

3. Stix, C. (2021). Foundations for the future: Institution building for the purpose of artificial intelligence governance. *AI and Ethics*. https://doi.org/10.1007/s43681-021-00093-w
4. Koniakou, V. (2022). From the "rush to ethics" to the "race for governance" in Artificial Intelligence. *Information Systems Frontiers*. https://doi.org/10.1007/s10796-022-10300-6
5. Jelinek, T., Wallach, W., & Kerimi, D. (2020). Policy brief: The creation of a G20 coordinating committee for the governance of artificial intelligence. *AI and Ethics, 1*. https://doi.org/10.1007/s43681-020-00019-y
6. Coeckelbergh, M. (2024). Artificial intelligence, the common good, and the democratic deficit in AI governance. *AI and Ethics, 5*. https://doi.org/10.1007/s43681-024-00492-9
7. Papagiannidis, E., Enholm, I. M., Dremel, C., Mikalef, P., & Krogstie, J. (2022). Toward AI governance: Identifying best practices and potential barriers and outcomes. *Information Systems Frontiers, 25*. https://doi.org/10.1007/s10796-022-10251-y
8. Himmelreich, J. (2022). Against "democratizing AI". *AI & Society*. https://doi.org/10.1007/s00146-021-01357-z
9. Emery-Xu, N., Jordan, R., & Trager, R. (2024). *International governance of advancing artificial intelligence*. AI & Society. https://doi.org/10.1007/s00146-024-02050-7
10. Schmitt, L. (2021). Mapping global AI governance: A nascent regime in a fragmented landscape. *AI and Ethics, 2*. https://doi.org/10.1007/s43681-021-00083-y
11. Hung, H. T. (2025). Exploring China's cyber sovereignty concept and artificial intelligence governance model: A machine learning approach. *Journal of Computational Social Science*. https://doi.org/10.1007/s42001-024-00346-8
12. Popa, D. M. (2024). Frontrunner model for responsible AI governance in the public sector: The Dutch perspective. *AI and Ethics*. https://doi.org/10.1007/s43681-024-00596-2
13. Kim, J., Kim, S. Y., Kim, E.-A., Sim, J.-A., Lee, Y., & Kim, H. (2024). Developing a framework for self-regulatory governance in healthcare AI research: Insights from South Korea. *Asian Bioethics Review*. https://doi.org/10.1007/s41649-024-00281-w
14. ÓhÉigeartaigh, S. S., Whittlestone, J., Liu, Y., Zeng, Y., & Liu, Z. (2020). *Overcoming barriers to cross-cultural cooperation in AI ethics and governance*. Philosophy & Technology. https://doi.org/10.1007/s13347-020-00402-x
15. Wong, P.-H. (2020). *Cultural differences as excuses? Human rights and cultural values in global ethics and governance of AI*. Philosophy & Technology. https://doi.org/10.1007/s13347-020-00413-8
16. Zaidan, E., & Ibrahim, I. A. (2024). AI governance in a complex and rapidly changing regulatory landscape: A global perspective. *Humanities and Social Sciences Communications*. https://doi.org/10.1057/s41599-024-03560-x
17. Gill, A. S., & Germann, S. (2021). Conceptual and normative approaches to AI governance for a global digital ecosystem supportive of the UN Sustainable Development Goals (SDGs). *AI and Ethics*. https://doi.org/10.1007/s43681-021-00058-z
18. Hine, E. (2024). Governing Silicon Valley and Shenzhen: Assessing a new era of artificial intelligence governance in the United States and China. *Digital Society, 3*. https://doi.org/10.1007/s44206-024-00138-7
19. Zhang, J., & Zhang, Z.-M. (2023). Ethics and governance of trustworthy medical artificial intelligence. *BMC Medical Informatics and Decision Making, 23*(1), 7.
20. Pierson, J., Kerr, A., Robinson, C., Fanni, R., Steinkogler, V., Milan, S., & Zampedri, G. (2023). Governing artificial intelligence in the media and communications sector. *Internet Policy Review, 12*(1), 28.
21. Wang, X., Oussalah, M., Niemilä, M., Ristikari, T., & Petri, V. (2023). Towards AI-governance in psychosocial care: A systematic literature review analysis. *Journal of Open Innovation: Technology, Market, and Complexity, 9*, 100157.
22. Liu, Y., Lu, Q., Zhu, L., Paik, H.-Y., & Staples, M. (2023). A systematic literature review on blockchain governance. *Journal of Systems and Software, 197*, 111576.

23. Lu, Q., Zhu, L., Xu, X., Whittle, J., Zowghi, D., & Jacquet, A. (2022). Responsible AI pattern catalogue: A collection of best practices for AI governance and engineering. *ACM Computing Surveys, 56*, 1–35.
24. Sidorova, A., & Saeed, K. (2022). *Incorporating stakeholder enfranchisement, risks, gains, and AI decisions in AI governance framework*.
25. Wirtz, B. W., Weyerer, J. C., & Sturm, B. J. (2020). The dark sides of artificial intelligence: An integrated AI governance framework for public administration. *International Journal of Public Administration, 43*(9), 818–829.
26. Knight, S., Shibani, A., & Vincent, N. (2024). Ethical AI governance: Mapping a research ecosystem. *AI and Ethics, 1–22*, 841–862.
27. Solomon, J. (2020). *Corporate governance and accountability*. Wiley.
28. Weill, P., & Ross, J. W. (2004). *IT governance: How top performers manage IT decision rights for superior results*. Harvard Business School Press.
29. Abraham, R., Schneider, J., & vom Brocke, J. (2019). Data governance: A conceptual framework, structured review, and research agenda. *International Journal of Information Management, 49*, 424–438. https://doi.org/10.1016/j.ijinfomgt.2019.07.008
30. Ocasio, W. (1997). Towards an attention-based view of the firm. *Strategic Management Journal, 18*, 187–206.
31. Eitel-Porter, R. (2021). Beyond the promise: Implementing ethical AI. *AI and Ethics, 1*(1), 73–80. https://doi.org/10.1007/s43681-020-00011-6
32. Benjamins, R. (2021). A choices framework for the responsible use of AI. *AI and Ethics, 1*, 49–53. https://doi.org/10.1007/s43681-020-00012-5
33. Ibáñez, J. C., & Olmeda, M. V. (2022). Operationalising AI ethics: How are companies bridging the gap between practice and principles? An exploratory study. *AI & Society, 37*(4), 1663–1687. https://doi.org/10.1007/s00146-021-01267-0
34. Butcher, J., & Beridze, I. (2019). What is the state of artificial intelligence governance globally? *The RUSI Journal, 164*(5–6), 88–96. https://doi.org/10.1080/03071847.2019.1694260
35. Schneider, J., Abraham, R., & Meske, C. (2020). *AI governance for businesses*. arXiv:2011.10672 [cs]
36. Gasser, U., & Almeida, V. A. F. (2017). A layered model for AI governance. *IEEE Internet Computing, 21*, 58–62. https://doi.org/10.1109/MIC.2017.4180835
37. Yeung, K., Howes, A., & Pogrebna, G. (2020). AI governance by human rights-centered design, deliberation, and oversight: An end to ethics washing. In M. D. Dubber, F. Pasquale, & S. Das (Eds.), *The Oxford handbook of ethics of AI* (pp. 75–106). Oxford University Press. https://doi.org/10.1093/oxfordhb/9780190067397.013.5
38. Floridi, L. (2018). Soft ethics, the governance of the digital and the general data protection regulation. *Philosophical Transactions of the Royal Society A: Mathematical, Physical and Engineering Sciences, 376*(2133), 20180081. https://doi.org/10.1098/rsta.2018.0081
39. Winfield, A. F. T., & Jirotka, M. (2018). Ethical governance is essential to building trust in robotics and artificial intelligence systems. *Philosophical Transactions of the Royal Society A, 376*, 20180085. https://doi.org/10.1098/rsta.2018.0085
40. Gahnberg, C. (2021). What rules? Framing the governance of artificial agency. *Policy and Society, 40*, 194–210. https://doi.org/10.1080/14494035.2021.1929729
41. Kaplan, A., & Haenlein, M. (2019). Siri, Siri in my hand, who's the fairest in the land? On the interpretations, illustrations and implications of artificial intelligence. *Business Horizons, 62*(1), 15–25.
42. Hevner, A. R., March, S. T., Park, J., & Ram, S. (2004). Design science in information systems research. *MIS Quarterly, 28*, 75–105. https://doi.org/10.2307/25148625
43. de Almeida, P. G. R., de Almeida, P. G. R., dos Santos, C. D., & Farias, J. S. (2021). Artificial intelligence regulation: A framework for governance. *Ethics and Information Technology*. https://doi.org/10.1007/s10676-021-09593-z
44. Turner, J. (2018). *Robot rules: Regulating artificial intelligence*. Springer.

45. Pierson, P. (2000). Increasing returns, path dependence, and the study of politics. *The American Political Science Review, 94*(2), 251–267.
46. Thelen, K. (1999). Historical institutionalism in comparative politics. *Annual Review of Political Science, 2*(1), 369–404.
47. Floridi, L., Cowls, J., Beltrametti, M., et al. (2018). AI4People—An ethical framework for a good AI society: Opportunities, risks, principles, and recommendations. *Minds and Machines, 28*, 689–707. https://doi.org/10.1007/s11023-018-9482-5
48. Stahl, B. C., Andreou, A., Brey, P., Hatzakis, T., Kirichenko, A., Macnish, K., LaulhéShaelou, S., Patel, A., Ryan, M., & Wright, D. (2021). Artificial intelligence for human flourishing – Beyond principles for machine learning. *Journal of Business Research, 124*(2), 374–388. https://doi.org/10.1016/j.jbusres.2020.11.030
49. Stahl, B. C., Antoniou, J., Ryan, M., Macnish, K., & Jiya, T. (2021). Organisational responses to the ethical issues of artificial intelligence. *AI & Society, 37*. https://doi.org/10.1007/s00146-021-01148-6
50. Taddeo, M., & Floridi, L. (2018). How AI can be a force for good. *Science, 361*, 751–752. https://doi.org/10.1126/science.aat5991
51. Bilchitz, D. (2016). Corporations and the limits of state-based models for protecting fundamental rights in international law. *Indiana Journal of Global Legal Studies, 23*(1), 143–170. https://doi.org/10.2979/indjglolegstu.23.1.143
52. Kampourakis, I. (2019). CSR and social rights: Juxtaposing societal constitutionalism and rights-based approaches imposing human rights obligations on corporations. *Goettingen Journal of International Law, 9*(3), 537–569.
53. Lane, L. (2018). The horizontal effect of international human rights law in practice: A comparative analysis of the general comments and jurisprudence of selected united nations human rights treaty monitoring bodies. *European Journal of Comparative Law and Governance, 5*(1). https://doi.org/10.1163/22134514-00501001
54. Zamfir, I. (2018). Towards a binding international treaty on business and human rights. In *EPRS | European Parliament Research Service* (November). https://www.europarl.europa.eu/RegData/etudes/BRIE/2018/620229/EPRS_BRI(2018)620229_EN.pdf
55. Facebook. (2020). *Facebook's five pillars of responsible AI*. Retrieved October 27, 2021, from https://ai.facebook.com/blog/facebooks-five-pillars-of-responsible-ai/
56. IBM. (2020). *AI ethics | IBM*. IBM Cloud Learn Hub. https://www.ibm.com/cloud/learn/ai-ethics
57. Microsoft. (2017). *Responsible AI principles from Microsoft*. Our Approach. https://www.microsoft.com/en-us/ai/responsible-ai?activetab=pivot1%3Aprimaryr6
58. Pichay, S. (2018). *Our principles—Google AI*. https://ai.google/principles/
59. Pinjušić, T. (2022). *The Atos blueprint for responsible AI – Atos*. ATOS. https://atos.net/en/lp/cybersecurity-magazine-ai-and-cybersecurity/the-atos-blueprint-for-responsible-ai
60. Partnership on AI. (2020). *Partnership on AI*. https://partnershiponai.org/
61. Radu, R. (2021). Steering the governance of artificial intelligence: National strategies in perspective. *Policy and Society, 40*(2), 178–193. https://doi.org/10.1080/14494035.2021.1929728
62. Deva, S. (2017). Conclusion: Connecting the dots: How to capitalize on the current high tide for a business and human rights treaty. In *Building a treaty on business and human rights* (pp. 472–494). Cambridge University Press. https://doi.org/10.1017/9781108183031.019
63. Greenstein, S. M. (2015). How the internet became commercial: Innovation, privatization, and the birth of a new network. In *The Kauffman foundation series on innovation and entrepreneurship*. Princeton University Press.
64. Lyytinen, K., & Rose, G. M. (2003). Disruptive information system innovation: The case of internet computing. *Information Systems Journal, 13*(4), 301–330. https://doi.org/10.1046/J.1365-2575.2003.00155.X

65. Black, J., & Murray, A. (2019). Regulating AI and machine learning: Setting the regulatory agenda (complementar). *European Journal of Law and Technology, 10*(3), 1–17. http://eprints.lse.ac.uk/102953/4/722_3282_1_PB.pdf
66. Fukuda-Parr, S., & Gibbons, E. (2021). Emerging consensus on 'ethical AI': Human rights critique of stakeholder guidelines. *Global Policy, 12*(S6), 32–44. https://doi.org/10.1111/1758-5899.12965
67. Jobin, A., Ienca, M., & Vayena, E. (2019). *The global landscape of AI ethics guidelines.* arXiv:1906.11668.
68. Zeng, Y., Lu, E., & Huangfu, C. (2018). *Linking artificial intelligence principles.* arXiv:1812.04814
69. Dafoe, A. (2019). *AI governance: A research agenda, working document, v1.0.* Governance of AI Program Future of Humanity Institute University of Oxford.
70. Jelinek, T. (forthcoming 2021). The artificial intelligence governance gap: a barrier to intelligent decarbonization. In: Inderwildi, O., Kraft, M. (eds.) *Intelligent decarbonization – Can artificial intelligence and cyberphysical systems foster the achievement of climate change mitigation targets?* Springer Nature and Cambridge CARES.
71. Wallach, W., & Marchant, G. E. (2019). Toward the agile and comprehensive international governance of AI and robotics. *Proceedings of the IEEE, 107*, 505–508. https://doi.org/10.1109/JPROC.2019.2899422
72. Gill, A. S. (2021). The changing role of multilateral forums in regulating armed conflict in the digital age. *International Review of the Red Cross,* No. 913, March 2021.
73. United Nations. (2019). The age of digital interdependence. In *Report of the UN Secretary-General's High-level Panel on Digital Cooperation*. United Nations.
74. Lakner, C., Yonzan, N., Mahler, D. G., Aguilar, R. A. C., & Wu, H. (2021). *Updated estimates of the impact of Covid-19 on global poverty: Looking back at 2020 and the outlook for 2021.* World Bank.
75. Coeckelbergh, M. (2022). *The political philosophy of AI.* Polity.
76. Zimmermann, A., Di Rosa, E., & Kim, H. (2020). Technology can't fix algorithmic injustice. *Boston Review.* http://bostonreview.net/science-nature-politics/annette-zimmermann-elena-di-rosa-hochan-kim-technology-cant-fix-algorithmic. Accessed 09 Jan 2020.
77. Tutt, A. (2017). An FDA for algorithms. *Administrative Law Review, 69*(1), 83–124.
78. Mikalef, P., & Gupta, M. (2021). Artificial intelligence capability: Conceptualization, measurement calibration, and empirical study on its impact on organizational creativity and firm performance. *Information Management, 58*(3), 103434. https://doi.org/10.1016/J.IM.2021.103434
79. Amershi, S., Begel, A., Bird, C., DeLine, R., Gall, H., Kamar, E., Nagappan, N., Nushi, B., & Zimmermann, T. (2019). Software engineering for machine learning: A case study. In *2019 IEEE/ACM 41st International Conference on Software Engineering: Software Engineering in Practice (ICSE-SEIP).*
80. Smuha, N. (2019). The EU approach to ethics guidelines for trustworthy artificial intelligence. *Computer Law Review International, 20*(4), 97–106.
81. Trocin, C., Hovland, I. V., Mikalef, P., & Dremel, C. (2021). How artificial intelligence affords digital innovation: A cross-case analysis of Scandinavian companies. *Technological Forecasting and Social Change, 173*, 121081.
82. MacIntyre, J., Medsker, L., & Moriarty, R. (2021). Past the tipping point? *AI and Ethics, 1*, 1–3. https://doi.org/10.1007/s43681-020-00016-1
83. Bostrom, N., & Yudkowsky, E. (2014). The ethics of artificial intelligence. In K. Frankish & W. M. Ramsey (Eds.), *The Cambridge handbook of artificial intelligence* (pp. 316–334). Cambridge University Press. https://doi.org/10.1017/CBO9781139046855.020
84. Veale, M., Van Kleek, M., & Binns, R. (2018). Fairness and accountability design needs for algorithmic support in high-stakes public sector decision-making. In *Proceedings of the 2018 CHI Conference on Human Factors in Computing Systems, New York* (pp. 440:1–440:14). https://doi.org/10.1145/3173574.3174014

85. Cave, S., Nyrup, R., Vold, K., & Weller, A. (2019). Motivations and risks of machine ethics. *Proceedings of the IEEE, 107*, 562–574. https://doi.org/10.1109/JPROC.2018.2865996
86. Turchin, A., & Denkenberger, D. (2020). Classification of global catastrophic risks connected with artificial intelligence. *AI & Society, 35*, 147–163. https://doi.org/10.1007/s00146-018-0845-5
87. Ó hÉigeartaigh, S. S., Whittlestone, J., Liu, Y., Zeng, Y., & Liu, Z. (2020). Overcoming barriers to cross-cultural cooperation in AI ethics and governance. *Philosophy and Technology, 33*(4), 571–593.
88. Rotenberg, M. (2019). The AI policy sourcebook 2019. *Electronic Privacy Information Center (Epic).*
89. Schiff, D., Biddle, J., Borenstein, J., & Laas, K. (2020). *What's next for AI ethics, policy, and governance? A global overview* (pp. 153–158). https://doi.org/10.1145/3375627.3375804
90. Shi, Q. (2020). *AI governance in 2019—A year in review: Observations from 50 global experts.* Shanghai Institute for Science of Science.
91. Dafoe, A.: AI governance: A research agenda (2018).
92. Carlisle, K., & Gruby, R. L. (2019). Polycentric systems of governance: A theoretical model for the commons. *Policy Studies Journal, 47*, 927–952. https://doi.org/10.1111/psj.12212
93. Biermann, F., Pattberg, P., van Asselt, H., & Zelli, F. (2009). The fragmentation of global governance architectures: A framework for analysis. *Global Environmental Politics, 9*, 14–40. https://doi.org/10.1162/glep.2009.9.4.14
94. Cihon, P. (2019). *Standards for AI governance: International standards to enable global coordination in AI research & development.* Future of Humanity Institute, University of Oxford. https://www.fhi.ox.ac.uk/wp-content/uploads/Standards_-FHITechnical-Report.pd
95. Hudson, R. (2019). France and Canada move forward with plans for global AI expert council. *Science Business.* https://sciencebusiness.net/news/france-and-canada-move-forward-plans-global-ai-expert-council. Accessed 27 Dec 2017.
96. Access Now. (2018). *Human rights in the age of artificial intelligence.* https://www.accessnow.org/cms/assets/uploads/2018/11/AI-and-Human-Rights.pdf
97. IEEE [The IEEE Global Initiative on Ethics of Autonomous and Intelligent Systems]. (2018). *Ethically aligned design: A vision for prioritizing human well-being with autonomous and intelligent systems.* IEEE. https://standards.ieee.org/content/dam/ieee-standards/standards/web/documents/other/ead1e.pdf
98. Raso, F., Hilligoss, H., Krishnamurthy, V., Bavitz, C., & Kim, L. (2018). *Artificial intelligence & human rights: Opportunities & risks.* Berkman Klein Center Research Publication No. 2018–2016. https://ssrn.com/abstract=3259344
99. Latonero, M. (2018). Governing artificial intelligence: Upholding human rights & dignity. *Data & Society.* https://datasociety.net/library/governing-artificial-intelligence/. Accessed 20 Nov 2024.
100. AI HLEG [High-Level Expert Group on Artificial Intelligence]. (2019). *Ethics guidelines for trustworthy AI.* https://ec.europa.eu/digital-single-market/en/news/ethics-guidelines-trustworthy-ai
101. ARTICLE 19. (2019). Governance with teeth: How human rights can strengthen FAT and ethics initiatives on artificial intelligence. Available Online at: https://www.article19.org/wp-content/uploads/2019/04/Governance-with-teeth_A19_April_2019.pdf
102. Macioce, F. (2016). Balancing cultural pluralism and universal bioethical standards: A multiple strategy. *Medicine, Health Care and Philosophy, 19*(3), 393–402.
103. Macioce, F. (2018). Charters of rights and bioethical principles: A multicultural challenge. In C. Caporale & I. R. Pavone (Eds.), *International biolaw and shared ethical principles: The universal declaration on bioethics and human rights* (pp. 40–57). Routledge.
104. Bloom, I. (1998). Fundamental intuition and consensus statements: Mencian Confucianism and human rights. In W. T. de Bary (Ed.), *Confucianism and human rights* (pp. 94–116). Columbia University Press.

105. Allen, D., Hubbard, S., Lim, W., Stanger, A., Wagman, S., Zalesne, K., & Omoakhalen, O. (2025). A roadmap for governing AI: Technology governance and power-sharing liberalism. *AI and Ethics*. https://doi.org/10.1007/s43681-024-00635-y
106. Angwin J., Larson J., Mattu S., & Kirchner L. (2016). *Machine bias. ProPublica*. https://www.propublica.org/article/machine-bias-risk-assessments-in-criminal-sentencing
107. United Nations AI Advisory Body. (2024). *Governing AI for humanity*. https://www.un.org/sites/un2.un.org/files/governing_ai_for_humanity_final_report_en.pdf
108. Gov.UK. (n.d.). *International scientific report on the safety ofadvanced AI*. https://www.gov.uk/government/publications/international-scientific-report-on-the-safety-of-advanced-ai#:~:text=Future%20advances%20in%20general%2Dpurpose,could%20result%20in%20catastrophic%20outcomes. Accessed 20 Nov 2024.
109. Marr, B. (2023). The 15 biggest risks of artificial intelligence. *Forbes*. https://www.forbes.com/sites/bernardmarr/2023/06/02/the-15-biggest-risks-of-artificial-intelligence/. Accessed 20 Nov 2024.
110. Golbin, I., et al. (2020). Responsible AI: A primer for the legal community. In *Proceedings IEEE international conference on Big Data* (pp. 2121–2126).
111. Calo, R. (2017). Artificial intelligence policy: A primer and roadmap. *The UC Davis Law Review, 51*, 399–435.
112. Schwalbe, N., & Wahl, B. (2020). Artificial intelligence and the future of global health. *Lancet, 395*, 1579–1586. https://doi.org/10.1016/S0140-6736(20)30226-9
113. Gibbons, E. D. (2021). Toward a more equal world: The human rights approach to extending the benefits of artificial intelligence. *IEEE Technology and Society Magazine*. https://doi.org/10.1109/MTS.2021.3056295
114. Leslie, D., et al. (2024). 'Frontier AI', power, and the public interest: Who benefits, who decides? *Harvard Data Science Review*, 1–20.
115. United Nations. (2023). *Interim report: Governing AI for humanity*. Published by advisory body on artificial intelligence. Accessed 20 Nov 2024.
116. United Nations. (2023). *International community must urgently confront new reality of generative, artificial intelligence, speakers stress as security council debates risks, rewards*. https://press.un.org/en/2023/sc15359.doc.htm. 20 Nov 2024.
117. IBM. (2023). *AI alliance launches as an international community of leading technology developers, researchers, and adopters collaborating together to advance open, safe, responsible AI*. https://newsroom.ibm.com/AI-Alliance-Launches-as-an-International-Community-of-Leading-Technology-Developers,-Researchers,-and-Adopters-Collaborating-Together-to-Advance-Open,-Safe,-Responsible-AI. Accessed 20 Nov 2024.
118. United States Department of State. (2023). *Artificial intelligence for accelerating progress on the sustainable development goals: Addressing society's greatest challenges*. https://www.state.gov/artificial-intelligence-for-accelerating-progress-on-the-sustainable-development-goals-addressing-societys-greatest-challenges/. Accessed 20 Nov 2024.
119. Cha, S. (2024). Towards an international regulatory framework for AI safety: Lessons from the IAEA's nuclear safety regulations. *HSSC, 11*, 1–13.
120. Strous, L. (2019). Should artificial intelligence be more regulated? In L. Strous & V. G. Cerf (Eds.), *Internet of things. Information processing in an increasingly connected world* (pp. 28–34). Springer.
121. Trager, T., et al. (2023). *International governance of civilian AI: A jurisdictional certification approach*. 1–51.
122. Lee, J. (2022). *Artificial intelligence and international law*. Springer.
123. Ratcliff, C. J. (2023). Who will write the rules for AI? How nations are racing to regulate artificial intelligence. *The Conversation*. https://theconversation.com/who-will-write-the-rules-for-ai-how-nations-are-racing-to-regulate-artificial-intelligence-216900. Accessed 20 Nov 2024.
124. Hars, A. (2022). AI and international law—Legal personality and avenues for regulation. *Hungarian Journal of Legal Studies, 62*, 320–344. https://doi.org/10.1556/2052.2022.00352

125. Veale, M., Matus, K., & Gorwa, R. (2023). AI and global governance: Modalities, rationales, tensions. *The Annual Review of Law and Social Science, 19*, 255–275. https://doi.org/10.1146/annurev-lawsocsci-020223-040749
126. Nindler, R. (2019). The United Nation's capability to manage existential risks with a focus on artificial intelligence. *International Community Law Review, 21*(1), 5–34. https://doi.org/10.1163/18719732-12341388
127. Burri, T. (2018). International law and artificial intelligence. *GYIL, 60*, 91–108. https://doi.org/10.3790/gyil.60.1.91
128. Besson, S. (2016). State consent and disagreement in international law-making. Dissolving the paradox. *LJIL, 29*, 289–316. https://doi.org/10.1017/S0922156516000030
129. Franzie, B. (2018). *Does international law change state behavior? Submitted in partial completion of the requirements for departmental honors in political science*. Bridgewater State University.
130. Dellapenna, J. W. (2000). Law in a shrinking world: The interaction of science and technology with international law. *Kentucky Law Journal, 88*, 809–883.
131. Governatori, G., et al. (2022). Thirty years of artificial intelligence and law: The first decade. *Artifical Intelligence and Law, 30*, 481–519. https://doi.org/10.1007/s10506-022-09329-4
132. Sartor, et al. (2022) Thirty years of artificial intelligence and law: The second decade. Artifical Intelligence and Law 30:521–557. doi:https://doi.org/10.1007/s10506-022-09326-7
133. Villata, S., et al. (2022). Thirty years of artificial intelligence and law: The third decade. *Artifical Intelligence and Law, 30*, 561–591. https://doi.org/10.1007/s10506-022-09327-6
134. Chinen, M. (2023). *The international governance of artificial intelligence*. Edward Elgar Publishing.
135. Gantzias, G. (2020). Dynamics of public interest in artificial intelligence: 'Business intelligence culture' and global regulation in the digital era. In S. H. Park, M. A. Gonzalez-Perez, & D. E. Floriani (Eds.), *The Palgrave handbook of corporate sustainability in the digital era* (pp. 259–281). Springer.
136. Zekos, G. I. (2021). *Economics and law of artificial intelligence: Finance, economic impacts, risk management and governance*. Springer.
137. Payne, K. (2018). Artificial intelligence: A revolution in strategic affairs? *Survival, 60*, 7–32. https://doi.org/10.1080/00396338.2018.1518374
138. Garcia, E. V. (2021). *Multilateralism and artificial intelligence: What role for the United Nations?* https://www.researchgate.net/publication/350193708_Multilateralism_and_Artificial_Intelligence_What_Role_for_the_United_Nations. Accessed 20 November 2024.
139. Maas, M. (2019). International law does not compute: Artificial intelligence and the development, displacement or destruction of the global legal order. *Melbourne Journal of International Law, 29*, 1–29.
140. Alschner, W. (2021). The computational analysis of international law. In R. Deplano & N. Tsagourias (Eds.), *Research methods in international law: A handbook* (pp. 203–227). Edward Elgar Publishing.
141. Liu, H. Y. (2018). The power structure of artificial intelligence. *Law, Innovation and Technology, 10*, 197–229. https://doi.org/10.1080/17579961.2018.1527480
142. Burchardt, D. (2023). Editorial to the special issue "the impact of digitalization on international law". *GLJ, 24*, 435–437. https://doi.org/10.1017/glj.2023.32
143. Chache, E. G., Dremlyuga, R. I., Tret'yakova, N. A., & Neznamov, A. V. (2023). System approach to the study of state policies and formation of ethics of application of artificial intelligence technologies: Global atlas of regulation. *Doklady Mathematics, 106*, S65–S69. https://doi.org/10.1134/S1064562422060059
144. Walz, A., & Firth-Butterfield, K. (2019). Implementing ethics into artificial intelligence: A contribution, from a legal perspective, to the development of an AI governance regime. *The Duke Law & Technology Review, 18*, 176–231. https://scholarship.law.duke.edu/dltr/vol18/iss1/17
145. Council of Europe. (2024). *Framework convention on artificial intelligence*. Human Rights.

146. Cyberspace Administration of China. (2023). 生成式人工智能服务管理暂行办法 (Interim Measures for Generative Artificial Intelligence Service Management). https://www.cac.gov.cn/2023-07/13/c_1690898327029107.htm. Accessed 20 Nov 2024.
147. Schwarz, E. C. (2019). Human vs. machine: A framework of responsibilities and duties of transnational corporations for respecting human rights in the use of artificial intelligence. *Columbia Journal of Transnational Law, 58*, 232.
148. Smuha, N. A. (2021). From a 'race to AI' to a 'race to AI regulation': Regulatory competition for artificial intelligence. *Law, Innovation and Technology, 13*(1), 57–84. https://doi.org/10.1080/17579961.2021.1898300
149. Talimonchik, V. P. (2021). The prospects for creating instruments for the coordination of activities of international organizations in the regulation of artificial intelligence. In E. Osaba et al. (Eds.), *Artificial intelligence: Latest advances, new paradigms and novel applications*. InTech Open.
150. Musch, S., Borrelli, M., & Kerrigan, C. (2023, August 23). The EU AI Act As Global Artificial Intelligence Regulation. *SSRN*. https://doi.org/10.2139/ssrn.4549261
151. Erdélyi, O. J., & Goldsmith, J. (2018). Regulating artificial intelligence proposal for a global solution. In *2018 AAAI/ACM Conference on AI, Ethics, and society (AIES '18), February 2–3, 2018, New Orleans, LA, USA*.
152. Follesdal, A. (2022). The significance of state consent for the legitimate authority of customary international law. In P. Merkouris, J. Kammerhofer, & N. Arajärvi (Eds.), *The theory, practice, and interpretation of customary international law*. Cambridge University Press.
153. Krisch, N. (2014). The decay of consent: International law in an age of global public goods. *The American Journal of International Law, 108*, 1–40. https://doi.org/10.5305/amerjintelaw.108.1.0001
154. Lister, M. J. (2011). The legitimating role of consent in international law. *Chinese Journal of International Law, 11*, 663–691. https://scholarship.law.upenn.edu/faculty_scholarship/317
155. Bodansky, D., & Watson, J. S. (1992). State consent and the sources of international obligation. *Proceedings of the Annual Meeting, 86*, 108–113. https://www.jstor.org/stable/25658621
156. Anzini, M. (2021). *The artificial intelligence act proposal and its implications for member states*. European Institute of Public Administration. https://www.eipa.eu/publications/briefing/the-artificial-intelligence-act-proposal-and-its-implications-for-member-states/. Accessed 20 Nov 2024.
157. Taeihagh, A. (2021). Governance of artificial intelligence. *Policy and Society, 40*(2), 137–157. https://doi.org/10.1080/14494035.2021.1928377
158. Pesapane, F., et al. (2021). Legal and regulatory framework for AI solutions in healthcare in EU, US, China, and Russia: New scenarios after a pandemic. *Radiation, 1*, 261–276. https://doi.org/10.3390/radiation1040022
159. Robles Carrillo, M. (2020). Artificial intelligence: From ethics to law. *Telecommunications Policy*. https://doi.org/10.1016/j.telpol.2020.101937
160. Anastassov, A. (2021). Artificial intelligence and its possible use in international nuclear security law. Papers of BAS. *Humanities and Social Sciences, 8*, 92–103.
161. Sari, O., & Celik, S. (2021). Legal evaluation of the attacks caused by artificial intelligence-based lethal weapon systems within the context of Rome statute. *Computer Law and Security Review, 42*, 105564. https://doi.org/10.1016/j.clsr.2021.105564
162. Deeks, A. (2020). High-tech international law. *George Washington Law Review, 88*, 574–653.
163. Galceran-Vercher, M. (2023). *Artificial intelligence and cities: The global race to regulate algorithms*. CIBOD 50. https://www.cidob.org/en/publications/publication_series/notes_internacionals/286/artificial_intelligence_and_cities_the_global_race_to_regulate_algorithms. Accessed 20 Nov 2024.
164. Rai, R., & Murali, S. A. (2020). *Global standards on artificial intelligence: a report on global legislation & policy positions governing AI technology*. INDIai. https://indiaai.gov.in/documents/pdf/global-standards-on-ai-report.pdf. Accessed 20 Nov 2024.

165. Jacobi, C., van Atteveldt, W., & Welbers, K. (2016). Quantitative analysis of large amounts of journalistic texts using topic modelling. *Digital Journalism, 4*(1), 89–106. https://doi.org/10.1080/21670811.2015.1093271
166. Weston, S. J., Shryock, I., Light, R., & Fisher, P. A. (2023). Selecting the number and labels of topics in topic modeling: A tutorial. *Advances in Methods and Practices in Psychological Science, 6*(2), 1–13. https://doi.org/10.1177/25152459231160105
167. Attard-Frost, B., & Lyons, K. (2024). AI governance systems: A multi-scale analysis framework, empirical findings, and future directions. *AI and Ethics, 5*. https://doi.org/10.1007/s43681-024-00569-5
168. Liebig, L., Güttel, L., Jobin, A., & Katzenbach, C. (2022). Subnational AI policy: Shaping AI in a multi-level governance system. *AI & Society, 39*, 1477–1490.
169. Wilson, C. (2022). Public engagement and AI: A values analysis of national strategies. *Government Information Quarterly, 39*(1), 101652.
170. Peretz-Andersson, E., Tabares, S., Mikalef, P., & Parida, V. (2024). Artificial intelligence implementation in manufacturing SMEs: A resource orchestration approach. *The International Journal of Information Management, 77*, 102781.
171. Innovation, Science and Economic Development Canada: Voluntary code of conduct on the responsible development and management of advanced generative AI systems. Government of Canada. (2023, September). Retrieved from https://ised-isde.canada.ca/site/global-innovation-clusters/en
172. Innovation, Science and Economic Development Canada: Global Innovation Clusters. Government of Canada. (2023). Retrieved from https://ised-isde.canada.ca/site/global-innovation-clusters/en
173. Bolgov, R. (2023). Artificial intelligence politics and sanctions: Comparing the cases of Russia and Iran. *Digital International Relations*. https://doi.org/10.1007/978-981-99-3467-6_4
174. Government AI Readiness. (2021). *Oxford insights*. https://www.oxfordinsights.com/s/Government_AI_Readiness_21.pdf.
175. Nature Index. (2020). *Artificial Intelligence*. https://www.natureindex.com/supplements/nature-index-2020-ai/tables/countries.
176. Global AI Index. (2021). *Tortoise Media*. https://www.tortoisemedia.com/intelligence/global-ai/.
177. Bolgov, R., Chernov, I., Katsy, D., & Ivannikov, I. (2019). Battle in twitter: Comparative analysis of online political discourse (cases of Macron, Trump, Putin, and Medvedev). In *International Conference on Electronic Governance and Open Society: Challenges in Eurasia, EGOSE (2018). Communications in Computer and Information Science, 947* (pp. 374–383). https://doi.org/10.1007/978-3-030-13283-5_28
178. Tkachenko, S., Zhiglinskaya Wyrsch, N., & Zheng, C. (2021). Technology platform competition between the United States and China: Decoupling and sanctions against Huawei. *Vestnik of Saint Petersburg University. International Relations, 14*(4), 378–392.
179. Nakayama, S. (2012). Techno-nationalism versus techno-globalism, East Asian Science. *Technology and Society: An International Journal, 6*(1), 9–15.
180. Bezrukov, A., Mamonov, M., Suchkov M., & Sushentsov, A. (2021). *International competition and leadership in the digital environment*. Valdai Club. https://valdaiclub.com/files/33065/
181. Decree of the Government of the Russian Federation. (2018). No. 1415. http://government.ru/docs/34831/
182. Bolgov, R., Chugunov, A., Filatova, O., & Misnikov, Y. (2014). Electronic identification of citizens: Comparing perspectives and approaches. In *ACM International Conference Proceeding Series. 8th International Conference on Theory and Practice of Electronic Governance, ICEGOV 2014; Guimaraes; Portugal; 27 October 2014 through 30 October 2014* (pp. 484–485). https://doi.org/10.1145/2691195.2691245
183. Korean National Institute of Health. (2023). *Research ethics guidelines for AI researchers in healthcare*. Korea Disease Control and Prevention Agency.

184. National Commission for the Protection of Human Subjects of Biomedical & Behavioral Research. (1978). *The Belmont report: Ethical principles and guidelines for the protection of human subjects of research*. National Commission for the Protection of Human Subjects of Biomedical & Behavioral Research.
185. European Commission. (2021). *Proposal for a regulation of the European Parliament and of the council laying down harmonised rules or artificial intelligence (artificial intelligence act) and amending certain union legislative acts*. Brussel, 21 Apr 2021.
186. European Parliament. (2024). *AI act*. https://www.europarl.europa.eu/doceo/document/TA-9-2024-0138-FNL-COR01_EN.pdf
187. Bernasco, et al. (2024). *Artificiële intelligentie, justitie en veiligheid. 1/24/Wetenschappelijk Onderzoek- en Datacentrum*. Ministerie van Justitie en Veiligheid en Boom juridisch.
188. Adams, R., Adeleke, F., Florido, A., de Magalhaes Santos, L. G., Grossman, N., Junck, L., & Stone, K. (2024). *Global Index on responsible AI 2024* (1st ed.). South Africa: Global Center on AI Governance. Evidence Explorer. Public participation and awareness. https://www.global-index.ai/thematic-areas-Public-Participation-and-Awareness
189. Roberts, H., Cowls, J., Hine, E., Mazzi, F., Tsamados, A., Taddeo, M., & Floridi, L. (2021). Achieving a 'good AI society': Comparing the aims and progress of the EU and the US. *Science and Engineering Ethics, 27*(6), 68. https://doi.org/10.1007/s11948-021-00340-7
190. Roberts, H., Cowls, J., Hine, E., Morley, J., Wang, V., Taddeo, M., & Floridi, L. (2023). Governing artificial intelligence in China and the European Union: Comparing aims and promoting ethical outcomes. *The Information Society, 39*(2), 79–97. https://doi.org/10.1080/01972243.2022.2124565
191. *Artificial intelligence: Advancing innovation in the national interest*. (2023). Tech Policy Press. https://techpolicy.press/transcript-house-hearing-on-ai-advancing-innovation-in-the-national-interest/
192. Hine, E., & Floridi, L. (2022). Artificial intelligence with American values and Chinese characteristics: A comparative analysis of American and Chinese Governmental AI policies. *AI & Society, June*. https://doi.org/10.1007/s00146-022-01499-8
193. Münch, R. (2001). *The ethics of modernity: Formation and transformation in Britain, France, Germany, and the United States*. Rowman & Littlefield.

Index

A. Carnevale, *The AI Ethics Advisor*,
https://doi.org/10.1007/978-3-032-05526-2

FSC
www.fsc.org
MIX
Papier aus verantwortungsvollen Quellen
Paper from responsible sources
FSC® C105338

If you have any concerns about our products,
you can contact us on
ProductSafety@springernature.com

In case Publisher is established outside the EU,
the EU authorized representative is:
Springer Nature Customer Service Center GmbH
Europaplatz 3, 69115 Heidelberg, Germany

Printed by Libri Plureos GmbH
in Hamburg, Germany